DECONSTRUCTING
THE RAT PACK:
JOEY, THE MOB, AND THE SUMMIT

By Richard A. Lertzman
With Lon Davis

Stories From Classic Hollywood
THE LIFE & TIMES OF Hollywood

PRESTIGE

Prestige Press, Cleveland, Ohio
Library of Congress Cataloguing-in-Publication Data:
Deconstructing the Rat Pack / By Richard A. Lertzman with Lon Davis

ISBN 978-1-09834-161-9

Front cover illustration: (left to right) Sammy Davis Jr., Dean Martin, Frank Sinatra, and Joey Bishop in a publicity photograph for Ocean's 11 (Warner Bros., 1960). Photo by Sid Avery.
Back cover illustration: The iconic photo of the Rat Pack members standing beneath the Sands' marquee, 1960.

This book is dedicated to my late wife, Diana Christine Lertzman. Diana is my shining light and guiding star. Her spirit lives on through this book.

de·con·struct / ˌdēkən'strəkt/verb/ past tense: deconstructed; past participle: deconstructed

To analyze (a text or a linguistic or conceptual system) by deconstruction, typically in order to expose its hidden internal assumptions and contradictions and subvert its apparent significance or unity.
To reduce (something) to its constituent parts in order to reinterpret it.

Table of Contents

Introduction

Why Bother Writing a Book on that *mashugana*?
—Sheldon Leonard

My introduction to Joey Bishop began in the spring of 1996. I was in Los Angeles doing interviews on a planned book about actor Robert Cummings. I was also kicking around the idea of a biography on Joey Bishop that would touch upon the Rat Pack. I thought it was perfect timing. Sammy had died in 1990. Dean had just passed away at Christmas in 1995. Peter Lawford had ceased to exist more than a decade earlier, in 1984. Frank Sinatra gave his last performance in February of 1995 and the rumor was that he was suffering from dementia. Joey was basically the last man standing.

I was enjoying a leisurely lunch at the old-school Valley Inn Restaurant in Sherman Oaks, California, with sitcom writing guru Austin "Rocky" Kalish and the legendary actor/producer/director Sheldon Leonard. Over the years, my greatest pleasure was listening to these accomplished raconteurs. Writers always know the inside scoop on the comics and can expose every gory detail. And the topic of Joey Bishop opened the floodgates.

I asked for their thoughts about my writing a book about Joey Bishop and the Rat Pack.

"Shoot yourself first," cracked Leonard in his unforgettable side-of-the-mouth, New Yorkese, gangster voice. Leonard was far from being a streetwise hood, however. A graduate of Syracuse University, Sheldon Leonard Bershad was an erudite partner and producer (with Danny Thomas) of some truly classic sitcoms. One of the lesser shows under the Danny Thomas umbrella was *The Joey Bishop Show*. With Leonard's help—and despite the hiring and firing of writers, directors, actors and with several format changes—it lasted four seasons on two networks for an astonishing 123 episodes.

"Why bother writing a book on that *mashugana?*" Leonard continued.

My dear friend Rocky Kalish was my Sensei. Rocky and his wife (and writing partner), Irma (who became a prominent leader at the Writers Guild), spanned decades in television. Rocky had the unfortunate experience of writing for the Bishop show as a favor to Sheldon.

Rocky was never one to mince words. "That son of a bitch isn't worth a paragraph . . . talentless motherfucker. He couldn't score a role on *Sunrise Sermon.*"

I was hoping that Sheldon could wrangle an interview with the Chairman of the Board as he had been friendly with him and had co-starred (as Harry the Horse) in *Guys and Dolls* in 1955. Leonard said with a wry grin, "Not a chance."

Under Rocky's tutelage, I met countless other great writers, performers, and legends of film and television. A wonderful documentary entitled *Lunch* (2012), lovingly created by Donna Kanter (daughter of comedy legend Hal Kanter), shows Rocky in his full splendor. As Jannette Catsoulis of the *New York Times* wrote in her November 8, 2012, review:

> It's all knishes and kibitzing in "Lunch," Donna Kanter's charming documentary about a Hollywood institu-
> tion more enduring than most sitcoms. . . . Every other Wednesday for 40 years a bunch of legendary comedy writers and directors—whose career highlights alone would fill a showbiz encyclopedia—have been meeting for a prandial catch-up session. The location may change (currently it's Factor's Famous Deli), but the diners remain constant, give or take the odd family or medical event. And though the gathering usually kicks off with health updates —the so-called "organ recital"—these guys (and they are all guys) would rather not focus on hip-replacement humor.

These lunches, several of which I attended as Rocky's guest, featured top comedy writers, directors, and television personalities: Hal Kanter, Irving Brecher, Sid Caesar, Carl Reiner, Gary Owens, director Arthur Hiller, Mel Brooks, Matty Simmons, Arthur Marx, Monty Hall, and writers Ben Starr and John Rappaport. I sat there like the proverbial fly on the wall, soaking up these great stories as they flew, fast and furious, around the table.

Inevitably, at almost every lunch I attended over several years, stories about working with Joey Bishop came up—war stories. It seemed that at one time or another Joey fired virtually every legendary comedy writer. It became a sort of badge of honor, a Purple Heart. Harry Crane, Fred Freeman, Marvin Marx, Bill Persky, Sam Denoff, Irving Ellison, Fred Fox, Danny Simon . . . the list seemed endless.

After each lunch, I went back to my hotel room and recorded these unforgettable stories, carefully including the anecdotes about the perils of working with Joey Bishop.

Joey's head writer of his ABC talk show, Trustin Howard (a.k.a. Slick Slavin), told the author, "I believe I was the longest-surviving writer to stick with Joey [nearly three years]. While I was grateful for the job, Regis and I lived through a constant reign of terror."

It was a call from both Sheldon and Rocky that unlocked the door to Joey. I called him and, at first, he sounded rather old and crotchety.

"I'm not talking about the fucking Rat Pack," he warned me.

Nonetheless, I wangled an invitation to his home, which was in the Newport Beach area, about an hour from where I was staying in the Valley. I had my eldest son, Matthew, with me as he was on spring break. Matthew had no idea who (or even *what*) Joey Bishop was. It had been almost thirty years since Joey had walked off his ABC late-night talk show in 1969. For all intents and purposes, when his talk show was canceled, so was he.

I was hoping that a book about the Rat Pack, fronted by Joey, would be saleable. It wasn't Joey I was interested in, but a fresh, insider's glimpse at Frank, Dean, and Sammy (and Peter) by "the hub" (as Joey called himself) of the wheel.

Joey had lived for nearly thirty years in a gated community in Newport Beach. Lido Isle is a man-made island located in the harbor, which is linked to the city by a small bridge. It's a crowded, residential area with townhouses, condominiums, and small homes. Joey, who loved the water, had also docked his boats (*Son of a Gun I, Son of a Gun II,* etc.) near the condo. I believe he had sold his last boat just prior to our initial meeting.

I set up the meeting for about 11 A.M. with his assistant, Nora Garibotti. Joey lived in an older condo with Sylvia, his wife of nearly sixty years. Although it was a crowded residential complex with a marina setting, it had a spectacular view of the ocean/harbor. I met Sylvia, and then Joey, who looked much older and far more disheveled than I had expected. He was wearing a sweat suit dotted with food stains. The house was a throwback to the early 1970s "Jewish schmaltz" that I remembered from my youth. Joey took us upstairs to his study, which he called the "trophy room." It was basically a shrine to himself. There were plaques, framed photographs, statuettes (awards), and books lining the shelves.

As it turns out, my visit was hardly an "exclusive." A parade of writers and reporters had already made the pilgrimage to Lido Isle after the deaths of the other Rat Pack members, hoping to squeeze out some hitherto-unexplored memories. As our conversation progressed, Joey grew angrier as he began to realize that our interest was clearly in Frank, Dean, and Sammy—and that he was just an afterthought.

What attracted us to this subject was far more complex than just the man's talent—or lack thereof. In fact, I don't consider Joey Bishop to be much more than a competent comedian. He was not unlike baseball player Bob Uecker, who made himself the butt of many jokes concerning his mediocre career. "If a guy hits .300 every year, what does he have to look forward to?" Uecker asked. "I always tried to stay around .190 with three or four RBI. And I tried to get them all in September. That way I always had something to talk about that winter."[8]

Thus, we compare Joey to that utility player. That guy on the bench—a journeyman. Dependable. Adequate.

So why write a book about an adequate comedian?

Joey took his ordinary skills and landed himself in the middle of the phenomenon known as the Rat Pack. His inclusion, though, had far less to do with his comic skills and more with his neutrality. There is a Yiddish expression, *"Ir Nit Shtinken ader schkm,"* which translates as "You neither stink nor smell." In essence, it means you can get along with everybody. You don't stand out in a loud way. Joey knew how to be liked and blend in. He could kiss ass.

While perfecting his craft as a comic in the 1930s and '40s, he was also making the right friends—mobsters such as Moe Dalitz, Billy Weinberger, Carl Cohen, Mickey Cohen, Louis Roth-kopf, Frank Costello, Benjamin "Bugsy" Siegel, Meyer Lansky. He became the fair-haired boy of Murder, Inc. He worked their joints, kept his nose clean, handled hecklers, looked the other way when needed, and always, *always* kept his mouth shut. And when they thought the time was right, they paired him with the most impact-ful artist of his generation, Frank Sinatra. As the author will uncover through his research, it was Joey, not Frank, who was tight with the mob. It was Joey who testified at the murder trial of Mickey Cohen.

Frank certainly had the connections, yet his talent was culti-vated by bandleaders like Tommy Dorsey, record executives like Manie Sacks, arrangers like Nelson Riddle, movie moguls like Louis B. Mayer and Harry Cohn, and public-relations guru George Evans.

Joey, on the other hand, was cultivated by the legendary agent Abe Lastfogel of the William Morris Agency, who worked hand-in-hand with Joey's pals Bugsy, Meyer, Moe, and Mickey. As Frank's comic, Joey knew his place. Frank could trust him never to carry any backstage tales. And Joey did a great job of entertaining an audience, warming them up for the headliner, but not tiring them out like Jerry Lewis, Buddy Hackett, Shecky Greene, Jack E. Leonard, or Don Rickles would.

And when all the elements fell into place for the Rat Pack, Joey was in the right place at the right time—(As Joey would say, using his one catchphrase, "Son of a gun!") The straight man to three of the biggest dynamos ever to grace a nightclub stage—Frank, Dean, and Sammy. Joey didn't stink or smell. He was there to keep the rhythm, keep the beat going, as any good straight man would, whether it was Bud Abbott or Dan Rowan. He tossed in an occasional ad-lib, but he would never outshine his partners. Although he was by no means in their class of performance, the rewards for his mediocrity were great. He became a Vegas head-liner, appeared in films, and starred for four seasons in his epony-mous sitcom and late-night talk show.

This book, written in tandem with film historian, author, and editor Lon Davis, will take an in-depth look at the life and times of the Rat Pack, told through the eyes of Joseph Gottlieb, a.k.a. Joey Bishop. It will follow his slow rise to the top, his inclusion in a quintet notorious for its misogyny, his own position at the top of the heap, and his slow, sad return to obscurity.

Strap yourself in and enjoy the ride.

Richard A. Lertzman

Chapter 1
Growing Up in South Philly

Joseph Gottlieb's Formative Years

Philadelphia, PA, c. 1915.

Joseph Abraham Gottlieb was a South Philly boy through and through, except he was born in the Bronx, into an already large Jewish brood. His parents, Anna and Jacob, were part of the large Jewish enclave that congregated around or near Delancey Street in New York's Lower East Side at the beginning of the 20th century. Many of the European Jews who immigrated to New York lived in the tenements along with Greeks, Hungarians, Poles, Romanians, Russians, Slovaks, and Ukrainians. The Jewish neighborhood was estimated to have a population of nearly four hundred thousand. The streets were loaded with merchants—mainly of the pushcart variety, but also shop owners and ragmen. In addition, Yiddish theaters proliferated along Second Avenue, featuring such well-known personages as Molly Picon, Jacob Adler, Mischa Auer, and Leon Liebgold.

Joseph's father, Jacob, was born in Austria in 1885 and spoke broken English and fluent Yiddish. As was the case with many Jewish émigrés, he entered the United States through Ellis Island. Born Yankel Gottgottlick, his name was quickly Americanized as Jacob Gottlieb. Similarly, his future wife, Anna, born in 1891, escaped with her family to New York when she was ten, due to the rising anti-Semitism in Romania. Anna was a tough, serious young woman. According to Joey, she suffered from partial blindness in one eye, the result of an encounter with a deranged street cleaner in Romania.

"'Jew?' the street cleaner asked my mother," Joey recalled. "She was about seven, and he towered over her in his horse and wagon. When my mother said, 'Yes,' the street cleaner cracked his whip and caught her in the eye, leaving a scar that curled down the side of her face forever."

Jacob was a tinkerer with the knowledge of an engineer. As Joey remembered, "He loved to take apart things and put them back together . . . I wish I had his skills." At first, Jacob worked in factories in New York. He was a slight man, Joey recalled, "Very quiet and rarely raised his voice." Anna was a rather harsh woman, due possibly to her experiences in Romania. Large and husky, "She was definitely the boss," her son recalled. "She ruled with an iron hand. My older brothers got the brunt of her anger, thank God. But you always did things her way."

Anna and Jacob met and married in 1906. Surprisingly, they did not have children right away, as was common in that period. Jacob was offered a job at an uncle's factory in Milwaukee, Wisconsin, where they relocated in 1908. In 1910, they had their first child, Clara. Both Jacob and Anna disliked the bitter cold of Wisconsin's winters and insisted that the family return to New York shortly after Clara's birth. They found a better neighborhood in the Bronx, where Jacob's brother had recently relocated. In 1912, the family welcomed a son, Morris; in 1913, another son, Harry; daughter Rebecca in 1915; and Freddy in 1916. The youngest child, Joseph, made his entrance on February 3, 1918. Nicknamed Joey, the runt of the family weighed just two pounds, fourteen ounces, according to his records at Fordham Hospital in the Bronx.

"I was the smallest baby ever born there," Joey said. "I told Buddy Hackett what I weighed, and he asked, 'Did you live?'"

Little Joey was only twelve weeks old when his parents, with the encouragement of yet another uncle, packed him up with the other children and settled in South Philadelphia, where there was already a congregation of Gottlieb family members.

South Philly is the section of Philadelphia that is bounded by South Street to the north, the Delaware River to the east and south, and the Schuylkill River to the west. A diverse community, "It was loaded with every dago, mick, spade, and kike," Joey said, jokingly referring to the large Italian, Irish, Black, and Jewish populations. Joey remembers that his family was the poorest on the block. Jake Gottlieb earned just $21 a week at the old Fidelity Machine Co., in Northeast Philadelphia.

"We were poor," Joey recalled. "But—how can I explain it?—we were *happy*."

With a growing family to support, Jacob left his unlucrative position and, with the financial aid of his relatives, bought a building at 332 Snyder. The lower level became The Gottlieb Bicycle Shop, and the family lived in the two-bedroom apartment above the store ("Until the rent was due," he joked). Joey, his brothers, and sisters shared one room; Anna and Jacob, the other. "All five kids were always up at seven o'clock—because my father was up at five minutes to seven, coughing," Joey explained. "It was a warm, secure, kosher Jewish family. My mother won't even let a Paper Mate Pen in her house because it has a piggy-back refill."

Besides repairing and selling bicycles, Jacob rented them out at fifty cents a day. Everyone helped out at the shop, including Joey and Anna. "My mother would ask the people who rented the bikes, 'What's your name?' and scribble in the book. Who knew she couldn't write English?" For that matter, he said, "Here was my father selling bicycles in a poor neighborhood. Who the hell needed bicycles?"

On hot summer days, Joey and his buddies would strip off their clothes and dive from Pier 98 into the Delaware River. Even in the 1930s, the Delaware was discolored with pollution, but no one could have enjoyed himself more as the South Philadelphia summers closed in on the tiny bedroom Joey shared with his four siblings.

"Times were bad," Joey said. "Our recreation was to walk around, hitting awnings. As a boy, I was forced to rely on my own ingenuity for amusement."

During one of the author's interviews, Joey stated just how important his South Philly neighborhood was in shaping his view of the world. He explained that sitting on the stoop of his home was a colorful way of understanding what made people laugh— "I'd listen to these stories in the neighborhood and got a good understanding of human nature," he asserted.

Those same South Philadelphia streets also spawned Frankie Avalon, Fabian, Eddie Fisher, Jack Klugman, Mario Lanza, and Bobby Rydell.

Joey never forgot his old South Philly gang, nor did they forget him. "He was just the nicest, funniest guy," said man-about-town and longtime Bishop friend Harry Jay Katz. Katz recalled that Joey would call him every December 25th, his birthday. "He would always sing, and he had a horrible voice," Katz said. "He would sing 'Happy Birthday' and say, 'Can you guess who this is?'"

"Unfortunately, I had no voice," Joey concurred. "The way I sing, some of the notes I hit, only Jewish dogs can hear me. I naturally fell into clowning around. I was nine years old before I cut my hair. When I came home from the barber, was my mother shocked! So was the kid who carried my books."

South Philadelphia was a melting pot and, unlike the deep divides that exist today, people of different ethnicities and races learned to coexist, and lifelong friendships were forged. Joey maintained an unlikely friendship with a nun named Sister Joan Marie, who was a teacher at the nearby Our Lady of Mount Carmel parochial school. Joey, who like many of his buddies was an avid handball player, preferred the high wall at Mount Carmel.

"I went over to play there, and the sister came out. I was about to leave, before I got in any trouble, and she told me I could stay. I said, 'But, Sister, I don't go to this school—I'm Jewish.' And she looked at me and said that it was okay, I could play there. We became lifelong friends," Joey said with pride. In 1996, when the ninety-three-year-old Sister Joan Marie became ill and knew she was dying, she told her friends to alert Joey immediately.

Of the five future Rat Pack members, Joey was the only one who *almost* graduated from high school. He was educated at Furness Junior High and South Philadelphia High. He recalled, "It became clear to me that my life plans didn't include higher education. I went to South Philadelphia High School but left a semester short of graduation." Joey was actually a good student. While he always downplayed that he was a studious kid ("I flunked sandpile," he joked), in fact, he was a voracious reader. Joey once won fifty cents in a spelling bee contest and his father beat him with a leather belt as he thought the boy had stolen the money. In Jacob's eyes, winning money through education was unheard of.

Joey had no aspirations to become a "lawyer, an engineer, or a doctor—much to the chagrin of my mother." He decided that high school was not a necessity on his path to success, nor did his parents insist he remain in school. Without a steady paycheck or job, he dropped out.

When Joey was seventeen, he left home and went to New York to live with an uncle.

"He got me into an amateur contest, and I lost," Joey recalled. "He then got me a job in a hat factory at five dollars a week. When that didn't work out, I got a two-week gig as an emcee at a Chinese restaurant on Broadway. I wore a tuxedo, which I rented from my cousin, and rode the subway to work. I always kept on my makeup, as I wanted people to know that I was in the business. So, I picked up a couple of sandwiches, as the owners of the Chinese restaurant wouldn't feed the help, and I was paid thirteen dollars a week."

It was that Eastern European work ethic that created the expectation that every family member contribute to the family's funds. Joey's older brothers and sister all did odd jobs to help support the family. As for Joey, he made pastrami sandwiches at a deli at 5th and Dickinson; he sold magazines door to door; he handed out playbills; put in time in the warehouse of Gimbel's Department Store; dipped candles at the Pine Wax Works; swept sidewalks in front of stores; sold peaches and tomatoes off a pushcart; worked the counter as a soda jerk at the corner drugstore; and acted as a messenger boy.

"In those days," Joey recalled, "most of the families did not have phones yet, so if you didn't send a telegram—like they did if there was a death in the family—they would call the corner drugstore to get a message to someone in the neighborhood. It was cheaper, too! So, the drugstore hired me as a runner and I would take them a message. I got a nickel a message. And I got stiffed at times for that nickel."

"It was the Depression," he said matter-of-factly. "Pennies mattered, so you did what there was to be done."

Joey recalled, incorrectly, that "there had been no performers in my family before me, none of my brothers and sisters were so inclined." In fact, his brother Harry, who was two years older and looked like a taller version of Joey, was enamored of show business. While Harry never found anything compared to the success of his brother, he eventually worked as a dialogue coach on *The Joey Bishop Show* and other projects.

"As early as I can remember," Joey said, "I wanted to be in show business. I used to hang around in front of the Earl Theatre for a glimpse of the celebrities, like Benny Davis or Ted Lewis, coming out of the vaudeville. Just to let them pass close to me was a thrill. *Thrill?* I pretended I was leaving the theatre myself all the way home." Like many of that era, he also had fond memories of his family's old Philco radio, at which he sat for hours and listened to the comedic headliners of the time: Fred Allen, Jack Benny, and Eddie Cantor.

Joey schooled himself in comedy at local amateur shows. At the Grand Theatre at 7th and Snyder, at the Colonial Theatre at 11th and Moyamensing, and at the Admiral Theatre at 5th and Lehigh, he picked up extra cash with a repertoire of impressions that included the distinguished British actor George Arliss; Broadway entertainers Jimmy Durante, Al Jolson, Cantor; radio comic Joe Penner; even the brilliant pantomimist Harpo Marx. In 1936, he performed his impressions in an amateur show and won the three-dollar first prize.

"From then on, I was a professional."

In addition to his talent for mimicry, Joey was a superb tap dancer. As he said, "Of course, everybody in South Philadelphia could tap dance—'cause when it was cold outside, it would keep us warm. Our group at 4th and Snyder were considered excellent dancers when it came to the Jitterbug. I remember when we used to travel over to Strawberry Mansion or West Philadelphia, the girls would say, 'Oh, the South Philadelphia guys are coming ...'"

Dancing was the rage then, and Joey and his pals would lie in ambush for better-heeled boys on their way from dancing school and held them in ransom for the steps they had learned. It worked. In 1936, Joey won the "Benny Goodman Jitterbug Contest," which entitled him to passes that year to the Steel Pier in Atlantic City, making him the envy of his buddies on Snyder Avenue.

At the age of eighteen, Joey Bishop was dancing and joking his way into show business.

Chapter 2
The Bishop Brothers

Joey Sticks His Toe in Show Business

Young Joey Bishop, standing in front of the Jewish Neighborhood House, at Sixth and Mifflin, in Philadelphia, PA, mid-1930s.

Dancing momentarily overshadowed Joey's true calling in life. "I'm not a dancer," he said definitively. "I'm a comic by nature, by instinct."

Joey worked up an act with a couple of pals from the old neighborhood, Morris Spector and Sammy Reisman (who soon dropped out because of illness and was replaced by Mel Farber), billing themselves as "The Bishop Brothers." The trio specialized in sendups of the "Irish Nightingale" Morton Downey Sr., the Ink Spots, radio serials, and followed the sound of laughter through an unending cycle of sparse hotel rooms, lunch-counter food, and echoing train depots.

Morris Spector—nicknamed "Rummy," which was short for Rum Nose—was interested in joining an act that Joey was forming at the Jewish Neighborhood House, a forerunner of the Jewish Community Center (JCC). "Everybody in South Philly had nick-names," explained Spector. "Once I got hit in the nose by a snow-ball and it turned very red. Thus, Rum Nose."

"Everybody met up at the Jewish Neighborhood House on Sixth and Mifflin," Rummy recalled. "I lived only a couple blocks away from Joey and everyone hung around the guys in their own area. If you lived within one block, you knew everybody, but if you lived *two* blocks away, you didn't know those guys."

When Rummy told Frank Tonkin, who put together the dra-ma club at the Neighborhood House, that they were looking to expand the team, Tonkin suggested a guy on Snyder Avenue who did impressions. His name was Joseph Gottlieb. Joey joined the act, and Ramie Needleman dropped out.

"We were then back to three," Rummy continues. "And we needed transportation. This Black kid named Glenn Bishop was a pal of ours. Joey always said that he had a car we could borrow, but he was as poor as we were. But it was Glenn who suggested that we call ourselves the Bishop Brothers, using his name. He said it didn't sound too Jewish—obviously!"

And that is how Joseph Gottlieb became Joey Bishop.

"Our first gig was a one-nighter at a place in Philly called O'Shea's Wagon," Rummy recalled. "But it was a big deal. The newspaper had a story and our pictures were in it. We were big heroes in the neighborhood and to our families."

That may be. But when her son was introduced as Joey Bishop, Anna stood up in the audience and said loudly and indignantly: "No . . . Joey *Gottlieb!*" From that time on, he and Rummy continued to use Bishop as their own name. "I tried using Gottlieb for a while," Joey said, "but they thought I was an owner."

The newly christened Bishop Brothers kept rehearsing their act at the Jewish Neighborhood House, located upstairs from a poolroom, and auditioned in saloons for whatever coins the customers would throw at them. Finally, they began to get some bookings—one-nighters in the wilds of Jersey and Pennsylvania.

Joey later said that Rummy "is still my closest friend, and in a way, I suppose we *are* brothers." They did satires on radio programs *We the People, Gangbusters,* and *Doctor I. Q.* ("We did our impression of a Russian hunger strike," recalls Rummy. "We marched and marched and moaned and groaned, and then someone burped. The rest of us turned on him and said: 'You cheated!'")

The young comic did impressions of Edward G. Robinson, Jimmy Cagney, and Ted Lewis. But Rummy was more uninhibited and got most of the laughs, particularly with his ability to perform slapstick.

"I stood around and said 'Attaboy, Rummy!'" Joey remembers. "The truth is anybody can tell a joke. I enjoyed doing the straight lines."

"It was Frank Palumbo who gave us our first real break," remembered Rummy. "He ran a joint over on Catherine Street called—what else?—Palumbo's. It was pretty well known in Philly and had some big stars play there, like Jimmy Durante. We got good money for those times—I think it was like forty-five dollars for the team. We were thrilled."

The stint at Palumbo's helped them to "get their chops" as performers and learn to play to an audience. "It was like taking a grad course," Rummy said. "You learned the business on the fly." It also led to other gigs around town, including Mike Dutkin's Rathskeller on Broad and Girard, which led to another longstanding gig.

"Joey was the business manager, our agent," recalled Rummy. "He talked the business and arranged the gigs. So, when we got hired at the Rathskeller, he arranged for us to get top billing, which was a smart move. But the club owner tossed us out. The great thing is that we met another act we traveled with to play the Havana Casino, in Buffalo."

In the summer of 1938, the trio was booked into the mountains. The offer was $25 a week, or $8 apiece, with room and board. The day after Labor Day, they went to collect their salary and found the place deserted—office, kitchens, everything. "I was glad I had taken a stand," says Joey. "I insisted laundry had to be included. They said okay, because they knew they weren't going to pay us anyway, and in the end, it worked out about even."

Soon after the big break at the Havana Club, the Bishop Brothers received a booking at $45 a week for a long engagement at the Town Casino in Buffalo. From there, they went to the Glen Park Casino where, for some reason or other, *Variety* reviewed their act and gave them a rave notice. On the strength of this, the hot new comedy team received a wire asking them to come to Chicago. When they arrived, they found it was only for an audition. "The boss said we were only kids and that the mob would murder us," said Rummy. They didn't make it. They hung around Chicago, looking for work, picking up one-nighters, and quickly running out of funds.

"One of us had to stay in the room all the time for fear they'd lock us out," Joey explained. "We used to sit around in a delicatessen nearby and eat the bread and pickles and sauerkraut on the tables. When they came for the order, we'd just say we were waiting for someone."

Finally, money arrived from home and they retreated to Philly, but they didn't allow this discouragement to get the better of them. They occasionally played Palumbo's and then picked up more and more small clubs, some vaudeville houses like the Court Square in Springfield, Massachusetts, and even a burlesque theater on the eastern wheel of the Hurst Circuit.

"Joey used to worship comics named Mike Sachs and Maxie Furman," says Rummy. "He used to stand in the wings and watch them night after night. Me, I was having a good time, but he was always trying to learn how to be better."

The year 1940 found the Bishop Brothers at the Nut Club in Miami, making $150 a week. When the season was over, they went north for the Mercury Brothers, who also owned a spot in Pittsburgh. By then, the trio had dwindled to a double; first Sammy, and then his replacement, Mel, had been drafted. In Pittsburgh, both Joey and Rummy registered for the draft. Back they went to Miami, where Rummy received his notice. The owner of the club got him temporarily deferred on the claim that without Rummy, the show would collapse and put all the employees of the club out of work. The U.S. Army waited until after the season was over; it wasn't until April of 1942 that Uncle Sam broke up the act.

Chapter 3
Mobbed Up

A Wise Ass Meets the Wise Guys

Rondelli's Italian Restaurant, Sherman Oaks, CA, 1959

Joey had served his apprenticeship. Now he began his residency. At the age of twenty-one and without his partners, Joey Bishop played his first solo gig in Cleveland, at a club inauspiciously named El Dumpo. Originally a Chinese restaurant called the Butterfly Inn, it was owned in the 1930s by Jacob Hecht. He opened his large basement room as a nightclub and, from 1934 to the 1940s, presented full floor shows with a house band led by Marion Sears. The name of the place was later upgraded to Cedar Gardens.

"I was nervous at first," Joey later admitted. "Rummy had always supplied the punchlines, but as soon as I walked out there, I knew it was going to be all right. I felt free, relaxed, how do you say?—liberated. I suddenly realized how uncomfortable I had been trying to adhere to an act. Working alone, I didn't need a routine. The humor came out of the situation, the weather, the owner, the customers, the girls in the show. I just stood up and talked and it came out funny."

The self-assured young comic soon became friendly with the owners of the club, all of whom were leaders of the Cleveland Jewish mob run by noted racketeer/bootlegger Max Diamond and his partner, the murderous Shondor Birns. (Birns was portrayed by Christopher Walken in the 2012 film *Kill the Irishman*). As part of the notorious Maxie Diamond gang, Birns was soon recruited by Maxie Diamond, leader of the E. 55th Street and Woodland mob. Diamond was an associate of Teamsters leader William Presser and was once referred to by the local newspapers as "Cleveland's Number-One Racketeer." Birns became a ranking member of Diamond's gang during the battles for control of the city's dry cleaners and launderers in 1933, shortly after he hooked up with the Maxie Diamond gang. Diamond narrowly escaped death from gunfire by rival gangsters in what the police department called "a continuation of the city's dry-cleaning racket war." Birns was among those who were picked up for questioning. He was released, but only after paying two dollars for two overdue traffic tickets. Both Diamond and Birns were part of a reported 120 mob hits over the next few years in northeast Ohio.

The author was well acquainted with Diamond, who had "retired" from the mob after accumulating a fairly substantial sale of his properties following his conviction by the Cleveland safety director, Eliot Ness of "The Untouchables" fame. Diamond claimed that Ness was getting a cut of his casinos and bars and wanted a larger share. When Maxie turned down Ness's request, he arranged to have Diamond convicted and sent to prison. This allowed Ness to install mob boss Joe Lonardo in his place. When Diamond returned from prison and "sold" his assets, Diamond decided to live a quiet life. He went to work for the author's grandfather Barney Lertzman and his father Ronald Lertzman in a legitimate business (The Barney Lertzman Auction Group) to kill time.

Philly mobster Frank Palumbo stated that he had given the Bishop Brothers their big break by booking them into his club, which led to a tour of the Eastern burlesque circuit—booked alongside other burlesque comics, including B. S. Pully (*Guys and Dolls*), Joe E. Ross (*Car 54, Where Are You?*), and Mickey Rooney's father Joe Yule—Joey became a solo act when Rummy entered the service.

During his extended stay at El Dumpo, Joey became acquainted with the management, a veritable roll call of Murder, Inc. El Dumpo was one of a set of the Cleveland-based nightclubs used as fronts for casinos throughout the Midwest. There was the main casino in Geauga County, Ohio, called the Piedmont Club; the Casablanca in Shaker Heights; the Beverly Hills Club in suburban Cincinnati, among others. The ownership was based in New York City, with Meyer Lansky, Benjamin "Bugsy" Siegel, and Charles "Lucky" Luciano at the helm. Meyer Lansky installed a trusted friend, Morris "Moe" Dalitz, at the helm of the Midwest operations based in Cleveland. Dalitz was nicknamed "Mr. Las Vegas" due to his ownership in the Desert Inn and the Dunes, along with being the force behind building the Las Vegas Convention Center and Sunrise Hospital.

Dalitz was extremely important to the mob as he was clean— he had no criminal record, unlike Lansky, Luciano, and Siegel. He was able to be licensed. Though he admitted under oath that he had been a bootlegger and had operated illegal gambling houses, Dalitz was never convicted of a crime and remained pure even after he appeared before the committee investigating organized crime. In November 1950, the first major U.S. Senate investigation of organized crime was underway. Chaired by Estes Kefauver—a tall, broad-shouldered, courtly senator from Tennessee—the Kefauver Hearings were broadcast live on television from May 30, 1950 to May 3, 1951.

In all, the Kefauver Committee heard testimony from six hundred witnesses, several of whom were high-profile godfathers of La Cosa Nostra in Chicago, New York City, Cleveland, Detroit, and ten other U.S. cities. Many of the country's leading gangsters, including Meyer Lansky and his brother Jake, were on the committee's hit list.

Some of the out-of-state gangsters the committee named as actively controlling gambling in Florida resorts included Joe Adonis, Frank Erickson, Vincent Jimmy "Blue Eyes" Alo, Mike "Trigger Man" Cappola, all of New York; Sammy "Game Boy" Miller of Cleveland; and Jose Massei and Willie Bischoff, the latter of whom went by the alias "Lefty" of Detroit. Kefauver wrote that his committee came away "shocked and disgusted" by the various testimonies, although Moe Dalitz came away clean, thereby opening the door for licensing in Las Vegas.

Under Dalitz, in Cleveland, were many of the familiar names who eventually ran Las Vegas, including Alfred "Big Al" Polizzi, who ran the Sands; Sammy "Game Boy" Miller; Shondor Birns; and Mickey Cohen, who became the notorious Los Angeles mob boss and co-owner of the Flamingo.

According to a biography of Mickey Cohen—*Hollywood Celebrity Gangster* by Brad Lewis (BookSurge Publishing, 2009)—Joey Bishop was friendly with the leading gangsters of the era, particularly so with Cohen.

> When Mickey Cohen was in prison for tax evasion, one of the few people who wrote him consistently was Joey Bishop. They also called Joey Bishop to testify in a retrial of a murder against Mickey Cohen—the shooting of Jack Whelan. They called Joey Bishop as a witness. Ironic. Of all the Rat Pack, the only one to ever testify in a murder trial was Joey Bishop.

Author Brad Lewis also contends that Cohen helped to promote many other entertainers and politicians.

> The "Boys" took a liking to the tough kid from Philadelphia. He had an attitude they admired. And like Cohen, Miller, Lansky, and Dalitz—he was Jewish. After all the "Dago" singers the Cleveland boys pushed—Sinatra, Dean Martin, Dean's roommate Sonny King (born Luigi Antonio Schiavone), Perry Como, and others—it was nice to push a "Yid."

> While Joey was appearing at Cleveland's El Dumpo during 1941, Dean Martin—a.k.a. Dino Paul Crocetti, from Steubenville, Ohio—was making a name for himself in Cleveland with the Sammy Watkins orchestra. He married a girl, Betty MacDonald, in Cleveland and lived in nearby Cleveland Heights in the early 1940s. Watkins had Dino change his name to a more American-sounding Dean Martin. The "Boys" loved Dino. He had it all, the cool attitude, he was an ex-boxer, and the broads loved him too.

"I met Dean in Cleveland the first time," Joey recalled for the author in 1998. "He was at the first-class joints in Cleveland like the Theatrical for Mushy Wexler and the boys. Maybe at the Hollenden, too. They used to tote him out to the casino way out in the boonies [to the Piedmont Club]. I knew he was going to hit it big. I loved his casual style and I took note. I added that [trait] to my repertoire."

By the time Joey was a solo act, he already had the mob's seal of approval. The Bishop Brothers had worked the "Eastern Wheel" of mob clubs, booked by the mob-influenced, Chicago-based MCA—the same MCA that eventually bought Universal Pictures.

The brains behind MCA was Jules Stein, a Chicago ophthalmologist who discovered that he could make more money booking bands. When Stein and an associate, Billy Goodheart, founded the Music Corporation of America in 1924, they began empire building. They had plenty of help from James Petrillo, the head of the American Federation of Musicians, with whom MCA maintained a sweetheart labor-management relationship. According to Justice Department documents, Petrillo was paid off in return for favors to MCA. Taft Schreiber and Sonny Werblin were among the first two top MCA assistants, followed by Lew Wasserman, who was groomed as Stein's heir and was named president of the company in 1946; Stein then became MCA's chairman of the board. MCA's aggressive agents were known as "the black-suited Mafia."

The rise of MCA and its move to Hollywood paralleled the rise of the Chicago Mafia and its infiltration of the motion picture industry. While MCA was representing some of the top motion picture stars, Chicago mobsters took control of the International Alliance of Theatrical Stage Employees (IATSE), the major Hollywood labor union, through Willie Bioff, a small-time hood who was supervised by Chicago mob lieutenant Johnny Rosselli. The studios made payoffs to the underworld for labor peace—and to keep their workers' wages and benefits at a minimum. But when the studios' payoff man was caught evading federal income taxes, he plea-bargained with the government, implicating Bioff, but not the Mafia, in the extortion scheme. Bioff was indicted and convicted—and then turned state's evidence against his cohorts, who were also convicted and sent to prison.

The Chicago Mafia's role in Hollywood did not end with the convictions; it simply changed. Chicago's new liaison in the motion picture industry became attorney Sidney Korshak, backed by MCA and Stein, who had represented Bioff. Charles Gioe, a top Chicago Mafia figure, had told Bioff that Korshak was "our man . . . any message he may deliver to you is a message from us."

MCA needed the right performers to put bodies in the clubs they booked. These performers needed the approval of the owner/front for the venues, such as Jules Podell at the Copacabana, Mike Fritzell at the Chez Parée in Chicago, Billy Wilkerson at Ciro's in Los Angeles, The Latin Quarter in New York run by Lou Walters (Barbara Walters's father), and Moe Dalitz at the Piedmont in Cleveland.

The clubs needed performers who could not only pack them in their showrooms, but who also were able to follow the rules.

They needed, as Bishop said, to "keep their fucking mouths shut. Don't make waves. Don't fuck the showgirls two by two..." Joey was a self-admitted politician, a schmoozer. He came from the streets of South Philly. He knew how to play the game. Joey was a wiseacre, a smart-ass, the mob's version of S. J. Perelman. He was their type of wit. A wise guy from the street. They got his humor.

Joey remembered that, during his year at El Dumpo in Cleveland, he was unaware that the clubs were filled with some of the most notorious mobsters.

"You know who the bartender there was?" Joey asked us. "Remember Leo Gorcey in the *Dead End Kids?* His father [Bernard Gorcey, who later played Louie in the Bowery Boys movies]. He saved me from getting killed there one night. "Out in the audience was a guy named 'Game Boy' Miller, who—unbeknownst to me—was one of the top-ten most-wanted men in America. Here he is with five other guys and some broads, and just as I was preparing to step on stage, the owner of the club [Moe Dalitz] comes up and whispers to me, 'Game Boy Miller is here celebrating his birthday. Wish him a happy birthday.' So I say 'Okay.'

"I walk up on stage and say, 'Ladies and gentlemen, we have the celebration of a birthday tonight.' And I start singing: 'Happy birthday to you, happy birthday to you, happy birthday dear Game Boy ...' No sooner did I get out the words *'Game Boy'* than a bottle flew past me. The guys he was with grabbed me and were taking me into the washroom when the bartender [Gorcey] stepped in and said, 'Listen, the kid did not know.'"

The life of a solo artist was not only tough, it could be downright deadly. The audiences, fueled by alcohol, could be brutal. You had to obviously deal with hecklers as well as other. More dangerous, circumstances. In August 1945, Joey was working the Casablanca Roadhouse in South Jersey when thieves wielding Tommy guns entered through the rear of the building. One of them ordered Joey to "keep talking," and Joey did just that, even as one of the intruders cracked a woman in the jaw with the butt of his gun. "She spit a ring out on the table," says Joey, who remembers that he stood up there on the stage and "did the same Edward G. Robinson impression thirty-five times."

In a 1987 interview with the author, former bootlegger Moe Dalitz recalled his friendship with Joey Bishop. In the early 1930s, Dalitz ran the Midwest bootlegging operations out of Cleveland. His associate was the Lertzmans' family friend, Maxie Diamond. Through Maxie, Rick became acquainted with Dalitz. After serving as an officer in World War II as a laundry quartermaster in New York City (and living in the Hotel Savoy-Plaza), he took over construction of Wilbur Clark's Desert Inn in 1950. However, Dalitz, who had seen what unconstrained publicity could do to those with checkered backgrounds, was smart enough to stay out of the limelight. In addition to helping to create the modern Las Vegas, Dalitz supported a host of charitable causes and helped to establish what is now the University of Nevada, Las Vegas; reportedly, he was the first thousand-dollar contributor and helped collect money to build the $100,000 football field.

He also helped engineer a million-dollar loan from the Teamsters Union pension fund to build Sunrise Hospital, setting the stage for other Teamster loans to Las Vegas commercial projects and, ultimately, through the mob's control of the pension fund, to mob infiltration of casinos in Las Vegas. Along with the Desert Inn, Dalitz helped fund and run two other casinos in Las Vegas: the Showboat and the Stardust. The former appeared to be free of mob infiltration, but the latter became synonymous with a massive "skim" of profits that went to Midwestern mobsters.

In the 1960s, Dalitz continued to develop some of the premier institutions of modern Las Vegas, including what is now the Las Vegas Convention and Visitors Authority, the Las Vegas Convention Center, and the Nevada Resort Association. In 1967, he sold his interest in the Desert Inn to reclusive billionaire Howard Hughes, who had moved into the top floor of the hotel. In 1969, Dalitz sold his interest in the Stardust to a mob associate, which would turn out to be a smart move, as the hotel ultimately became a target of federal and state investigators.

By the 1970s, Dalitz was fêted by Nevada's governors, state Supreme Court justices, and other community leaders. But he was still publicly associated with the mob. In 1975, *Penthouse* magazine ran a story that suggested Dalitz was using mob-controlled Teamsters money to build a resort in California. Dalitz sued the magazine for defamation. He won an apology from *Penthouse* but dropped the suit. As late as 1980, Dalitz was involved in the development of a hotel-casino in downtown Las Vegas called the Sundance, but he had to defer management of the property to others when he realized he could not get a license from the Nevada regulators because of his mob contacts. The Sundance later became Fitzgerald's, and today is the D Resort.

Joey, the master politician, had dealt with these characters all of his life and was well liked by the mobsters who ran Vegas, starting with Moe Dalitz, Louis Rothkopf, Gus Greenbaum, Carl Cohen, Meyer Lansky, and, of course, Mickey Cohen—the Jewish arm of Murder, Inc.

Los Angeles mob boss Jack Dragna was infuriated by the Jewish mobsters taking control of Vegas. The Desert Inn, which opened April 24, 1950, symbolized the fulfilment of assorted dreams. Characteristically, the name in lights above the $5 million casino was not that of any member of the Cleveland Syndicate. Indeed, if the Kefauver Committee had not come to Cleveland and Los Angeles, the involvement by the Cleveland boys might not have become common knowledge. The name that they put in lights, the front man, was Wilbur Clark. It was Wilbur Clark's Desert Inn, in 1950, that the source of Clark's capital became known—and only then because certain members of the Cleveland Syndicate applied to the Nevada Tax Commission for gambling licenses. No syndicate member doubted that, if necessary, proper arrangements could be made in West Virginia, or anywhere else, to operate illegally. But the very concept of legal gambling held a fascination. For a quarter of a century, the leaders of the syndicate had operated in the shadows. They had made plenty of money, and perhaps had a lot of fun in the process, but they were pushing middle age now. There was an increasing yen for respectability.

In Newport, Kentucky, the syndicate surrendered nothing of value. In Las Vegas, it gained the Desert Inn and all that it symbolized. With Rothkopf's name out, the Nevada Tax Commission took a deep breath and accepted his partners. Respectability had been achieved at last. Shortly thereafter, a Rothkopf family member appeared. Lou Rothkopf, his nephew, along with Allan Rosen, represented the second generation, college-trained and clean. Bernard had attended Ohio's Wesleyan University. While he had obtained solid experience working in syndicate clubs around Cleveland, he had never been arrested. Married and the father of two daughters, he was the personification of respectability. Given minor administrative duties at first, he soon advanced.

Not unlike Mario Puzo's *The Godfather*, wherein Don Corleone wanted his son Michael to become a college-educated, respected member of society, Moe Dalitz, Gus Greenbaum, Lou Rothkopf, Carl Cohen, and the rest of the Cleveland Mafia sought to accomplish this within their own families in Las Vegas. This was the world that Joey Bishop was a part of when he was taken under the wing of noted mob bosses who were steadily taking control of Las Vegas.

At the top of the heap and in control of the highest-grossing hotel/casino, the Desert Inn, was Moe Dalitz. In an extended interview with the author, Dalitz fondly recalled Joey Bishop. "He was a good kid," Dalitz said. "Very bright. His mind was very fast and he was always quick on his feet. He worked for a couple of years for Maxie [Diamond] at the Casablanca Club [in Shaker Heights, Ohio] and at the Mounds. He always was quite popular. He traveled the circuit of clubs that I was associated with in Chicago, Cincinnati, Detroit, Youngstown, and Pittsburgh. I enlisted in the Army in 1942—I became an officer. I helped Joey get into Special Services when he was drafted. He was assigned to Fort Sam Houston in San Antonio . . . never any trouble. A good family man. We watched over Joey."

It seems that Dalitz was implying that Joey was protected by the "boys" even in the military by receiving a cushy position in Texas, out of the action in Europe and Japan. Joey spent three years entertaining the troops in hospitals near Fort Sam Houston in San Antonio.

Dalitz continued: "After the war, Joey played many of the clubs that guys like Danny Thomas spent time at, such as Chez Parée [in Chicago]; Joey and Sylvia were always good people. He drew good crowds and he was well liked. Club bosses took a liking to him as he kept his nose clean and his material didn't ruffle any feathers . . . I never heard a bad word about Joey."

Joey was the fair-haired boy of the mob club owners. While they were acknowledged as "independent," the truth is that they worked for the syndicate. For example, while first Monte Proser, then Jules Podell, were called the "owners" of New York's famed Copacabana, they essentially worked for Frank Costello and his gang.

Maxie Diamond was one of the leaders of the Mafia-owned clubs based in Cleveland in the 1930s and '40s. He was behind placing William Presser as head of the Teamsters Union. He also was part of the group that financed Clevelander Billy Weinberger's takeover of Caesars Palace in Las Vegas, first under the created title of "Food and Beverage Manager" and, in 1968, as president of Caesars. He later became president of Bally Manufacturing (they built slot machines and owned casinos). Maxie was also one of the owners of the clubs (with Moe Dalitz), such as El Dumpo, where Joey Bishop got his start with the syndicate.

Diamond was a close family friend of the author and worked for the Lertzmans' family business for over twenty years after he "retired" from the "rackets." Maxie recalled, "It was important to us that we had top-notch entertainment. It was all part of the ambience we tried to create. While he would be appearing at our clubs in the inner city, Joey would work the late shows out at the Mounds Club."

The Mounds Club was a full-scale casino that was adjacent to a racetrack in the "horsey country" county of Geauga County—about thirty-five miles east of Cleveland. It had the full protection of local law enforcement and was run very much like a Las Vegas casino.

According to Shecky Greene, it was part of the job of a nightclub comic to accommodate the "bosses" and appear at their illegal casinos, private clubs, and special events.

"You did it, or else," recalls Greene. "You always made those special favors, and much of it was gratis. They might toss a girl at you for compensation, but not much more. They counted it as part of the salary you got at the club. And they were fronts—clubs in Chicago were owned by guys like Sam "MoMo" Giancana. New York had Frank Costello owning the joints like the Copacabana, Latin Casino. Whether you were booked by Jules Stein at MCA or Abe Lastfogel at William Morris—they were all linked together. It was a network. Hey, listen—you had no fucking choice. You either worked for them or you didn't work. They owned the machines and vending with Bally, the food and beverage—they controlled everything. You learned to get along and you did good. However, I've always heard guys like Danny Thomas, Joey, Eddie Fisher, and the rest talk about how great these wise guys were to work for. That's just not true. Many were *meshuga*. Catch them on the wrong day, you got slapped around. Make the wrong remark—you could walk out limping. It was no piece of cake . . . Look at Joe E. Lewis. He went to work for a competing mob in Chicago and they cut his vocal cords. He nearly died. Yet he went back to work for them for the rest of his life."

This was corroborated by Joey, who told the author, "When they called, you did your job. I was the emcee at one of Sam Giancana's daughters' weddings. I think I was appearing at the Chez Parée at the time, but his daughter's wedding took priority. Who am I to argue?"

The fear that had been placed so prominently in the comics came from witnessing an occasional act of horrific violence at the hands of one of these wise guys. Charles Dayton, the son of actor/comic/singer/producer Danny Dayton, told the author of a shared, traumatizing experience involving his father and Joey:

"My dad and his then-wife, Dagmar, were on the bill with Joey Bishop at the Copacabana. At the end of each show, they would sometimes meet and greet celebrities or known mobsters between shows as the bosses wanted to make them feel like a big deal. So, Joey and my dad went over to say hello to this mob guy and Frank Costello and his goon push them out of the way. They start slamming this guy's head on the table and blood is flying everywhere. Joey and my dad are just standing there, stunned. Then Costello cuts out the guy's tongue. Seriously. Joey and my dad just slink away.

"The next day, the NYC detectives call them in for questioning on what they saw. It turns out that both Joey and my dad had amnesia. As my dad said, 'You kept your mouth shut and your eyes closed. And the mob trusted them to do that—or else. My dad said there were lots of times he saw violence happen—just not to him or Joey. They loved the comics."

Joey learned the business from the ground up. As he explained: "Working the small dumps and clubs was my apprenticeship. My college. I earned my B.A. in comedy in clubs like the El Dumpo. Those club bosses were my professors." Joey slowly built his act by trial and error. He carefully honed his timing and stage persona that evolved over the years through what Joey called "the school of hard knocks."

What made his journey worthwhile was that he had the luxury of being one of the comics that the head of the William Morris Agency, "Uncle" Abe Lastfogel, kept a watchful eye on. Like Lastfogel's other fair-haired boy, Danny Thomas, he thought that Bishop—who was endorsed by Moe Dalitz and Billy Weinberger—was destined for national exposure. He assigned one of his best agents (and one of his closest friends), Harry Kalcheim, to help guide Joey's career. They had Joey hire another Philadelphia native, Charles "Chubby" Goldfarb, as his road manager.

Despite their needed connection to the mob owners, Lastfogel was quite conservative. A square in stature, he wore conservative suits, his signature bow tie, was always smoking a cigar, and was rather soft-spoken. Often at his side was his wife, Frances, who was the yin to his yang. She was a short, heavyset woman whose vocabulary could make a sailor blush. She was an ex-vaudeville star, so she had that loud stage voice she projected as well. Blunt and loud, she sometimes got Abe's point across without having to raise his voice. When the legendary Hearst newspapers' Broadway gossip columnist Walter Winchell, a well-known scandalmonger, wrote some unkind remarks about Joey in a column, many feared for Winchell's well-being. According to Joey, Frances went at Winchell until he was nearly shriveled up into a ball, until "Uncle" Abe called off his wife. Being with Lastfogel made Joey feel safe and protected.

Sylvia was especially thrilled when her husband was booked into the Vine Gardens Inn, on Chicago's North Side. This was Sylvia's former haunt, and much of her family still lived there. Joey was originally booked for a two-week stand at the club, which stretched into a record-breaking forty-nine weeks. Much as it did for Danny Thomas, word spread quickly about Joey, and in no time, he had gained a solid following. When he went to see the popular bandleader Russ Carlyle at Chicago's big-time mob-run club, Chez Parée, he learned that this establishment had a hidden, adjacent casino as well.

Carlyle played an important part in promoting Joey's career. He had caught Joey's act at the Vine Gardens. Bishop worked clean, which Carlyle liked. The bandleader needed a comic and they tried out some *schtick* and banter, which clicked. Joey could do a "give and take" with the band, and audiences loved it. Thus, Joey was booked in the Chez Parée and, according to Irv Kupcinet, became the first comic in Chicago nightclub history to make the jump from a neighborhood club—the Vine Gardens—directly to the big time. Joey, with the Russ Carlyle Band and noted singer Tony Martin, starred in their own show for forty-nine straight weeks. Twenty-eight-year-old Joey had gone from being a $250-per-week comic to $1,000-a-week headliner, seemingly overnight.

"I even fit in earlier gigs at the Oriental [Theatre] when Chez Parée was dark one night," Joey recalled. "Sylvia was happy—She was by her family and we were living like kings."

Joey was happy to have Sylvia with him on the road. She had been in fragile health since undergoing surgeries at the beginning of their marriage in 1941. She was also pregnant, years after the couple had given up hope of having children. Their son, Larry, was born on August 4, 1947, in Philadelphia, near Joey's family, who looked after Sylvia and the baby while Joey continued to work in Chicago. Joey's niece Marlene, the daughter of his older brother Morris, also helped Sylvia. After receiving his honorable discharge in 1945, Joey rented a second-floor apartment over Kaplan's butcher shop. It was a great location, as it was across the street from his parents' apartment and bicycle shop in the old South Philly neighborhood. With Joey and his new baby son under the watchful eye of his parents and the rest of the clan, he could relax and focus on his career for the first time since being in the service.

In Chicago, Joey started to hit his stride. He struck a chord with audiences and established the persona for which he would become known. Not quite deadpan, his face was nevertheless unsmiling; his sardonic attitude had a touch of Rodney Danger-field's "I don't get no respect," along with the flippancy of Mort Sahl, the self-deprecating humor of Jackie Vernon, and the dour wittiness of the great Fred Allen. This was the unique mix that became Joey Bishop. He soon gained more recognition and a larger following. He was even being copied by other comics.

It was at Chez Parée in 1948 that Danny Thomas had gained a following, just as Abe Lastfogel had planned. Like Thomas, Last-fogel rightly believed Joey was seasoned enough for a big-time venue, as a review in *Variety* had pointed out. Joey's straight man was Jack Soo, who would later be known as the harried, Japanese American detective Nick Yamana on the television series *Barney Miller* in the late 1970s. Irv Kupcinet, whose "Kup's Column" was a popular feature in the *Chicago Sun-Times*, nicknamed Joey "The Frown Prince of Comedy," based on the fact that the "dour comic has a world-weary demeanor."

Another of author Lertzman's family friends was former Cleve-lander Carl Cohen (1913–1986), a Cleveland-based associate of Moe Dalitz. Like Dalitz, Cohen began his career as a bookie and operator in illegal gambling clubs operated by the Mayfield Road mob in Cleveland. "These were the very clubs where Bishop worked.

The mob moved Cohen to Las Vegas, where he became casi-no manager for the El Rancho in the 1940s and, in the following decade, the Sands Hotel and Casino. Cohen had a controlling interest in both resorts. He advanced to senior vice president of the Sands and, in 1973, became senior vice president of the newly opened MGM Grand Hotel.

Cohen would gain national notoriety in 1967 for an altercation at the Sands, during which he responded to Sinatra's drunken and aggressive behavior by punching him in the mouth, knocking out the caps from his front teeth. Cohen was a former professional boxer and stood about six four; Frank, by contrast, was five seven and scrawny.

Cohen took over the Sands with Jack Entratter, another Dalitz protégé. Cohen was instrumental in upgrading the resort amenities to make the Sands "the most magnetic and sparkling operation on the whole of the booming Strip." His efforts included the 1959 introduction of a high-stakes baccarat table and that much-publicized "floating crap game in the swimming pool." Cohen had one of the largest followings of high-stakes players, giving them preferential treatment, such as "secret rooms where there were no betting limits."

Cohen recalled his Cleveland days for the author: "Much of what we learned in the clubs we brought out to Vegas. At the Mounds Club [an illegal casino], we always brought in the top-notch entertainment and bands. We made it an experience. We had comics like Joey Bishop, Joe E. Lewis, Fat Jack [Leonard], and lots of guys who were just getting started. We had Dean, who was appearing at the Hollenden House with the Sammy Watkins Band. Dean lived in 'Little Italy' [in Cleveland] for a few years; he met and married Betty [his first wife] there."

Beyond his Las Vegas connection, Cohen's son, Allen Cohen (a.k.a. Cory Allen) was best known for his role as gang leader Buzz Gunderson in the 1955 James Dean film *Rebel Without a Cause*. In addition to doing supporting roles, he also became a leading director of such television shows as *Dallas*, *Hawaii Five-O*, *Hill Street Blues*, *The Rockford Files*, and *Star Trek*. He even won a Best Director Emmy for a 1981 episode of *Hill Street Blues*.

Allen Cohen, who passed away in 2010, once recalled for the author his years in Vegas with his father: "He was a no-nonsense guy. I do remember that one of his dearest friends from his Cleveland years was Moe Dalitz. He was also very close to others, like Benny [Bugsy] Siegel, Gus Greenbaum, and Jack Entratter. I later went to the University of California to study drama and left that life behind. However, many of Dad's friends in the business—from Dean Martin to Joey Bishop—were always helpful over the years."

The entertainment world and the underworld were seemingly entwined in a symbiotic relationship. If you wanted to succeed as an entertainer, you simply needed those connections. You needed a Moe Dalitz, or a Carl Cohen, or a Jack Entratter in your corner. And Joey Bishop became a master at courting the favors of these men.

Frank Sinatra's reputation as the beloved godson of the Mafia has become a part of his legend. While some of it is factual, much of it is not. *The Godfather*, which included the fictional character Johnny Fontane, who was supposedly "based" on Sinatra, was strictly a literary invention by the novel's author, Mario Puzo. Sinatra started to achieve fame in a big band that was more removed from the mob clubs. His game-changing Oscar-winning role of Maggio in *From Here to Eternity* (1953) was more the result of the campaigning of his superstar wife, Ava Gardner, and his agents at MCA, rather than Harry Cohn waking up with a horse's head in his bed.

While Frank loved the aura of being "Mafia-friendly," it was Joey Bishop who had close relationships with many in the underworld. The story of the murder of the Mafia hit-man Jack Whelan is emblematic of Joey's loyalty to the "boys," becoming involved in one of their noted hits that made headlines in Los Angeles for several years. The story of Joey's involvement as a witness for Mickey Cohen was a real-life *film noir*. Joey was used as the decoy to cover up a murder—a hit on one of the local enforcers.

The site of this murder was Rondelli's Italian Restaurant, a popular eatery co-owned by Mickey Cohen, located at 13359 Ventura Boulevard in Sherman Oaks. It also was a hangout for those in organized crime. On December 2, 1959, a prominent mobster named Jack "The Enforcer" Whalen, a.k.a. Jack O'Hara, was shot between the eyes at a booth occupied by Mickey Cohen. At that time, Mickey was cultivating publicity and had become L.A.'s most famous and media-friendly criminal. Chief of Police William Parker took personal charge of the Whalen murder investigation, which turned up such evidence as a gun belonging to Cohen's late bodyguard Johnny Stompanato in a trash bin behind the restaurant. Waiting outside the restaurant was Cohen's six-foot-five-inch-tall bodyguard, Max Baer Jr. (the actor who later portrayed Jethro Bodine on the long-running CBS sitcom *The Beverly Hillbillies*).

Cohen was booked for the murder, released when an associate copped to the deed, and later indicted on new evidence. His trial ended in a hung jury.

Johnny Stompanato, whose gun was used in the murder and found in the restaurant's trash bin, was the boyfriend who had been stabbed to death the year before (1958) in the *boudoir* of actress Lana Turner, allegedly by her daughter, Cheryl Crane.

Also questioned was Los Angeles TV anchor Baxter Ward, who later had a long elective career on the Los Angeles County Board of Supervisors. Ward was married to Whalen's daughter, Karen.

Joey Bishop was supposed to be having dinner with Cohen that night, but he claimed he had played forty-five holes of golf that day and asked for a raincheck. The chair next to Cohen, where Whalen was shot, was being held for Joey. Bishop, supposedly ignorant of what had occurred, called Cohen at the restaurant to apologize for the "no-show" and invited Cohen and his friends to catch his act later that night at Cloister's (formerly the Mocambo on the Sunset Strip), which had been run by mobster Charley Morrison. Bishop was leaving the next day for Las Vegas to take part in the shooting of *Ocean's 11*. Joey loved Rondelli's *gnocchi*, which was made fresh every Wednesday. It was the closing night at Cloister's for him and Cohen usually tagged along to watch his buddy perform. Joey's agent, Joe DeCarlo, was to drive Joey to Rondelli's, then to Cloister's.

Joey testified that Cohen was supposed to spend the evening with him and that he had absolutely no idea what happened to Whalen. In the end, the hit was made by Cohen flunky Sam LoCigno, who would take the rap for a $50,000 payday and a promise to secure him a short sentence, as they would claim self-defense. The story all but mirrors that of Michael Corleone in *The Godfather* when he pleaded self-defense (after hiding in Italy for a year) for the murder of a corrupt police captain and a mobster at a Manhattan restaurant.

Joey Bishop proudly related to the author that Mario Puzo had personally told him that he had based the dinner scene between Michael Corleone, Police Captain Mark McCluskey, and "Turk" Sollozzo on the killing at Rondelli's. Puzo said he studied the picture of Whelan's dead body at the restaurant, shot between the eyes, when he wrote that episode in his book.

"I was definitely the cover," Joey said emphatically. "I never lied in my testimony. It was the *emmes* [Yiddish for *truth*]. I owed a certain loyalty to Mickey. He was always helpful. I worked in many of his clubs, and he was good to me."

Chapter 4
The Voice:

Frank Sinatra and the Midas Touch

Francis Albert Sinatra lights up a Chesterfield, c. 1945.

For two decades (or more), whatever Ol' Blue Eyes touched turned to gold. A film project that included Frank was guaranteed to reap box-office gold. He took Capitol Records to new heights just as they hit their stride. Las Vegas and the Sands Hotel's neon lights shone even more brightly when he was headlining. If the Chairman wore a cardigan sweater, sales went through the roof. Any actress that was rumored to be involved with Sinatra became suddenly bankable—Angie Dickinson, Shirley MacLaine, Juliet Prowse, and Mia Farrow, to name but a few. Martinis became the drink of choice for the white-collar working man when Frank uttered, "I feel sorry for people that don't drink, because when they wake up in the morning, that is the best they are going to feel all day."

As Shawn Levy colorfully wrote in *Rat Pack Confidential*:

> He concocted an intoxicating brew of money, power, talent, romance, gall, a nexus of showbiz and muscle, politics and glamour, a brilliant netherworld spinning at 33 1/3 with himself stock-still at the center, conducting it all with his mind.

By 1952, Joey personified the Webster definition of a journeyman: "a worker or sports player who is reliable, but not outstanding." Reliability was an important job requirement in the mercurial world of nightclub entertainment. As the quantity and quality of the nightspots multiplied and expanded following World War II, it was getting tougher to fit the slots with solid performers who could fill the showrooms, sell the drinks, and keep their noses clean. Much of the time, the comic was booked not only for his skills as a monologist, but also as the M.C.—the master of ceremonies. In many of the bigger clubs, like the Chez Parée or The Latin Quarter, it wasn't enough just to employ a comic. They needed a popular orchestra leader (it was an "orchestra" in the clubs whether you had a six-piece band or thirty-five musicians), a singer, and the M.C., or comic. Those comics, singers, and musicians lived on the road. Their hours were hardly typical as they worked the night shift and slept much of the day. They called their venues of employment "saloons" and were there, as Rose Marie told the author, "to sell the booze, get 'em drunk, and get them to the tables." Many of the clubs, of course, were fronts for casinos.

Back in the forties, according to comedy historian Kliph Nesteroff, "nine out of ten venues that stand-up comedians would play were controlled or owned by the mob." Mobs also controlled boxing rackets where reliable fighters were deemed "stand-up fighters." Those titles were also used for other specialists, including comedians. Thus, the birth of the "stand-up comedian." Ask anyone who has plied this profession and he (or she) will tell you it is anything but easy.

"There isn't a lonelier life in the world," Joey admitted. "I was always the 'stranger' in town. I missed Sylvia and the kid. I'd spend eight, ten weeks playing clubs, came home, got a new toothbrush, then headed out again."

"My dad just loved Joey," remembered Sandy Hackett, Buddy Hackett's son. "They would spend hours swapping stories when they were on the road. They both loved what they were doing, but it was hard on the road. They really missed their families."

A great many comics, regardless of their level of talent, have been forgotten. Case in point: Charlie Manna. Born in the Bronx in 1920, he and Joey were only two years apart. Manna, like Joey, kicked around the business starting in the late 1930s. He worked in the Catskills and later played the same circle of clubs. His style of comedy was conceptual, based on incongruity, such as the routine in which an astronaut balks at being launched until someone finds his box of crayons, containing "a green, an orange and two blacks." He also used his musical training in such routines as "Alcatraz—the Musical," and "La Bonanza," an opera parody based on the popular TV Western. Manna hit the national spotlight with appearances on *The Tonight Show, The Perry Como Show, The Garry Moore Show, The Ed Sullivan Show, The Jackie Gleason Show*, and many others. He died at the age of fifty-one in 1971.

Phyllis Diller, who started playing the club circuit in the early 1950s, told the author, "It was Manna who taught me the basics of standup and helped me structure my routine when I was the new kid on the block. It was at New York's Bon Soir nightclub that Charlie gave me the greatest advice about how to get on: Quickly tell five of your hottest jokes and then run with them. Get the audience laughing for real; don't make it a phony deal. He taught me there are two varieties of comedy: funny and not funny."

Manna is used as a comparison to Bishop as a respected, dependable comic with a similar career path. Both comics were liked by the mob bosses. But there was one major reason that Joey's career took off and why he is remembered today: The Voice. The link, that connection between Joey and Frank, was born in 1952, just prior to Frank's reemergence as a superstar.

That historic meeting between the singer and the comic took place at The Latin Quarter, located at 1580 Broadway and 47th Street in Manhattan.

"Frank and I clicked," Joey said. "He liked that I didn't take bullshit from the audience. When a joke fell flat or if there was a rowdy crowd, I just kept plowing through. You know, by then I was doing my act for about fifteen years, so I knew the rhythm, the crowd, and I took no prisoners. Frank told me that night, 'What you got is your own. Don't change it.'"

Frank and Joey had much in common. Frank was only two years Joey's senior and they had both started in the business in their teens. Joey's quick wit soon became legendary in the comic underworld.

Shecky Greene told the author, "Frank once told the story about Joey following Danny Thomas at New York's Policemen's Benefit Show at Madison Square Garden in 1946. Thomas was at the top of his game and his stories had the crowd in tears from laughter. I mean, he was *killing* them. You never want to follow that. I mean, it's a graveyard. So, what did Joey do? He walked out onto the stage, coat over his shoulder and leaned into the mike and said, "What Danny Thomas said goes for me, too," and then he just slowly walked off the stage. It was a perfect comic moment to understand it, but Joey had that quick comeback and the other comics respected that."

By 1952, Abe Lastfogel, the high and mighty guru of the William Morris Agency, thought Joey was ready for bigger things. Frank was set to play Bill Miller's Riviera Club in Fort Lee, New Jersey, a very plush establishment that attracted the headliners. Bill Miller would soon make the jump to Las Vegas, where he would get a 10% ownership in the Sahara, and then set about to turn the hotel/casino into a great venue for entertainers.

Norm Brokaw, the future head of the Morris Agency, recalls, "I was sent to Abe to watch over Joey's act. He was quite nervous being the [opening act] for Frank for the first time. Joey was by that time being introduced as 'The Frown Prince of Comedy,' and, somehow, it was great chemistry. I mean, Joey was the perfect opener. And by the second night, Joey was coming out and trading barbs with Frank. I think Frank asked Joey to come back out and it clicked. Not a long bit, but it worked."

Joey remembered, "I didn't know the Riviera stage revolved, and on opening night, Frank pushed me on the stage. And when the stage didn't stop, Frank told the crowd, 'Place your bets, 'cause I don't think he's gonna stop!'"

Joey continued, "Frank spoke of my talents when you couldn't get a good argument. He saw me working in some third-rate joint and he took me into his act at the Riviera. It's the first time I was in a 'class' club and the first time the right people saw me work. Frank knew I'm not a fast act. I need time. On different occasions, Frank has talked a club manager into giving him less time on the bill and letting me have twenty-five minutes instead of eighteen."

Brokaw continues: "We knew they clicked, and Frank adored Joey. Joey started opening for Frank in clubs in the East, like D'Amato's 500 Club in Atlantic City and the Copacabana. Joey became known as 'Sinatra's comic,' and that was what ignited his career. We were able to book him as a headliner in clubs like the Copacabana because he had been blessed over by Frank. By that time, everything Frankie touched turned to gold. Fortunately, for Joey, he had Frank sprinkle stardust on him."

By 1955, Frank convinced Joey to hire Warren Cowan, of the Rogers and Cowan public relations firm, to become his publicist. Cowan had replaced the great George Evans as Frank's guru and was working magic for him. Warren Cowan became Joey's trusted friend and confidant for the rest of his life. As Cowan told the author in 2007, "Joey really had to be pushed into hiring us. He knew Frank was right. Frank was clicking on all cylinders by then when we took Joey under our wing. This was after he had been opening for Frank at clubs like the Copa and such. It was in 1956 that Frank was starring in a Western called *Johnny Concho*, which was shot at Paramount. We talked Paramount into opening the film at the old Paramount Theater in New York, where Frank had hit it big with the bobbysoxers in the forties. We would show the film, followed by Frank reuniting with his old bandleader Tommy Dorsey and his brother Jimmy Dorsey. The Dorsey brothers had not talked in years, and Frank convinced them to end the feud and reunite with him for a week at the Paramount. It became a huge event. We got loads of traction. Then Frank asked Joey to be the opening act. It was incredible exposure. Huge. He gets lots of press and buzz, lots of excitement. I remember being in a car with Frank and asking him why *he* didn't manage Joey. Get a cut. I told Frank, '*You* found him. *You* discovered him. Shouldn't you have piece of his future?' And Frank, to his credit, said, 'Nah, I don't want to get into that, but Joey's on his way. The kid deserves it. He earned it.' And that was that. Joey became a name, He got booked on *Ed Sullivan* and other shows and he really took off after that."

Joey felt he had hit the big time two years earlier, in 1954. He recalled, "Frank had asked me to open for him at the Copa. He had just won the Oscar for *From Here to Eternity* and was hot again. The place was mobbed. I came out, sized up the place, and said, 'Look at this crowd! Wait till Frank's following shows up.' In the middle of my act, Marilyn Monroe walks in all by herself, draped in a white ermine coat and, of course, all heads turn towards her. I looked at her and said, 'I told you to sit in the truck.' That stopped the show. At ringside, sitting together were Victor Jory and Gabby Hayes. I introduced them and said, 'For a minute, I thought I was watching the late, late show.' After the show, I went over to Lindy's and when I walked in, the whole place went crazy. After that, I was on my way."

Chapter 5
Setting the Trap

The Start of the Rat Pack

(Left to right): Frank, Dean, Sammy, Peter and Joey, 1960.

The final version of what became known as the Rat Pack was essentially a business association of comics and singers who were at the top of their game. Each of its members was successful on his own merits. It was not a publicist's concoction, and it lacked that stench of phoniness. It was a loosely based amalgamation of successful artists who saw an opportunity to capitalize on their individual success and collect a fat paycheck. While they absolutely enjoyed the camaraderie and friendship, which made the grind of doing the same show every night easier—and took the pressure off working as a single—it offered a great chance for publicity to enhance their careers. Each of its members was savvy in garnering great PR. It was guilt by association. They became trendsetters. They timed their peak at the ideal moment in American culture.

Frank Sinatra, much like others in the entertainment industry who would survive for decades, was a master of reinvention. He went from being a big band singer, then became the idol of the bobbysoxers. When that phase faded, he morphed into an award-winning character actor, followed by that of a romantic balladeer, then as a leading man and light comedian in films. His next phase was to become the leader of a cool pack of hip, middle-aged men who lived the lives that many married men envied and through whom they could live vicariously.

Entwined in the creation of the Rat Pack was the mob. And since it was based in Los Angeles, Mickey Cohen was part of the fabric. Despite all of Cohen's cumulative troubles and his problematic relationship with the Kennedys, Mickey still played his role as an honorary member of the developing Rat Pack. Whether it was social or political, his efforts never ceased, not even while he awaited his pending tax trial.

Let's start with Sinatra.

Frank did not like to be alone. Through his different manifestations, he had several groups, cliques to which he assigned a name. When he was with the Dorsey band, he had his bandmates. As a solo recording artist, he had an entourage that included Columbia Records executive Manie Sacks, composer Jimmy Van Heusen, and lyricist Sammy Cahn. Frank called the group "The Varsity." Like his other groups, The Varsity hit all the nightspots, golfed together, went to boxing matches, and fucked around with the broads they shared.

It was during this period in the late 1940s and early '50s that Frank gained the reputation for being "friendly" with the wise guys in New York City. Hanging out with The Varsity, Frank knew many of the mobsters and Times Square sharpies—not unlike his alter ego Nathan Detroit, the character he portrayed in the film version of *Guys and Dolls* (1955).

Also part of the clan was the earlier mentioned Jimmy Tarantino. Tarantino, one of Sinatra's pals on the East Coast, reacquainted himself with the Chairman in Los Angeles. Formerly a mob-connected boxing writer, he ran *Hollywood Night Life*, a precursor to the notorious *Confidential Magazine*, and later, *The National Enquirer*. Sinatra's supposedly good buddy Tarantino extorted (through Cohen) fifteen thousand dollars from Sinatra, a married man with children, to keep his philandering ways out of the scandal sheet. Frank was often the sucker for many of these hoods. Frank wanted to be liked and respected by the mobsters, and they saw him as an easy mark.

Cohen wrote about his friendship with Sinatra through his rough period in the early fifties and how he persevered with Frank for three decades. He also mentioned Joey Bishop, whom he called one of his "dearest and most loyal of friends. A brother."

While Joey seemed a bit more streetwise than Frank did about these gangsters, he remained loyal to those he respected and needed for their connections and protection.

It was inevitable that Joey and Frank, with their mutual acquaintances in the underworld, would allow each other a sense of familiarity. Both Frank and Joey had a streetwise swagger that gave them the Runyonesque charm that endeared them to audiences. Both had affected a "wise-ass" demeanor: Frank with his Hoboken attitude, and Joey with his similar South Philly cockiness.

Since he began his career in 1938, Joey had spent most of those twenty-plus years appearing in clubs. Obviously, many of the clubs were, as Joey called them, "second-rate joints," but as he steadily gained a reputation, he ascended to clubs such as the Chez Parée, the Latin Quarter, and the Copa-cabana. For the first decade, Joey stuck to the clubs in the Midwest or on the East Coast. The farthest he would travel would be to Miami to "get out of the cold in the winter." By the late 1940s, Vegas was expanding—due to Bugsy Siegel's Fla-mingo Casino, Moe Dalitz's the Desert Inn, Carl Cohen's the Sands, Gus Greenbaum's El Rancho—and they brought Joey out for long stints. From Las Vegas, it was a short jump to Los Angeles, where he would appear at the legendary Mocambo or at clubs like Slapsie Maxie's, fronted by ex-boxer and comic actor "Slapsie" Maxie Rosenbloom.

Melody Doff, the actress whose father was the talented pro-ducer/agent Red Doff (who handled Mickey Rooney for decades), and her mother was Marilyn Morrison, whose first husband was singing superstar Johnnie Ray. Melody's grandfather was the owner of the Mocambo, the mobbed-up Charlie Morrison.

"The Mocambo was the hot nightclub in Hollywood for nearly three decades," Morrison told the author. "It was the Rat Pack incubator. Dean and Jerry played there. Sammy Davis Jr. was a favorite, as was Joey Bishop. When my grand-father died in 1957, everyone knew that he had left tremendous debt. Frank Sinatra called my grandmother and said, 'Mary, I have nothing to do for twelve days,' so he came in with his orchestra and played for two weeks, sold out every night to raise money. They gave my grandfather a sendoff funeral in style and put a sign on the door that said, 'Gone Fishing.'"

The Mocambo was the "in" spot during Hollywood's golden era. The modern version of The Mocambo opened on January 3, 1941, becoming an immediate success. The club had a Latin-Amer-ican-themed décor by Tony Duquette, which cost $100,000 (the equivalent of $1,703,394 in 2020). Along the walls were glass cag-es holding live cockatoos, macaws, seagulls, pigeons, and parrots. They had their own big band, and the club became one of the most popular dance-till-dawn spots in town. On any given night, one could bump into some of Hollywood's leading movie stars.

By the mid-1950s, the nucleus of the Rat Pack—Frank Sinatra, Dean Martin, and Sammy Davis Jr.—had relocated to Los Angeles.

Frank and his second wife, film star Ava Gardner; Dean and his second wife, Jeanne; Peter Lawford and his wife, Patricia Kennedy—schmoozed at the Los Angeles clubs, watching their buddies perform and drinking the night away.

Frank felt right at home in a club. He always had his entourage, men with whom he could schmooze, gamble, drink, laugh, find some action at the bars, go to the horse races or the boxing matches. He was no different than the so-called celebrities of the 2020 generation who need their "crew" or "posse" or whatever the colloquial term *du jour* happens to be. It was part of the spoils. However, this time he would be the "Chairman of the Board." And, in 1959, he was looking for some new best friends. His original "Clan" had dissipated. The members of the Holmby Hills Rat Pack had scattered due to death, illness, and broken relationships. Members had included Sinatra (pack master), Judy Garland (first vice-president), Lauren Bacall (den mother), Sid Luft (cage master), Humphrey Bogart (rat in charge of public relations), Irving "Swifty" Lazar (recording secretary and treasurer), Nathaniel Benchley (historian), David Niven, Katharine Hepburn, Spencer Tracy, George Cukor, Michael Romanoff, and Jimmy Van Heusen. In *The Moon's a Balloon*, the first of his vivid memoirs, actor David Niven confirms that the Rat Pack originally included him, but not Sammy Davis or Dean Martin.

This time Frank sought a more tightly woven pack of similar-aged, like-minded "boys" who would benefit greatly from being knighted by Mr. S. Each was nearly at (or had crossed) that forty-year threshold, the mid-life-crisis age. All were in a tier below Frank. Each needed a career boost that could only be achieved by becoming part of an exclusive boys' club with Sinatra at the helm.

Frank and the rest of the "Pack" would often be seen at the clubs, watching Sammy and his "uncle" Will Mastin, and his father, Sammy Davis Sr. The Will Mastin Trio played all the Los Angeles hot spots.

In an interview with the author, actress Eileen Wesson recalled: "My father [actor-producer-writer Dick Wesson] and his brother [Gene Wesson] grew up with Sammy Davis Jr. They were White men, abandoned by their parents and were practically raised by

Sammy Davis Sr. and Will Mastin. To everyone, it was a frater-nity of performers. Everyone loved watching the others perform. The clubs were open all night, so it gave them the opportunity to check out the other acts. Frank loved Sammy, or he'd watch Martin & Lewis at the clubs, trying out new material. They loved the comics like Buddy Hackett, Don Rickles, Jan Murray, Alan King, and Joey Bishop. It was like a big fraternity. At the clubs, my father and his buddy Mickey Rooney would hang out all night with the 'boys.'"

As stated earlier, Bishop was rather reluctant to discuss "The Clan" during his several interviews with the author; he preferred focusing on his solo career. He would, however, frequently state that he was the backbone of the group, the "glue" that held the performances together.

One of the routines he devised involved his standing backstage with an open mic while Sinatra sang one of his many standards, such as "Try a Little Tenderness" (written by Jimmy Campbell, Reg Connelly, and Harry M. Woods). With perfect timing, Joey would inject some succinct dig at his famous colleague. It went something like this: "I'm not much to look at," sang Frank ("You can say that again," opined Joey.) "Nothing to see." ("If you stand sideways they'll mark ya absent.") "Just glad I'm livin'." ("Dean, he thinks he's alive!") "And happy to be. I've got a woman." ("He found a broad!") "Who's crazy 'bout me." ("She must be nuts.") "She's funny." ("She's queer.")

"Ya see, I could get away with *carte blanche*," Bishop boasted. "Frank liked it so much that he told me to do it every night. I didn't have to ask if it was all right."

Frank, Dino, Sammy, and Peter were labeled by a magazine writer as the "four kings." Joey is "the most regal joker, who shuf-fled the king's men in the wildest shows ever dealt from any night-club." Sinatra was quick to acknowledge this. At the end of every Rat Pack performance, Frank would ask the audience, "Did you like the show?" While the crowd applauded and cheered, Sinatra would give a theatrical wave of the hand to Joey and say, "Well, there's the guy who put it together . . . *son of a gun!*"

"Frank was Frank," Joey said. "There was no phoniness. When we were playing at the Fontainebleau Hotel in Miami Beach, I went to my suite and saw a nineteen-year-old girl ready to jump off the balcony if she didn't get to meet Sinatra. It was two-thirty or three in the morning, and she had given the bellhop ten bucks to let her in. I told her I'd see what I could do for her. I went to Frank's suite, but he was already in bed. Joe DiMaggio was playing cards with some people, though, so I told them. But Frank overheard what was going on and said he'd be right over. He came with flowers and a picture and invited her to the show with her mother and father. 'Joey, take care of the reservations,' he said. That's Frank Sinatra."

On the subject of the group's name, it seemed to vary with the times. An early moniker was The Clan, an unfortunate choice to be sure. Out of deference to Sammy Davis Jr., a Black man who had converted to Judaism, the name was dropped in favor of the Rat Pack. Sinatra always claimed that he disliked the term. He much preferred "The Summit." But whatever it was called, it could never be described as being politically correct.

"I gave Dean one of the finest lines ever," Joey claimed. "The whole world knew Sammy had converted, so I told Dean to walk out, pick up Sammy and say, 'I'd like to thank the NAACP for this award.' You never heard such screams." Joey also took credit for one of Dean's opening jokes: "When he came onstage, I told him the band would vamp for ten seconds. Then he would walk over there and ask, 'How long have I been out here?' He had just walked out! You never heard a laugh like that. I helped Dean a lot."

In one of our interviews, Joey said bluntly that the only reason Peter Lawford was part of The Rat Pack was because his brother-in-law JFK was president. Joey had been more diplomatic when he spoke to James Spada, the author of *Peter Lawford: The Man Who Kept the Secrets*: "Peter held his own, but he was well aware that a lot of people wondered, 'What is he doing up there with those four guys?' I mean, if you take anybody away from the show without hurting it, it would be Peter. He must have sensed that the only reason for being there was his relationship to Jack Kennedy. And that would make anyone feel ill at ease."

Joey devised a bit that Lawford was to perform during the show. Dressed as a busboy, he would walk through the audience and pick up a random plate from a customer's table. In a sly nod to his powerful brother-in-law, he would then comment, "Can you imagine what I'd be doing if he *didn't* win?" Joey was unhappy with Peter's line reading, and he told him so between performances. Lawford, an experienced actor, shot back: "Don't tell *me* how to read a line!" Sinatra, overhearing this exchange, walked over to Lawford and said coldly, "Say it the way Joey says or get the fuck out of the show." There was no further argument.

Sinatra's influence extended into virtually every area. Once, when the Pack was playing an engagement in Miami Beach, Frank, Dean, Sammy, and Peter were all ensconced in their plush suites at a five-star hotel. Joey, on the other hand, was stuck in a single room on the seventh floor. At one point, Frank asked Sammy where Joey was; "The seventh floor," Sammy answered. Frank angrily put in a call to the terrified hotel manager and said, "Unless Joey Bishop gets a suite, there will be *no* show this evening."

Moments later, there was an urgent knock at Joey's door. As he recalls it: "I opened it and a team of bellboys came running in. One removes the clothes from the closet, and another one packs up the bathroom, and a third one slides the drawers out and takes those. One word from Frank and I had a suite."

A major reason Joey was welcomed into Sinatra's circle was that he knew his place. For instance, Joey would never presume to dine at Frank's table unless he was expressly invited. Sinatra found this incredibly amusing.

"Goddammit," he said, laughing out loud, "How long does he have to be with me to know that he can eat with us?"

But Joey knew that he could not take undue liberties with the volatile singer.

"Maybe he was doing business, or he was angry at something," Joey said wisely. "I never, ever imposed, and I never thought I was his equal. He liked me, he hired me, and that was that."

Not many comedians could get away with doing jokes about the Chairman, but Joey knew how to draw a blow. Once, at a night spot in Miami Beach, the stage was occupied by three of show business's heaviest drinkers: Frank, Jackie Gleason, and Joe E. Lewis. All three performers were so gone that the manager became concerned that the show was quickly devolving into chaos. He went up to the comic and said, "Joey, *please*, you've got to do something." And he did.

"I walked out on the stage and said, 'Folks, this is the first time I've ever seen a stationary stage with revolving performers.'"

At their peak, during the winter months of 1959–1960, the Rat Pack shows were filling the Sands' Copa Room and the casino. Jack Entratter and Carl Cohen were wise enough to cut both Martin and Sinatra a piece of the pie at the hotel. He also gave each of them a cut of ownership in the Copa Room. Both men were pulling down a cool 100k weekly during their run at the Sands. In 1959 dollars, that was quite a haul, nearly $900,000 in today's currency. Reportedly, Sammy and Joey were getting about 25K weekly, although Joey claimed his cut was closer to 50k weekly. It was a win/win for everyone. And the mob bosses were thrilled with the grosses at the casino, which spilled over to the other casinos as well. It also created a larger market and garnered vast publicity for Las Vegas.

Former mayor and mob lawyer Oscar Goodman told the author, "More than anything, the Rat Pack period put Vegas on the map. It really made Vegas *the* hot spot. From that period, it spawned Caesars Palace, the Dunes, the Stardust, and many others. It moved from being a weekend spot for those in L.A. to an awareness internationally."

Shecky Greene, who held court for years in Las Vegas, said, "It helped everyone. The lounges where I played were jam-packed when the boys were in town. It helped guys like [Don] Rickles, even [Louis] Prima, hit their stride."

Joey Bishop was hitting his stride as well.

The Rat Pack epitomized the male-dominated era of the 1960s. It was far more than a loose amalgamation of friends in the entertainment business. It symbolized the attitudes of hipsters and cool cats. It effectively transformed a dusty cow town into a jet-age, adult theme park, complete with gambling and prostitution.

The group bestowed a Robin Hood–like admiration to murderous, underworld sociopaths who terrorized entire communities.

As for the key players, there was the ultimate entertainer and most influential singer of the 20th century. Then there was an insouciant singer of Italian songs, the ex-partner of the most popular film comedian of the day. Another was a short, Black, Jewish, one-eyed, singing-and-dancing sensation. Another is an upper-crust British pretty boy turned degenerate B-movie star actor—the brother-in-law to an ascendant politician. And holding them together is a stiff-shouldered comic with the quintessential Borscht Belt emcee's knack for needling one-liners. The architectonically sleek marquee of the Sands Hotel announces their presence simply by listing their names:

FRANK SINATRA
DEAN MARTIN
SAMMY DAVIS JR.
PETER LAWFORD
JOEY BISHOP

Around them an entire cast gathers: actors, comics, singers, songwriters, gangsters, politicians, willing women, as well as thousands of star-struck everyday folks who happily forked over pocketsful of money for the privilege of basking in their presence.

They had it all. Fame. Gorgeous women. A fabulous playground of a city and all the money in the world. The backing of fearsome crime lords and the blessing of the president of the United States. But the dark side, that razor-thin line between pleasure and debauchery, between swinging self-confidence and brutal arrogance, would take its toll. In four years' time, their great ride would be over, and show business would never be the same again.

Chapter 6
The Personals

Living the Suburban Life with Sylvia

Joey and Sylvia Bishop, c. 1965.

After Joey's triumphant engagement as Sinatra's comic at the Copacabana, William Morris and friends could pick and choose his gigs. His salary was inching up to nearly $2,500 for a week's engagement. Along with playing many of the better East Coast clubs in Chicago, New York, Miami, and Philadelphia, he even fit in a USO Tour at Travis Air Force Base in Northern California, along with Howard Keel, Keenan Wynn, and Debbie Reynolds.

Debbie Reynolds, the former MGM ingénue and a seasoned Las Vegas entertainer, told the author: "I first met Joey on that USO show. We met again when Eddie [Fisher, her husband at the time] and I were doing a tour for *Bundle of Joy* [their 1956 film]. Joey and Eddie became good buddies. Sylvia also became a good friend and was someone I stayed close with. Frank was absolutely always talking about how talented Joey was."

Joey's new publicist, Warren Cowan, was hard at work, pushing him in the press. The comic became a favorite of columnist Earl Wilson, who would use Joey's lines to pepper his column. In May 1954, Wilson wrote: "Joey considers himself an unlucky comedian; he asks, who else 'gets booked into Boston during Holy Week . . . into Las Vegas during the Atom Bomb tests . . . into Miami during August?'"

With the steady work and higher salary, Joey and Sylvia bought a seven-room, white-brick, Colonial home in the New York City suburb of Englewood, New Jersey, in Bergen County. It was there that Larry began his schooling. Englewood was the cradle of other Jewish comics, such as Buddy Hackett, Dick Shawn, Phil Foster, and Joey's later co-star and friend Corbett Monica. Instead of hanging out at the Hillcrest Country Club on the West Coast, the comics could be found at the Englewood Country Club, exchanging stories.

According to "Bergen: Comics' Haven," a feature in the *New York Times* by Jonathan P. Kraushar, on March 21, 1976:

> The idea that a comedian on television or in the nightclubs of New York and Las Vegas can get a laugh with a comment like, "If I do well here, they've promised to open me in Hackensack," is readily conceded by the comedians who live in Bergen County.

But in their opinions, there is nothing funny about New Jersey. It is, for them, something of a restful haven. The comedians who live here are not the ones to bring expectant smirks to the faces in the audience by opening a story with: "When I was in Hoboken last week, a funny thing happened." [. . .]

In the view of Phil Foster, [a star of the television comedy *Laverne and Shirley*], there is no such thing as New Jersey humor—that is simply a question of speaking slower."

Rather than having been affected by anything that might resemble such a thing as New Jersey humor, Mr. Foster believes that the New York brand has simply moved across the bridge.

"We changed the humor around here," Mr. Foster said. "You have pockets of people here typical of let's say, Brooklyn, the Bronx, or Manhattan. Like Fort Lee is simply a New York city. It's like the sixth borough now."

He reflected that once, when sitting in a Fort Lee diner, he noticed two women with baby carriages come in.

"One says to the other, 'How's Seymour?'" Mr. Foster remembered. "And I heard the name, Seymour, and I looked up. I haven't heard of a kid named Seymour since I left Brooklyn. And the other woman says, 'He fell out the window and now he won't eat.'

"I just listened to that sentence and I couldn't believe I heard it," he continued. "So, I realized that Jersey humor, at least in Bergen County, is becoming New York humor. And when I work in Jersey, I don't hide anything. I don't hold back anything. Everything I want to say I'll say just like I was on 54th Street and Seventh Avenue."

Ironically, for Mr. Foster, Mr. [London] Lee, Dick Shawn, Corbett Monica, Buddy Hackett, and Joey Bishop, all of them New Jerseyites at one time or another, the thing that attracted them to move here was that it enabled them, for at least part of the time, to leave New York behind.

"The last word is *roots*," said London Lee, the comic. "I sort of have a certain peace of mind out here. The property is beautiful, and I've built a wonderful home. Out here, we can relax. There's a certain tranquility about New Jersey—the state, the people."

Mr. Foster said that, before he moved, he was living on 54th Street in Manhattan, right over the Stage Delicatessen.

"I lived on the first floor," he said. "I used to open my closet to find out what item on the menu was going good for the day. I'd pound on the floor and yell down to Max, 'Pastrami today!' But I was losing hours trying to play golf."

When he learned about the Englewood Golf Club, just fifteen minutes by car from Manhattan, and visited the area, back in 1953, he recognized his suburban dream: spacious homes and new schools near the golf course.

"I said, 'What the hell, I'll give it a try,'" he remembered. "I'll make believe I'm on the road for a year." So, he moved with his then-pregnant wife to Bergen County, but soon she was lonely for her New York City friends.

A short time later, Mr. Foster persuaded Dick Shawn, recently seen on Broadway in *A Musical Jubilee*, to consider buying a house right on the Englewood Golf Club course. Mr. Shawn was so taken with the idea of playing golf right on his front lawn that he immediately put down a $500 deposit, not noticing that the house had just one bedroom and would be too small for his growing family.

"So, I talked Buddy Hackett, who was getting married, into taking the house," Mr. Shawn recalled with a laugh. "I said, 'Living is cheaper out here, and you can play the course.'"

Mr. Hackett bought the house, permitting Mr. Shawn to recover his deposit and to move to a larger house in Englewood. Joey Bishop and Corbett Monica followed. Mr. Hackett later moved to a Fort Lee mansion once owned by Albert Anastasia, the mobster, and lived there until he moved to California, as did Mr. Bishop.

For Mr. Shawn, this move from Forest Hills, Queens, about eighteen years ago was a step he regarded as a climb in social status.

"Most people came out to Bergen County for the same reasons we did," he said. "They were brought up on the Lower East Side and what not, and then suddenly their business starts to mushroom, and then they move up a level."

He continued: "None of these people—Buddy, Joe, me—ever had a fancy home before. I'm from a little town called Lackawanna, N.Y., a mining town. Joey Bishop's from a rough section of Philadelphia. Phil Foster's from a rough section of Brooklyn. Buddy Hackett's from ... well, I'm not so sure. It's been so long since people spoke the way he does that I forget where they're from. It could he Bangkok or something."

If moving to New York City was the first demonstration of success, moving their families to New Jersey was a further indication of prosperity, he said.

"Nobody knew what it meant to go outside and have grass around and have a yard to play in," Mr. Shawn explained. "We were all hustling for a buck at an early age. When we could afford it, and we had children, everyone wanted the ideal, which meant houses in suburbia."

Business for the comedians means frequent travel around the country to appear on television, at hotels, conventions, nightclubs or, occasionally, in films or theater. For that reason, their homes were often just home bases for them, while their families became part of the community.

"I just know how to get to the George Washington Bridge and back," said Mr. Shawn. "I mean, for me to go into Tenafly or places like that, I'd be afraid, because I know I'd get lost. Going to Montclair is like going to China."

For his children, it is different.

"The family across the street grew up with my kids," he said, "and with your neighbors, it's like anything else. When they see you walking around in your underwear, suddenly you're not a celebrity anymore. There's a great equalizer there."

Former members of the Englewood Golf Club are fond of telling legendary stories about the comics' days there. They are stories that the comics like to tell themselves.

"They had guys from the Mafia playing at the club," said Mr. Shawn. "I always knew not to yell at a foursome when the caddy was wearing a double-breasted pinstripe suit. Occasionally, we'd join them in a game. But we never bet too heavily with them. After all, how are you gonna collect?"

A favorite story about the comedians' golfing stars Buddy Hackett. During one round, the story goes, the portly comedian hit an awful drive into the woods and ran after the ball.

"A minute later," according to Mr. Foster, "Buddy comes running out from the trees—stark naked. And he's yelling, 'Locusts! Locusts!' Naturally, we all started laughing, but then Joey topped Buddy's act. He looks at Buddy, who's naked, remember, and he says—deadpan—"C'mon Buddy, stop fooling around. Just hit the ball."

With show business now, more than ever, concentrated in California, it is possible that some of the comedians will follow the lead of Mr. Hackett and Mr. Bishop and take the next step up in their professional lives by buying homes in California, Mr. Foster said. But even so, he added, it will not mean the end of Bergen County's drawing power for comedians.

"You've got a whole new generation of comics coming up," he said. "And they'll all follow in our steps. We may have started it, but for heaven's sake, it doesn't stop with us."

Jan Murray's son, Howard Murray, who became a noted television director in situation comedies (*The Big Bang Theory, Roseanne*, etc.) told the author, "I remember Buddy [Hackett] relocated to Fort Lee, New Jersey, before moving out to Los Angeles about the time that Joey did. Larry [Bishop] was older than I and went to another school."

"Larry was a pretty good baseball player," said Sandy Hackett, "and I remember Sylvia collected antiques and Faberge eggs."

Joey began to settle into a comfortable suburban life, hosting dinner parties with friends (most of whom were comics) and playing golf at Englewood. Said Sandy: "I remember they would bring other show-business friends out to the club, like Tony Bennett, Perry Como, Phil Silvers, Sammy Davis Jr., and Ed Sullivan."

"Joey was always an outsider to many of the comics out here [in Los Angeles]," said Howard Murray. "My father and Joey were friends, but I wouldn't say they were close. He wasn't around at many of the parties."

Joey, it turned out, was a homebody. By the late fifties, he started looking into the possibility of television work, so he could stay as close to home as possible. It was then that opportunity came knocking.

Chapter 7
Keep Talking

Television Comes for Joey

Three regulars from Keep Talking, a 1958 network panel show: Danny Dayton, Joey Bishop, and Mike Nichols.

"At first, I hated doing television as it ate up all my material," Joey stated. "I'd do a shot on *The Ed Sullivan Show* and needed to score. So, I used my best 'hard' five minutes. I figured that material was burned. I knew it was good for business [in the clubs], but if you did enough of those [variety] shows, it would kill your act that you work years to make solid. I didn't have a crew of writers like Gleason or Skelton and them. Then, I realized that I needed to do television, but I wanted to do what fit me."

The premise of *Keep Talking*, according to the show's producer, Danny Dayton, was as follows: "Six celebrity panelists, divided into two teams, would try to guess a secret word given to one player on each team. These two players would then proceed to tell a story to their team involving that word, yet not using that word. Narration of the story would jump from teammate to teammate, often leaving the new narrator at a loss as to how to continue the story. Little attention was paid to scoring and points—the point was for the panelists to build their ad-lib story seamlessly and entertainingly."

"It was, in essence, an improv gameshow," explained Charles Dayton, whose father Danny Dayton was the show's producer, writer, and panelist. Dayton had a long career as a comic and singer; he was also a veteran of television, working as an actor and director. While on Broadway, he replaced Phil Silvers in *High Button Shoes* and Zero Mostel in *A Funny Thing Happened on the Way to the Forum*. For years, he was on the nightclub circuit, appearing opposite his first wife, the voluptuous Dagmar, who later gained fame as the co-star (with Jerry Lester) on television's first talk show, *Broadway Open House*. Dayton was also paired for a time with burlesque comic Joey Faye. In later years, Danny had a recurring role as Hank Pivnik on the first season of *Archie Bunker's Place*. Danny scored a big role in *Guys and Dolls* on Broadway as Rusty Charlie and sometimes as Benny Southstreet. While making the 1955 film adaptation, Dayton established a lifelong friendship with co-star Frank Sinatra.

As Charles Dayton recalls: "Dad knew Joey Bishop, but his ties to Frank were probably the reason he asked him to be a panelist on *Keep Talking*. It was a verbal show and it needed the wittier comics to be able to do improvisation. Morey Amsterdam was another one asked to do the show. The panelists had to be able to keep the show flowing. Once, Errol Flynn came to my dad and actually *begged* to be on the show—as he was a viewer. Dad was frightened of Errol's reputation as an alcoholic, and since the show was done live, there were too many risks. So, he told Flynn he would have to audition. Shockingly, he agreed, and was great in rehearsal. Dad demanded that a "babysitter" stay with Flynn before the show to ensure he stayed sober [shades of *My Favorite Year*]. So showtime came and Flynn has ditched his babysitter and is at a bar near the studio, falling-off-a-barstool drunk. And Dad had to take his spot on the panel even though Flynn was announced as the guest star. Joey found that amusing and teased Dad about it for years."

Joey made a deliberate choice to do the show, saying at the time, "I've turned down four thousand a week from important club dates to do *Keep Talking*, where I was paid $850 a week. Money is not the most important to me, thank God. I'm thinking about a career now and I think being exposed on TV is the most important thing."

This TV racket fit Joey like the proverbial glove: "I could get out of bed in my house [in Englewood, New Jersey], commute to the city at a reasonable time and get home and sleep in my own bed. My wife is happy, and my kid is happy. And I'm happy."

The original host of *Keep Talking*, Carl Reiner, told the author, "It was a rather uneven show, but I liked doing it. It gave me some exposure and allowed me time to write. I took the place of Monty Hall, and then Merv Griffin took my place when the show moved to Los Angeles. Joey was a good panelist as he was quick and could think on his feet." Another comic on the show with whom Reiner became acquainted was Morey Amsterdam, who later played Buddy Sorrell on Reiner's *The Dick Van Dyke Show*.

Although appearing on *Keep Talking* was a gamble on Joey's part, it worked as he had envisioned. Verbal acuity was, after all, one of Bishop's strengths as a panelist. He exchanged quips with master panelists such as Ilka Chase, Peggy Cass, Pat Carroll, Mike Nichols & Elaine May, Orson Bean, Audrey Meadows, Danny Dayton, and Kitty Carlisle. Carlisle, Bean, and Cass later appeared for years on *To Tell the Truth*. Joey later became a recurring panelist on the granddaddy of those programs, *What's My Line?*, which featured such wits as Bennett Cerf (founder of Random House), Dorothy Kilgallen, Arlene Francis, and Groucho Marx. The experience he gained on these programs also prepared Joey in many ways for his later talk show. He was noticed by Jack Paar, who was just then hitting his stride as the second host of *The Tonight Show*, following Steve Allen. In later years, when Joey was hard pressed to find a spot on television, he was always welcomed as a panelist on shows like *The Match Game* and *Hollywood Squares*.

On *Keep Talking*, Joey perpetuated his image as "The Frown Prince of Comedy." His dour demeanor reminded some viewers of the late Fred Allen, who had been one of the kings of network radio. In those rare moments when Joey was caught off-guard, he would utter "Son-of-a-gun!" which soon caught on as his catchphrase.

Despite the short tenure of the program, it made a huge impact on Joey's career. He became a national phenomenon. *Keep Talking* only lasted two years on two different networks (CBS and ABC) and relocated from New York to Los Angeles for its second season, with the new host, Merv Griffin. For the time being, Carl Reiner remained in New York.

Joey recalled, "*Keep Talking* was my launching pad. No doubt. People got to know me and they liked that I wasn't a phony. I was a smart ass. It was an attitude. I needed to create that attitude to get noticed. I worked hard to create that. A genuine comic is a guy who is told by the audience that he is funny. The bad comic is the guy who tells the audience he is funny. Get it?"

Joey continued, "People liked my cynical attitude. It's reality, and the audiences appreciated that. You know, it's *all* like that today [on television]. When I did *Keep Talking*, the producers wanted me to smile when they did the sign off. It's like those newscasters today. I wouldn't do it. This is me and if they didn't like it, they could go fuck themselves . . . which they probably did anyway."

Joey shared some words of wisdom with Earl Wilson, which made their way into his column:

Viewers are getting a lot sharper and demanding more subtle material. What they accepted some years ago is old hat now. Look what happened to a lot of the comics who were on TV a while back—gone, that's what. And why? They were never developed into personalities, human beings. The performer who wants to get anywhere in TV has to be down-to-earth and real to viewers, like Jack Benny . . . overpowering nightclub comedy won't stand up on TV because you run out of material too fast. On television, you can't keep topping yourself.

Joey even physically changed his look at this time. Gone were his wavy locks. He now sported a close-cropped haircut. He ordered personally designed tuxedos to give him that "sophisticated look," and he was careful to stay tan. The new Joey was hitting center stage. And according to him, every bit of his success was calculated and planned. "I look at every aspect of my attitude, my style—how it all played into my demeanor. I wanted to be distinct."

Keep Talking might have been a misfire as a concept, but Joey was a hit with viewers. With his co-workers, not so much. Charles Dayton recalls an anecdote from his youth involving his father: "For the more than twenty years we lived in our home in Los Angeles, there was a sign planted at the end of our driveway that read: NO PARKING. THIS SPACE RESERVED FOR JOEY BISHOP. I always wondered why that sign was there, so one day, I asked my dad about it. He said, 'When I was producing *Keep Talking*, Joey Bishop was the world's biggest prick. He thought his shit didn't smell. One day when he was being a huge asshole to me, I yanked his sign from the studio parking lot and staked it on our driveway. It made me happy!'

Chapter 8
Joey Meets Jack Paar
The Art of Making an Impression

*Joey listens respectfully while Jack Paar
drones on, c. 1960.*

*K*eep *Talking* put Joey on the television map and into the national conscience. Kids were using Joey's catchphrase "Son-of-a-gun," which got them into far less trouble than "son-of-a-bitch." His theoretical plan to forsake revenue in clubs to gain the exposure on TV had worked perfectly. When the 1959 season of the show came to an end, the show moved to the West Coast, where it would be taped at ABC studios, the show's new network home, with Merv Griffin as the new host. Joey would not continue as a regular panelist, but he did agree to do the show on an occasional basis.

No longer tied to the show, he was back performing in clubs, earning far more than the $850 pittance he made for appearing on *Keep Talking*.

"I came, I saw, and I conquered," he boasted.

His good luck continued when talk-show host Jack Paar came calling. Paar was a former radio disc jockey (starting in Cleveland in 1938 on WGAR Radio) and, after the war, he began to gain notice on the West Coast as an uncategorized broadcaster. He was not a comic like Steve Allen or Jerry Lester, the hosts of *The Tonight Show* and *Broadway Open House*, respectively. Neither was he an actor, although he tried to be for a time. He was not really a disc jockey, a newsman, or even a typical game-show host. What he could do was talk. He could conduct a wonderful interview and elicit humorous responses. He was quick-witted and had a rather mercurial personality, making him both highly emotional and quite unpredictable. He had impressed Jack Benny during the war in his stint as a disc jockey for the USO, so Benny hired him to host his summer-replacement show in 1947. He later hosted game shows such as *The $64,000 Question* and *Bank on the Stars*. He hosted *The CBS Morning Program*, with Walter Cronkite as his newsman. He even tried his hand as a standup comic on *The Ed Sullivan Show*. However, Jack was the round peg network executives were trying to fit into the square hole. He had talent, but no one knew how best to use it. Then, when Steve Allen was moved by NBC from *The Tonight Show* into a variety show in a primetime slot in 1956, they had a hard time replacing him. Allen first tried to do both shows, and Ernie Kovacs was the fill-in host, but he was more adept at visual comedy than he was at hosting a talk show.

They tried a new format with *Tonight After Dark*, which flopped. Desperate, Pat Weaver decided to take a chance on Jack Paar, who had been fired by CBS and was foundering. They changed back to the talk-show format and renamed it *The Tonight Show Starring Jack Paar* (renamed *The Jack Paar Show* in 1959). Paar was unlike anything the viewers had ever seen: a masterful raconteur who was emotional, funny, genuine, and inviting.

The format was far different from what Steve Allen had attempted, which was mostly comedy sketches. Paar brought on wits such as Elsa Maxwell, Alexander King, Oscar Levant, Groucho Marx, and comedy writer Jack Douglas. His writers were also more intellectual than Allen's group. Case in point, Dick Cavett was on the Paar writing staff, aiming toward a more satirical tone. Gone were Louis Nye, Gabe Dell, and Bill Dana. Paar brought on a new breed of comic, including Mort Sahl, Bill Cosby, the Smothers Brothers, Buddy Hackett, and Godfrey Cambridge. Paar instigated feuds with Walter Winchell, Dorothy Kilgallen, and the powerful Ed Sullivan. The audience never knew what to expect, night in and night out, from Paar. It became Must-See TV. The respectable ratings Steve Allen had generated were dwarfed by the Paar juggernaut that, at times, earned higher ratings in late night than the network's vaunted prime-time shows. Whether it was Jack walking out due to the network censors' objection to his infamous "water closet" joke, or perhaps to one of his personal stories, Jack was a television phenomenon. Every comic fought for a spot on Paar's show, as they knew it could ignite a career. Joey was keenly aware of this and set his sights on becoming a part of it. Appearing as a guest now and then allowed him the flexibility of keeping his lucrative club dates and still staying in the spotlight. In short, it was the best of both worlds. Jack had caught Joey on *Keep Talking* and first invited him on the show in 1958. Paar was intrigued by Joey's no-nonsense approach and his quick wit, which he knew would be perfect on a panel show like his.

In Paar's 1961 book, *My Saber is Bent*, he wrote,

> When Joey first came on our show, he had been knock
> ing around in clubs without getting anything on fire,
> including the crepe suzettes. In no time at all, it seemed,

he was a star, making pictures, joining Frank Sinatra's clan, getting his own TV series and acting as an emcee for the $100-a-head inaugural gala for President Kennedy.

He continues:

"I'm now working in places," he told me, "where a year ago I couldn't afford to go to."

. . . Joey has a wonderful knack for self-editing. One night, he sat for a half-hour on our panel without saying a thing. Finally, he raised his hand.

"Yes, Joey?" I inquired.

"Nothing, Jack," he said, "I just wanted you to know I was here."

Joey never forgot the impact his appearances on the Paar show had on his career. "Everybody was watching Jack then," Joey told said. "I mean, even talentless people like Peggy Cass were getting big. If you scored on his show, it was huge. A big deal. Every club date I had was mobbed. I was pulling down more money than I had ever seen. And the great thing with Paar was that I didn't have to burn any material. I sat on the panel and it just came naturally, from the topic or source of the conversation. And Jack treated me like a million bucks. He was such a great setup man. A straight man. He was instinctual. He knew how to make you look good."

"Joey was quick," Buddy Hackett told the author. "He could think on his feet. He listened carefully and had that instinctual, quick smart-ass comeback. And the audience waited for it. It was like the conversation was a setup for Joey's payoff of a remark. And Jack loved it. The thing is, Joey was never the initiator. He waited in the reeds and then just sprung out on the right beat. It was amazing."

Not only did Paar notice it, so did every television producer who wanted to cash in and get Joey to spice up their programs. By the end of 1959, he had done *The Perry Como Show* on four occasions, *The Garry Moore Show*, *The Dinah Shore Show*, specials with Sinatra, Esther Williams, and others. He even did a dramatic turn on the *Richard Diamond* detective show playing (what else?) a comic.

Bob Finkel, who produced both *The Dinah Shore Show* and *The Perry Como Show*, told the author: "Joey was easy. He hit his mark. He helped punch up his dialogue with the writers and added that comic touch. He made the host look good, which was goal number one. He became hard to book after the Sinatra hookup. I tried to get him on a Jerry Lewis special as he had requested him, and he was impossible to book. He was very dependable. You knew how to write for him, too!"

Jack O'Brian, who was the very particular and often harsh critic for *The New York Herald-American*, wrote about Joey Bishop in 1959:

> He works masterfully on "The Jack Paar Show," where he can exercise the greased lightning mentality which twinkles to whatever topic or random event is served-up, however casually. Behind that shrewd false front of big expression races a comic mind attuned to the topical call of impudent small talk. He is a comic counterpuncher, at his best in quick-phrased rejoinder, at his worst sermonizing or psychologizing.

Jack Benny would tell anyone within earshot that he thought Joey Bishop "was the smartest young comic around." He told Earl Wilson of the *New York Post*, "Joey Bishop is one of the funniest men I've ever seen. He's just a naturally funny man. Great ad-lib comedian. Thinks fast. A lot of people think he worries too much; I do too; but then this you can't stop. That's his style, but then he's great."

In the middle of one show when Joey was appearing at the Sands in Las Vegas, Benny stood up, looked around at the audience and said, "I'm going home. You're too funny and too young," and he walked out. When the lines were growing with each show at the Sands, Joey learned that his famed admirer was advising his audience at the Desert Inn to head over to see "the funniest comic in the business."

Joey still opened for Frank whenever the call came, but now he was headlining the showrooms like the Copa, and the Sands in Las Vegas. While guys like Buddy Hackett, Shecky Greene, and Don Rickles were still openers and working the lounges, Joey was becoming a featured attraction, almost in the same league as Danny Thomas, Jack Benny, George Burns, and Red Skelton. Joey now had acts that opened for *him*. One was a singer, Judy Scott, a Jerry Lewis discovery. "He was drawing huge crowds," Scott told the author. "Much younger crowds, too, than Jack [Benny] would get. They liked it. A good gambling crowd. Joey was easy to work with then. I did the material I picked, and Joey gave me that leeway."

Joey was handpicked by Paar for his first time as a guest host of *The Tonight Show*. This was the host's way of legitimizing his arrival as a major star. Jack had tried to get Joey to pinch-hit for him earlier, but Joey turned him down, feeling he was not quite ready. In May 1959, Joey accepted Jack's offer.

Joey told Bob Williams of the *New York Post*, "Now that I've had some exposure on Paar's show, I will do it on the basis of doing a favor for a friend who's away on vacation. I'm a little like Paar in a few respects, I think. One of the things that makes him interesting to viewers is his attitude of tiredness and boredom. So as long as I keep things informal, I think I'll be alright. I plan to play it like I do when I'm a guest on the program—the reluctant-to-be-here attitude. Actually, I'm dreading it a bit for one reason. For the past twenty years I've been telling all my friends, 'If I can ever help you out, let me know.' Now I'm in the spot where I can and, boy, has my phone been ringing!"

True to his word, Joey even had on his old partner Rummy Bishop. Rummy was a less-than-stellar guest, but Joey did his best to keep him afloat.

Luckily, Joey's other guests that first week included his New Jersey friends Phil Foster, Buddy Hackett, Larry Storch, Faye Emerson, and Joey's co-star from the movie *Onionhead*—Andy Griffith.

Rocky Kalish was working for Danny Thomas in 1959 and thought that Joey's biggest break-out performance, which was televised on the *Kraft Music Hall* in mid-1959 as an all-star roast of Dean Martin, who was now *sans* his partner Jerry Lewis. It was held in Los Angeles and Joey wanted to be included. He was told he had to pay his own airfare to the event, which he did gladly. Like many of his gambles at that time, it paid off.

On the dais that night was the cream of show business: George Jessel, Jimmy Durante, Joey Bishop, Tony Martin, George Burns, Dinah Shore, Mort Sahl, Judy Garland, Sammy Cahn, Danny Thomas, Sammy Davis Jr., Bob Hope, Frank Sinatra, and Dean Martin.

Rocky Kalish, who wrote for the roast, remembered it well: "Joey was absolutely an insignificant ant to these guys. He begged to get on and we were told not to write him any lines. He was on his own. They had no room on the dais, so they seated him at the end, behind palm trees. Literally behind these potted palms. It was hysterical. So, he had one of the first slots and I think they gave him only four minutes. It was a comic's nightmare to be the warm-up. They are usually still serving. But as much as I learned to dislike Joey, he was fast that night. He shocked everyone—and they were all biggies—but he was hard to top."

The only surviving element from that evening is a record album. The following is a direct transcription of what Joey had to say once he was introduced.

> They put me on the end chair . . . I had the choice
> between speaking to a Spanish waiter or to Mort Sahl,
> who I understood less than I understood the waiter. .
> . . I also sat next to sweet, wonderful Dinah Shore and
> she spoke to me all night. Things like, "Pass the butter,"
> "Where's the salt?" . . . [turning toward Danny Thomas]
> You had so much faith in your nose. You wouldn't have
> it operated on. So now I heard they are going to film the
> Durante story and who's got the lead? Dean Martin!" .
> . . [to Steve Allen] I've never worked for you, nor do I
> intend to. I've seen what'd happened to your people on
> TV. Don Knotts is a nervous wreck, Tom Poston can't
> remember his own name, Skitch Henderson hasn't time

to shave. If you're *that* kind of taskmaster—*no thanks!* . . .
And thanks to what I *thought* was my friend, Mr. Sinatra.
He arranged my seat for me behind a palm tree!

Rocky Kalish remembered, "Joey then went on about how unimportant he was to be seated behind a palm tree, and everyone was in tears. After that, he was the talk of the night. Everyone knew Joey Bishop, among all these legends at the dinner, and he made his bones there and then."

Rocky was right. Hal Wallis called with a movie offer. Four of the West Coast-filmed shows called Joey to make appearances. A record company called with an offer to do an album. But the biggest whopper was something that was right up Joey's alley. His mentor, Frank Sinatra, called. He wanted Joey to be a guest on a special he was doing for Timex. Besides Frank and Sammy, another singer would also be on—some guy named Elvis.

Chapter 9
Joey Gets Hot

Will Success Spoil Joey Bishop?

Joey with his comedic idol, Jack Benny.

On May 12, 1960, the ABC television network aired a now-legendary episode of *The Frank Sinatra Timex Show*. The guests included Rat Pack members Sammy Davis Jr., Peter Lawford, and Joey Bishop, as well as Frank's daughter Nancy Sinatra. The special's official title is *It's Nice to Go Trav'lin'*, which was also the title of one of the tunes on Sinatra's hit 1958 Capitol album, *Come Fly with Me*. However, the only title by which this program is known today is *Welcome Home, Elvis*. It marked the first television appearance by Presley since leaving on a highly publicized U.S. Army tour of duty in Germany in 1957. This major network special was also the perfect vehicle to plug Elvis's comeback movie, appropriately titled *G.I. Blues*. As far as Sinatra was concerned, his presenting (and crooning with) Elvis would be a way to make him relevant to Elvis's youthful (and highly vocal) fan base. The hour-long show was taped at the Fontainebleau Hotel in Miami Beach, Florida, on March 26, 1960. It was Sinatra's fourth, and final, Timex special of the 1959–1960 season.

In a nod to the cultural clash of Elvis and the Rat Pack, Frank jokingly referred to the show's theme as "twitch boy meets the men." It was something that Sinatra relished as Elvis was now playing on Frank's turf. For his client's eight-minute appearance, Elvis's manager, Colonel Tom Parker, wangled a $125,000 appearance fee, which the network and Timex quickly covered. Watching the Voice in a duet with the King singing "Love Me Tender" while Elvis warbled "Witchcraft" remains a true classic, at least in a bizarre way. Sinatra and Presley had been thought to be rivals in the media, but all was jovial on set. The ratings went, as expected, through the roof—drawing nearly 67.7% of the overall television audience. The remaining viewers were apparently watching a special hosted by Tennessee Ernie Ford with his guests Johnny Cash and Groucho Marx.

In her book, *Elvis For Dummies*, Susan Doll notes how important this television special was to Presley's career. She writes, "Appearing with Sinatra suggested that Elvis was following the same career path [as Sinatra] and was therefore the natural heir to The Voice." She also points out that Presley's singing style and appearance on the show "clearly signaled that Elvis was courting a mainstream, adult audience."

As for his contribution to the program, Joey managed a few good lines, such as when all the females started screeching as Elvis was about to take the stage. Joey asked Frank, "What are they all screaming about? Are the rates too high in Florida?" Another Joey line to Sinatra: "You know, I had the feeling all along that Elvis was going to reenlist. Some very important people were hoping he'd stay in. People like Fabian, Ricky Nelson, Tab Hunter . . ." Mostly, however, it was great for Bishop just to be included in the hottest special of the season, with the majority of the country watching. Even still, Bishop felt unimportant in his subordinate role.

Conveniently, the Rat Pack was doing a gig at the Fontaineb-leau Hotel as well. *Ocean's 11* was not set to premiere until August, but the frenzy surrounding the group of middle-aged playboys was nearing its peak.

"Frank asked me to do the special," Joey recalled. "I never let the boys [the deal makers at the William Morris Agency] negotiate my fee when Frank asked. They'd fuck it up. Hurt feelings, you know. So, Frank goes, 'What's your price?' I say, 'I'd like to do the special but I gotta get my price—seventy-five hundred dollars.' He said, 'Nah,' and nodded his head. 'I can't get you seventy-five hundred. I can only get you eighty-five hundred.' You know, that's the thing Frank always did but you never hear about—always generous."

Joey knew that he was at a crossroads. He was, as he often said, a realist. He knew he was not big-screen material. Sure, he could make an appearance in a movie, but he was *made* for television. He scored on *Jack Paar, Ed Sullivan*, and other shows. During the 1959–1960 season the only non–Rat Pack appearance he made was on *What's My Line?* in the spring of 1960. The Rat Pack members also had cameos in *Pepe*, a film starring the Mexican comic Cantinflas. Joey, Sammy, Dean, and Frank were included, along with dozens of other show-business names, from Bing Crosby to Tony Curtis. Joey has one line, his catchphrase "Son-of-a gun."

"Since the line was hyphenated, I considered that I got paid three thousand dollars for one word," Joey said.

In a sudden burst of self-importance, Joey took a dangerous turn by rejecting an offer from the powerful Ed Sullivan to do ten appearances on his Sunday night variety show at $8,500 a shot. Not only did he refuse, he even spoke against the television institution to columnist Bob Williams of the *New York Post*: "You're booked for six or seven minutes, then suddenly you're cut to six or five. Then, just when you are getting ready to go on, you are cut to four."

The comments rankled Sullivan, who was notorious for his long-held grudges. His feuds with Jack Paar, Steve Allen, Walter Winchell, and Jackie Mason are legendary. And Sullivan's feuds were good for business. He knew the press, being a columnist himself, and never backed down from a battle.

Sullivan was quoted by the *Post*'s Bob Williams as saying: "This is completely untrue. Instead of relishing his success, with which all of show business is delighted, Bishop is getting too big for his breeches. He suddenly thinks he wrote the book. It makes a big man out of him to the hambones. I don't think we should be maligned by [someone] like this who, because of Sinatra's support, suddenly got hot. We played golf together and I never offered him a damn thing. What I resent is this guy stepping in as a great big man. Some guys start feeling their oats and decide they are going to dictate to TV shows."

Joey, who was, as earlier discussed, a world-class kiss-ass, rarely making waves and always being the good soldier, had made a sudden about-face. As he began to believe his own press, he also began his inevitable march to oblivion by burning bridges. A horrid air of invincibility and a lingering bitterness began to take hold, traits that would define him for the rest of his life. After twenty years of working his way from the small time to the national spotlight, he had turned cocky, a malady more common to overnight success stories.

Rocky Kalish told the author, "I knew Joey from writing for him on specials. We played golf. I later wrote for him for his television show for Thomas-Leonard. But he changed, almost overnight. He became arrogant in every way. He transformed into this diva, almost a monster in some ways. He thought show business revolved around him.

He forgot that the only reason he was hot was because of the Pope [Sinatra]. He was a dime-a-dozen comic who knew how to kiss a good *tuchus. No one* was about to kiss *his.*"

Warren Berlinger, the accomplished actor of stage and screen who would appear opposite Joey on his sitcom, told the author: "I worked with so many people in my career and most are rather decent. They appreciate their success and remember the hard-luck days. Joey had this arrogant attitude and it was all about Joey. Sometimes, if you have loads of talent, you can compensate for that kind of an attitude. My cousin [Milton Berle] had a bit of that, but he was one of a kind. Unfortunately for Joey, he was not in that class."

Abby Dalton, the lovely actress who played Joey's wife on his sitcom, said, "I worked with comedic actors throughout my career. Jackie Cooper [in *Hennessey*] was my co-star for four years. A wonderful man. So considerate of others. And that was why he was able to transition to a top-notch director. In Joey's case, he was neither a top-notch actor nor comic. He was never considerate of those he worked with."

While we consider these revealing comments about Joey, we return to the Sullivan "feud," which was quickly escalating in the press.

Joey insisted that he was offered a deal by Sullivan, despite the host's denials. As he attempted to clarify to Bob Williams of the *Post*, "What I was trying to say was that even a couple of years ago, when I *really* needed the money, I refused to go on variety shows unless I was integrated into the program."

Joey continued, employing more of this irrational logic: "I decided that it was just senseless to go on a program where everyone was merely interested in their show. Those shows go on forever, but the performer is in oblivion."

In a classic "he said/he said," Sullivan recalled Joey's first appearance on his show in 1956, just four years earlier: "He had made eight appearances on the show since then. He didn't have any complaints to me since. It certainly has taken him a long time to get angry."

Chapter 10
Vegas, Baby!
A Brief History

Las Vegas as it appeared before mobsters turned it into the world's gambling and entertainment mecca.

To better understand what fueled Joey Bishop and the Rat Pack (among other high-profile acts), it is vital to present a short history of the modern Vegas.

Las Vegas was truly a dusty small town prior to the end of World War II. There were casinos such as the Horseshoe, run by the nefarious Benny Binion, the Mont, and other clubs in downtown Las Vegas that allowed legal gambling. The proximity to Los Angeles made Vegas a fun short drive to be able to gamble without the prospect of a police raid. This caught the attention of the notorious Billy Wilkerson, who was, among other things, the owner of *The Hollywood Reporter* along with some of Los Angeles's chi-chi night spots, including Café Trocadero, Ciro's, and La Rue's. Everyone in Los Angeles whispered about Billy having the backing of the East Coast mob money while under the watchful eye of the ruthless Benny "Bugsy" Siegel, whose movie-star looks gave him entrée into the movie colony.

Benny Siegel was a founding partner of the Bugs and Meyer Mob, with Meyer being the brilliant money mind of Meyer Lansky, Bugs's boyhood pal. After the East Coast mob's Castellammarese War[1] Bugs and Meyer joined forces with another boyhood friend, Charles "Lucky" Luciano, to found Murder, Inc. Created by the business-minded Lansky, the organization was structured along the lines of a corporation, with strict rules and guidelines. A plan was implemented to launder the illegal profits through legitimate businesses. The entertainment industry was a prime outlet with the onslaught of nightclubs and entertainment venues and the need for escapism following World War II. Thus, as was explored earlier, most nightclub entertainers like Bishop, Sinatra, Martin & Lewis, Sammy Davis Jr., and Danny Thomas were all funded by Murder, Inc. or one of its affiliates. Territories and boundaries were formed, and "franchises" were awarded.

Thus, when Siegel sought to get out of New York and stake a claim in Los Angeles, he had the blessing of his partner Meyer. Along with the bookmaking, they infiltrated the unions in Hol-

---

1   According to Wikipedia: "The Castellammarese War was a bloody struggle for control of the Italian-American Mafia, from February 19, 1930, to April 15, 1931, between partisans of Joe 'The Boss' Masseria and those of Salvatore Maranzono. It was so called because Maranzono was based in Castellammare del Golfo, Sicily."

lywood and put a stranglehold on the studios. Siegel had good friends like tough-guy actor George Raft, along with his right-hand lieutenant Mickey Cohen, to watch after their interests in the clubs and the racing wire/bookie operation that was the main source of their funding.

It was Billy Wilkerson who approached Siegel with his concept of expansion in Las Vegas. The initial site eyed by Billy occupied forty acres originally owned by one of city's first settlers, Charles "Pops" Squires. Squires paid $8.75 an acre for the land. In 1944, Margaret Folsom bought the tract for $7,500 from Squires, and she later sold it to Billy Wilkerson. Wilkerson purchased thirty-three acres on the east side of U.S. Route 91, a mile south of the Last Frontier Hotel/Casino, in preparation for his vision.

Wilkerson then hired George Vernon Russell to design a hotel influenced by European architecture. Wilkerson also requested that the hotel be different than the "sawdust joints" on Fremont Street. He planned a hotel with luxurious rooms, a spa, a health club, a showroom, a golf course, a nightclub, an upscale restaurant, and a French-style casino. Because of high wartime materiel costs, Wilkerson ran into financial problems almost at once, finding himself $400,000 short and hunting for new financing.

Once World War II had ended in late 1945, Siegel, Lansky, and their partners visited Las Vegas. The city in the desert reportedly piqued Siegel and his mob's interest because of its legalized gambling and off-track betting. At the time, Siegel and Lansky held a large interest in TransAmerica Wire, a racing publication owned by Moses Annenberg and his son Walter.

Siegel and his pals first purchased El Cortez club in downtown Las Vegas for $600,000. His expansion plans were hampered by unfriendly city officials (strongly Mormon) who were aware of his criminal background, so Siegel began looking for a site outside the city limits. Hearing that Wilkerson was seeking extra funding, Siegel and his partners posed as businessmen and directly bought a two-thirds stake in the project. Siegel took over the final phases of construction and convinced more of his underworld associates—mainly Lansky—to invest in the project. Siegel reportedly lost patience with the project's rising costs, and he once mentioned to his builder, Del Webb, that he had personally killed sixteen men. Reportedly, when Webb reacted to this alarming statement with fear, Siegel reassured him, "Don't worry—we only kill each other."

Allegedly, Siegel named the resort after his gambling-loving girlfriend, Virginia Hill, nicknamed "Flamingo" due to her long, skinny legs. However, organized-crime king Lucky Luciano wrote in his memoir that Siegel once owned an interest in the Hialeah Racetrack in Miami and viewed the flamingos that populated nearby as a good omen. More likely, the "Flamingo" name was bestowed on the project at its inception by Wilkerson.

Siegel's trouble with the Flamingo began when, a year after its official groundbreaking, the resort had produced no revenue and drained the resources of its mob investors. Lansky was confronted at a major corporate/mob conference in Cuba, during which he was informed that either Siegel or Hill was skimming from the resort's building budget. This charge was amplified at a time when Hill was revealed to have taken $2.5 million and left for Switzerland, where the skimmed money was believed to be going.

"There was no doubt in Meyer's mind," Luciano recalled in his memoir, "that Bugsy had skimmed this dough from his building budget, and he was sure that Siegel was preparing to skip as well as skim, in case the roof was gonna fall in on him."

Luciano and the other mob leaders in Cuba asked Lansky what to do. Torn because of long ties to Siegel, whom he considered to be like a brother, Lansky nevertheless agreed that anyone stealing from his friends *had* to die. At first, Lansky persuaded the others to wait for the Flamingo's casino opening. If it was a success, Siegel could be persuaded in other ways to repay. Luciano concurred and persuaded the others to agree.

The splashy opening boasted such entertainers as Spanish bandleader Xavier Cugat, Toastmaster General George Jessel, Siegel's buddy George Raft, Rose Marie, and Jimmy Durante. Stars flocking in from Hollywood included Clark Gable, Lana Turner, Judy Garland, Joan Crawford, and Cesar Romero. Despite the push from Wilkerson in Los Angeles, the opening was a flop.

Rose Marie told the author, "It was an amazing opening. The first time I met Mr. Siegel was when I thought he was a hotel flunky and I asked for eighty-five bucks taken out of my paycheck. He was too good looking and charming for me to think that this was Benny Siegel. I knew all the boys and he did not fit. And *no one* called him Bugsy or Goodbye Charlie. He later paid me the eighty-five dollars and he was just charming. So good looking. Nothing was ready at the hotel, and it was a mess. I stayed under contract to the Flamingo and then Gus Greenbaum, who ran the hotel after Mr. Siegel. Later, Gus and his wife were killed—they cut off his head. I stayed loyal to them. They were good to me. If they wanted me for another date at another casino, I asked the boys at the Flamingo first—*or else* (*jokingly laughing*). Lots of years doing my act with Jimmy Durante—as he loved my impression of him. If you were good to the 'boys,' they treated you like a million bucks!"

Lansky managed to persuade the mob chiefs to reprieve Siegel once more and allow the Flamingo more time. But, by January 1947, Siegel had to order the resort closed until the hotel could be finished. The Flamingo reopened in March despite the hotel not being complete, and this time, the results proved different. By May, the resort reported a $250,000 profit, allowing Lansky to point out that Siegel was right about Las Vegas after all. But it wasn't quite enough to save Siegel. On June 20, 1947, relaxing in the Beverly Hills house he shared with Hill (who was away at the time), Siegel was shot to death. A memorial plaque adorns the Flamingo site, near the outdoor wedding chapel.

Unfortunately for Siegel, the Flamingo was extremely successful almost immediately after his death. In the year 1948 alone, it turned a $4 million profit (on paper, not including the skimmed cash).

Among the many entertainers who performed there between 1947 and 1953 were Martin & Lewis, Sammy Davis Jr., Tony Martin, dance team Marge and Gower Champion, Polly Bergen, Lena Horne, the Mills Brothers, Alan King, Betty Hutton, Billy Eckstein, Sophie Tucker, Pearl Bailey, Spike Jones, Rose Marie, and Jimmy Durante.

Tony Martin and his wife, the beautiful dancer Cyd Charisse, were headliners for decades at the Flamingo.

"I was the big draw for Vegas for years," Tony Martin told the author, "Cyd and I drew the gambling crowds they sought. I was rewarded a small piece of the owner from the boys. I knew Benny, Gus, and the others. They treated me and Cyd like a king and queen. Whatever we wanted . . . After the films dried up, it became our moneymaker . . . I always filled in wherever the boys needed me."

Once the Flamingo started turning massive profits, the mob started opening other such venues on the Vegas strip, out of the purview of the powers that be within Las Vegas city limits. The mob used Vegas as a perfect place to launder their illegal cash—which now included the sale of narcotics—along with being able to keep the boys happy in all the Murder, Inc. franchises through-out the country with their own, personal ATM machine. They regularly skimmed cash from the counting rooms with the help of their "collectors," one of whom was the notorious Tony "The Ant" Spilotro.

One of the other luxury resort/casinos that began appear-ing on the strip, the El Rancho, was built by businessman Wil-bur Clark. Clark then built the Desert Inn, which opened in 1950. When he ran into cash-flow issues, he turned to Moe Dalitz, of the Cleveland-based Mayfield Road Gang, who bought much of his interest (although Clark remained the "front man").

Then came the cradle of the Rat Pack. The Sands Resort/Casino.

Chapter 11
The Sands:

Headquarters for the Rat Pack

The Sands marquee, c. 1959.

In this construction boom on the Las Vegas strip, we finally get to the center of the Rat Pack universe—the Sands Resort/Hotel and Casino, which was designed to be the ultimate destination resort. In theory, a controversial group of investors fronted by Texas gambler and oilman Jake Freedman and New York night-club boss Jack Entratter built what was considered at the time to be one of the world's most lavish hotels and resort. Freedman purchased the land itself for $15,000 and spent $600,000 on the construction. Much of the actual money came from the Mayfield Road gang from Cleveland that was led by Moe Dalitz (who had also financed the El Rancho and the Desert Inn).

The Ohio mob, at the behest of Murder, Inc., included New York crime boss Frank Costello. Costello had owned clubs such as the Copacabana, employing the likes of Entratter and Jules Podell.

At first, they had difficulty obtaining the license from the Nevada Gaming Commission. Trying to avoid the public backlash, the commission was accused of shrouding ownership of the hotel with rumors of mob ties and dirty money. Thus, Dalitz put the hotel ownership (in name only) in the hands of Texas oilman Jake Freedman. As a result, the gaming commission allowed the establishment to open on December 15, 1952.

The original hotel was a fairly modest affair, at least by today's standards. The 212 guest rooms were situated in four buildings around a giant blue pool. The compound contained a thriving casino, immaculate dining rooms, and spaces dedicated to entertainment, the most prestigious of which was the Copa Room. The hotel was advertised by a giant pink, neon-lit sign (setting the look that would forever characterize the Vegas Strip) proclaiming "Sands: A Place in the Sun."

Although the Sands wasn't the largest hotel on the Strip, it did become one of the most well-known, thanks in large part to publicist Al Freeman. Freeman knew that he had to make a name for the hotel—and the up-and-coming town—in order to lure visitors.

Freeman looked for every angle. He convinced actress Rita Hayworth to marry her fourth husband, singer Dick Haymes (who was then booked in the Copa Room), in the hotel, complete with a camera-ready guest list. He staged stunts like that now-iconic photo in which a craps table was dropped into the hotel pool— with the Sands sign visible in the background—and surrounded by bathing suit-clad gamers who rolled the dice while half-submerged in the cool waters.

It was then that Freeman came up with the centerpiece of the Sands and Copa Room entertainment. In Freeman's words, "Frank Sinatra is the eye of the storm." Freeman already had the singer's attention after throwing everything at him. This included a $25,000 base salary with a cut of the receipts and a back-end ownership (some claim 9%, others much lower—and off the net) and other perks to convince the thirty-seven-year-old Sinatra to make the Sands his home base. Frank loved the location and the team, and beginning in October 1953, he began performing in the Copa Room. Sinatra brought an explosive dose of glamour, celebrity, and vice to the formerly dusty Strip.

While it is a common practice now, Freeman devised the idea of paying celebrities just to make "appearances" at the hotel for publicity purposes. The glitterati who made appearances around the casinos or on the stage over the years reflect the glamour that was once the entertainment industry: Lauren Bacall, Cary Grant, James Stewart, Carol Burnett, Lucille Ball, a pre-presidential John F. Kennedy, Marilyn Monroe, Marlene Dietrich, and Rosemary Clooney were paid, sometimes in cash, to be photographed and seen around the hotel at selected times.

It was Sinatra, as Freeman predicted, who was the main draw— and the creator of his own drama. The singer was known to gallivant around the property with his own entourage. George Levin, the maître d' of the Copa Room, remembers witnessing what happened when Sinatra was served mushrooms in his chow mein in the Garden Room, a white-glove restaurant specializing in Chinese cuisine.

"Everything was silver at that time, silver plates and silver toppings, coverings," Levin recalls. "Frank lifts the thing up and there are the mushrooms. He took the bowl and threw it over his head. I stepped on the side and I started to laugh. Frank gets up and he starts coming after me and I run into the kitchen. He comes after me into the kitchen and he says to me, 'You want to fight?' I said, 'I'm not a fighter; I'm a lover.' And he broke up! He hugged me, and that was it."

The Sinatra legend was also enhanced by Freeman. He presented him as a "tough guy," ready to fight anyone who crossed him, but he also fought for those who were being wronged. Beyond putting Las Vegas on the map, the singer played a large role in integrating the city.

Carl Cohen was installed to oversee the Cleveland mob money. Entratter was there to protect Frank Costello and his New York friends' interest. Eventually, Entratter and Cohen fully entrusted each other and a successful partnership was forged.

The Sands was designed by renowned California architect Wayne McAllister. The combination of Entratter's connections in the entertainment world (from his days at the Copacabana in New York), along with the hotel's lavish spending on entertainment, assured the Sands a preeminent place in show business for top-name entertainers and shows. After the death of Jake Freedman in 1958, Entratter and Carl Cohen, the casino boss, took over the hotel as president and vice-president, respectively.

In the University of Las Vegas's special collections archive is the Sands' public relations records; they document everything from expenses to personal memos during the years 1952 to 1977. The collection is essentially comprised of the files of Al Freeman, director of advertising and promotion at the Sands Hotel from 1952 until his death in 1972. Within these records is a documentation of the Copa Room and the Rat Pack. Also included are newspaper clippings, brochures, press releases, and interoffice memos relating to the advertising and promotional department. Materials also include reels of 16mm film of the Sands opening, various recordings of shows and events, including Frank Sinatra and Dean Martin's "Summit Meeting," and footage from various television productions featuring the Sands.

In a series of extensive interviews with the author, Carl Cohen, who along with Jack Entratter, ran the Sands hotel, cogently spelled out how the Rat Pack was created.

Cohen was born in Cleveland, Ohio, in 1913. A one-time boxer, he stood an imposing six-five. His size made him an ideal choice as a bodyguard for such notorious figures of the Mayfield Road Mob as Shondor Birns, who ran the numbers racket in Cleveland. Cohen was eventually awarded the position of bookie for the group, becoming involved with the clubs that they owned, including El Dumpo, which were merely fronts for the gambling casinos. Cohen had far more to offer than some big lug like "Slapsie" Maxie Rosenbloom. He possessed not only a mind for numbers, he also excelled at people skills. He rose quickly within the ranks, running the notorious Pettibone Club, a gambling club near Solon, Ohio, which had formerly been managed by Maxie Diamond. Diamond, who later worked for the author's father and grandfather, had this to say about Carl Cohen in 1975: "Carl was no slouch. Smart guy. He was more of an operations man, and everybody had lots of respect for him. Maybe because he was so big that it was hard to say no to him."

Cohen was adept at managing many types of personalities and maintaining complete control of casino operations. He was said to be "mild-mannered" and "slow to anger," but was "fast and skillful with his fists when provoked." He was always on call to eject unruly patrons from the casino and also to protect showgirls from male customers' advances.

As the Rat Pack concept was losing steam, so too was the Sands itself. It had been acquired by Howard Hughes, who exorcised many of the former mob demons that swirled in its soul. Megaresorts, such as Caesars Palace, effectively dwarfed the Sands. Carl Cohen, who had become a legend in Las Vegas, famously lost his cool with Sinatra, who fancied himself a "tough guy" after reading the Freeman publicity. Except that five-foot-seven-and-a-half, 119-pound Frankie didn't stand a chance against the six-foot-five, 280-pounder.

Stefan Andrews, of the *Vintage News*, wrote:

> Frank Sinatra was maybe not like Moe Dalitz, who put
> Las Vegas on the map, but he certainly played a part
> in making the city worth the trip. He was the one who
> brought the style, swing, and swagger into venues like

the Sands, the Sahara, or the Golden Nugget, to name just a few. So Frank was largely responsible for helping to create the Las Vegas image of a city as the ultimate adult playground.

Reportedly, the incidents with Sinatra at the Sands happened because the singer had been drinking and gambling to an unreasonable level for two long nights in a row without stopping.

[Once Sinatra had accumulated $200,000 worth of debt], Hughes had ordered his casino credit to be stopped.

It was a Saturday night, on September 9, 1967 when, in an outburst of rage, Sinatra walked out before a scheduled performance. He also yelled at the personnel, destroyed furniture in his room, and steered a baggage cart through a glass window before leaving the building and heading to Caesars Palace to immediately arrange a new contract. As that was the end of the cozy relationship the singer had with the Sands, more casualties followed when he returned to the resort in the early morning of Monday, the 11th of September, demanding to see Cohen.

The casino manager agreed to see him, but headed first to get breakfast, however. Frank was already there. Sinatra shot all sorts of curses and threats at Carl, including upending the breakfast table onto Cohen, spilling hot coffee on him.

It must have been a wild morning, as Cohen had responded with punches, a report on the incident reads: "At 6 A.M. today, Sinatra appeared at the Sands, made one hell of a scene and insisted on seeing Carl Cohen. He threatened to kill anyone who got in his way, used vile language, and said he would beat up the telephone operators if they did not connect him with Cohen, etc.

"In an effort to calm the situation, Carl agreed to meet him. Sinatra called Cohen every dirty name in the book, said he was going to kill him, pushed a table over on Carl, picked up a chair and attempted to hit Carl over the head. Carl ducked, took a pass at Sinatra and floored him."

Though everybody thought Sinatra had one of his front teeth knocked out, it was only the caps he had that had been dislodged. Surprisingly, the dramatic event only enforced Carl's reputation, making him somewhat into a local hero.

As municipal elections were scheduled for November that year, there was even one poster that appeared with a picture of Sinatra and his front teeth blackened out, reading a slogan: "Carl Cohen for Mayor."

Carl, who was the author's cousin, became the fair-haired boy of men like Moe Dalitz, Louis Rothkopf, and Morris Kleinman during the Prohibition era.

In 1957, Rothkopf and Max Diamond were convicted of tax evasion over liquor sales and sentenced to four years in prison; they were also ordered to pay a fine of $5,000. The trial showed they had failed to pay taxes on $150,000 worth of sales of illegal alcohol. Rothkopf operated the Pettibone Club, and was connected to the Jungle Inn, located near Youngstown.

When Rothkopf and Diamond were released from prison, they invested in the Desert Inn, as well as gambling establishments in Kentucky and Ohio. In 1936, he invested alongside Moe Dalitz, Morris Kleinman, Sam Tucker, and Max Diamond in River Downs in Cincinnati and Thistledown Racetrack in Cleveland, two legitimate enterprises. Carl Cohen quickly rose to operations manager and, by the time he was twenty-eight, he was the right-hand man to some of the most notorious underworld figures.

Max told the author, "After Eliot Ness (who became the safety commissioner of Cleveland) tried to set us up and take his own cut from the casinos, he turned on us and we were convicted. We decided to try to turn our money [to more legitimate ventures], and Vegas was legal. Racetracks were legal. Carl [Cohen] was the right guy to watch our money."

Note: Maxie Diamond, along with Morris Kleinman and Louis Rothkopf, was asked to testify before the Senate Crime Investigation Committee chaired by Tennessee Senator Estes Kefauver on bootlegging allegations in 1952. When both men refused because they didn't want the media to attend their hearing, they were first charged with contempt of Congress, but were later cleared.

When Moe Dalitz moved his operations from Cleveland to Las Vegas, he took along Carl Cohen in 1941 to become casino manager at the El Rancho, where he succeeded by being "respectful always to the prerogatives of the Boys and of such esteemed guests as Howard Hughes, for whom he kept a hotel cabin permanently reserved." In 1943, he became part owner of the resort.

His catering to Hughes resulted in his losing his job at the El Rancho Vegas in 1952 and gaining him a new position at the Sands. One night, El Rancho owner Beldon Katleman was inspecting the packed casino when he noticed a man dressed in jeans and tennis shoes sitting beside the well-heeled high rollers at the gaming tables. He ordered Cohen to eject the unsightly patron (it was Howard Hughes). Cohen refused, and their argument in the middle of the casino became physical when Katleman jabbed Cohen, and Cohen punched Katleman in the jaw, flooring him. Cohen then walked out, followed by half the dealers who were already disgusted by Katleman's behavior. A few hours later, Jakey Freedman, one of the operators at the Sands, invited Cohen to come in for an interview, and Cohen accepted the job of casino manager, along with a controlling interest of five points in the hotel operation. He brought along the dealers who had walked out with him and many of his wealthy clients, including Howard Hughes. Hughes later bought the Sands in 1967 and installed Cohen as the president of the hotel and casino.

Chapter 12
Do You Really Want to Know?

Rat Pack Fantasy vs. Reality

In the Sands' main showroom, Dean, Joey, and Frank perform their seemingly improvised—but actually well-rehearsed—comedy banter, 1960.

The author has no desire to reprint the false bravado, the manufactured characteristics or fantasies of the five members of the so-called Rat Pack. We assume the reader is aware of the illusions and fictions that have been peddled by other books that take them through the looking glass and into their Rat Pack/Alice in Wonderland world.

The Summit was a business proposition through and through. It was not Frank Sinatra's intent to create a situation to "hang out" with his buddies. However, due to Al Freeman, that was the story and he was sticking to it. Sinatra was nearly forty-five years old by the time of the Summit. Each supporting member was forty or older. They all had families, they had all been kicked around the business and knew its brutality and the short windows of fame that close quickly. This was their time to cash in on this sudden burst of infamy and then take their acts individually to exploit their good fortune.

Joey was about as close to Frank as Mike Pence is to Donald Trump. They each served a purpose. Despite the legend created for the past sixty years, Frank had his own coterie of friends. When he was working, he certainly would have dinner with Sammy, or say hello to Joey after he had warmed up the crowd for him, or played a round of golf with Dean, or held his nose as he used Peter to get closer to his charismatic brother-in-law. During their five-week engagement as the Summit, they obviously were thrown into proximity with one another. However, it was the meeting of five separate corporations merging to enhance their individual goals.

Al Freeman, as has been stated, was the master of creating an image that he could utilize to sell his product. Freeman's product was the Sands first; Las Vegas, second. The vehicle he used in this instance was The Rat Pack—and, yes, he used *that* term. We know the stories about Frank not liking it, but Frank liked whatever enhanced his 9% stake in the Sands. Don't sell Sinatra short. He knew his product and, for more than fifty years, he did what it took to perpetuate the legend and accumulate great wealth and power. He loved every minute of being Frank Sinatra. Frank was, in every respect, a true Machiavellian scholar. He carefully chose his Royal Court. His co-stars were each at the top of their game. First George Evans, then Warren Cowan, and his first lieutenant Guy McElwaine (eventually the head of Columbia Pictures) ran a masterful public-relations blitz throughout his career. Abe Lastfogel and Sam Weisbord and others managed his career, carefully charting its course. Nelson Riddle and other brilliant arrangers, composers, and musicians fought for his favor. Sinatra was the CEO of a carefully crafted organization.

And Frank had the Midas touch. Whomever he favored, and it would mainly be someone who could benefit *him*, would reap the benefits of his magical endorsement. And Joey knew it. Despite his later claims about his carefully crafted image, attitude, and career, he was at heart a journeyman comic who started his ascent when he became Frank's opening act, hit his stride as a member of the Rat Pack, and when Frank forgot about him, he spent nearly the last of his forty years in obscurity, only to resurface when the Rat Pack was mentioned. Sammy was a great talent, but he is mostly remembered for the Rat Pack films (singing the opening tune "Ee O Eleven," from *Ocean's 11*). Dean was also talented, but he hit fame almost entirely because of Jerry and then he may have disappeared after the split without becoming part of Frank's clan. Lawford is remembered for two connections: his marriage to a Kennedy and his time with the Rat Pack. His early appearances in films are mostly unremarkable and forgotten, his television shows are rarely shown, and his fame after the Rat Pack was as a derelict drug addict.

However, due to the master blueprint by Al Freeman for the five-week Summit at the Sands, Dean, Sammy, Joey, and Peter were anointed by Ol' Blue Eyes. As in the elements of a tornado, the gathering of the perfect components around Frank created a freewheeling attitude that prevails today. As mentioned earlier, the Rat Pack symbolized a harmless sense of misogyny, of women being subservient to men. There is enough nostalgia for those days to keep several tribute acts in business in the 21st century.

Work began on the actual preparation for the *Ocean's 11* film and the Summit when director Lewis Milestone and his more than forty advance men arrived in Las Vegas on January 12, 1960. Frank flew in five days later, followed by Dean and his wife Jeannie (and his sidekick Mack Gray), Peter and Pat Lawford (along with his manager Milt Ebbins), Sammy and his team. Joey came solo, with Sylvia and Larry still back in Englewood.

While the crews set up for the first shots, which were going to be at the Riviera, the performers began rehearsing their sets on January 18 for their debut of the Summit on January 20 in the Copa Room. The filming schedules were rigid and precise. There was very little room for error. Much of the filming took place between 3 P.M. and 6 P.M. Milestone said he felt a bit like prolific director William "One Shot" Beaudine. Their precise timing left little room for more than a couple of setups. But Milestone was an old pro who knew precisely what he needed. The legend that these middle-aged men filmed all day and partied all night was hardly a reality.

Meanwhile, Al Freeman and his other Vegas public relations gurus were on their toes. The town was overrun with journalists, photographers, newsreel cameras, and every other form of media to cover every minute of the Summit. It was like the Royal Wedding of Diana and Charles, only this event lasted for weeks. Every step was scheduled with precision and coordination by Al Freeman. Reading the transcripts in the archives and interviewing Carl Cohen, Moe Dalitz, and (to an extent) Mickey Cohen, the author was astounded by how much importance was placed on this event. And unlike *The Godfather* fantasy, these were goal-minded businessmen to the core.

The Summit, with its international focus, was eyed by others as a means of gaining personal attention. Most notably, presidential candidate Senator John Kennedy carefully planned to be a part of the hoopla for its attendant publicity. His father, publicity genius Joseph P. Kennedy, saw this event as a means of making his son the great White Knight—someone with whom the country could identify as "cool, hip, sophisticated" and attract those younger voters. While it was almost certain that Richard Nixon was to be the GOP candidate of 1960, he was stodgy and firmly entrenched in the establishment. Joe Kennedy had helped propel Gloria Swanson to superstardom. While he had little respect for his son-in-law Lawford, he became a handy tool to arrange the ultimate photo op for JFK. While he hardly needed Peter's help with the casino—he was, after all, a business partner of Frank Costello, Sam Giancana, Meyer Lansky, and Moe Dalitz during Prohibition—he used Peter's connections to set up Jack with Frank and the boys.

As JFK was preparing for his push to win the big primaries in the East, he scheduled some campaigns on the West Coast, with February 7 circled as his day at the Summit. It was beautifully choreographed. Jack had his huge entourage with him, including his baby brother Teddy. As the world's press watched, listened, photographed, filmed, and wrote, JFK held a press conference and was filmed with the Rat Pack paying homage to *him*. Jack was now one of the boys. He attended fundraisers that were conveniently arranged; he was filmed watching the Summit in the Copa Room, taking in shows in the lounge, and becoming an honorary member of the Rat Pack.

On the day of Kennedy's arrival, the boys did a show at the Moe Dalitz–built Convention Center for a benefit performance to mark "Four Chaplains Day," a local event that honored four clergymen who had been killed on a ship during World War II. The purpose of the benefit was to build a monument to these fallen heroes. And, of course, it was captured on film to expose the "big hearts" of the Rat Pack members.

For the nightly news, Frank introduced Kennedy from the stage with much reverence and even more bullshit. Kennedy took a bow. Then Dean, with his customary needle to puncture any bubble, joked, "What'd you say his name was?" Big audience laugh. It was precisely staged and planned, another masterful public-relations coup. Kennedy remained for more photo ops on February 8, then had a private reception in a room at the Sands before his plane departed for Oregon. Peter, Joey, Dean, Sammy, and (of course) Frank were there.

Shawn Levy wrote in *Rat Pack Confidential,*

> As Sammy remembered it, "Peter took me aside and
> whispered, 'If you want to see what a million dollars in cash
> looks like, go into the next room; there's a brown leather

satchel in the closet; open it. It's a gift from the hotel owners for Jack's campaign.' I never went near it. I was also told
that there were four wild girls scheduled to 'entertain him'
and I didn't want to hear about that either and I got out of
there. Some things you don't want to know."

The contribution was quite calculated. Murder, Inc. knew they
had a legal goldmine in Las Vegas and hardly wanted any inter-
ruption from the government. Taking care of the Kennedys with a
simple cash gift was the easiest way to placate the future president. They hardly foresaw his younger brother—Bobby, the attorney general—breathing down their necks in Senate hearings to
banish the Mafia.

The author also interviewed Judith Campbell Exner, who
became a mistress of both JFK and Giancana, for their book
on "Dr. Feelgood." (She had been one of the infamous Dr. Max
Jacobson's patients.) Campbell remembered the party: "I first
met Jack there. I knew all the boys and Frank."

Almost every A-list star migrated to the desert oasis to watch
the Summit. Kirk Douglas, Lucille Ball, Jack Benny, Cyd Charisse
and her husband Tony Martin, heavyweight boxing champ Inge-
mar Johansson, Milton Berle, Peter Lorre, Mexican star Cantinflas, Jack Lemmon, Marilyn Monroe, and countless others had
ringside seats. Even though there was not a ticket available anywhere, the Sands still ran ads that read "Star-Light, Star-Bright,
Which Star Shines Tonight?" Al Freeman and his team, despite
the press converging on the city, cranked out countless press
releases with every angle covered.

The theme of the Summit, at least in theory, was that each
night would feature one member of the group as the lead star.
The joke, according to Joey, was: "A couple of low rollers got tickets to the Summit and they are lined up outside the Copa Room.
One turns to the other and asks, 'Who's the star tonight?' and his
buddy says, 'With our goddamned luck, it'll be that Lawford.'"

As Joey told the author, "Peter was always so uncomfortable
onstage, it was quite visible."

The cost of the show and dinner was $5.95. The casino hardly
cared about the show's ticket prices—the tables and machines

would take care of the funding after the show. Other clubs were putting their best foot forward as well. The town was hopping, and the world was watching the party.

Chapter 13
The Rat Pack Blueprint: Part One

Frank interrupts Joey during his monologue, much to the amusement of ringsiders Marilyn Monroe, Elizabeth Taylor, and Dean Martin.

While several elements combined to create the cultural phenomenon known as the Rat Pack, there were two main ingredients. 1) Frank Sinatra, and 2) Al Freeman.

As discussed earlier, Sinatra was brought on board at the inception of the Sands by three of its creators, Moe Dalitz, Carl Cohen, and Jack Entratter. Jack set out to design a room similar to the club he had just left in New York, the legendary Copacabana. With the funding from Frank Costello and Meyer Lansky, the Sands had a "soft" opening in December of 1952. Trying to avoid the type of disastrous opening at the Flamingo four years earlier, they decided to work out the kinks before making their big splash.

With Moe Dalitz moving his base from the El Rancho along with his lieutenant, Carl Cohen (both Cleveland guys), the ambitious Sands Resort/Casino set out to be the ultimate Las Vegas destination. And as Frank Costello, Monte Proser, Jules Podell, and Jack Entratter had turned the Copacabana into *the* nightspot in New York City, they carefully plotted to turn the Copa Room—the main showroom at the Sands—into the Vegas "Ground Zero."

Al Freeman, the bright young publicist they enticed to join them from Los Angeles, was a protégé of the late George Evans. Since Evans's star client was Frank Sinatra, Freeman had one key suggestion: "Do whatever it takes to hire him." This was easier said than done. Sinatra was coming back from his deep slump. Using the launching pad of his eventual Academy Award–winning performance as Maggio in *From Here to Eternity*, Sinatra had turned things around. After a testimonial dinner given by Mickey Cohen, Frank had once again hit his stride.

In 1953, Sinatra was being courted by Capitol records. Those in charge were attempting to pair up Frank with Nelson Riddle, the brilliant arranger who had worked wonders with Nat "King" Cole (Riddle had arranged King's monster hit "Mona Lisa") and Doris Day. Sinatra initially tried to stay with Axel Stordahl, his collaborator from Columbia Records. When their first few Capitol sides fell flat, however, Sinatra relented and joined forces with Riddle. The debut product of their professional marriage was "I've Got the World on a String"—and they were off and running. Sinatra was not only setting the charts on fire; he became a box-office dynamo and was in demand for personal appearances. And now he had the gorgeous movie star Ava Gardner at his side.

When the author interviewed Carl Cohen in 1982, he asked him if the "boys" had pulled some strings to get Frank hired at the casino, as Mario Puzo's *The Godfather* suggested. "Are you *kidding*?" Cohen laughed. "Frank was all business. He had the protection of 'Uncle' Abe Lastfogel of William Morris, and we dealt with his first lieutenant, Sam Weisbord. Frank surrounded himself with the best advisors and Sam knew exactly his commodity. Frank was the best draw in Vegas. He drew the players. We were not looking for the family trade then. We wanted the gamblers from Los Angeles, and we wanted the best. We wanted a hopping lounge and the number-one showroom. And only Sinatra could guarantee us that. Frank wanted ownership. He wanted a piece of the action. He loved Jack Entratter and Al Freeman, so he felt at home at the Sands. We offered an opportunity for him to buy a 9% piece."

"In cash?" the author asked.

He shook his head. "It was structured against his salary, where he would pay it off. Once we had Frank, everyone else followed."

Sinatra made his first appearance as a Vegas headliner at the Desert Inn in 1950. From October 1953 until his disastrous face-off with Cohen in 1967, Frank was entrenched at the Copa Room at the Sands. The swinging, swaggering Sinatra style became a part of the fabric of Las Vegas. He alone defined the city's image as a sophisticated adult playground. And that one-of-a-kind blend of impeccable showmanship and anything-goes merriment that Sinatra embodied in his Las Vegas engagements established the city as a home to world-class entertainment. In fact, it's difficult to overestimate the impact that Francis Albert Sinatra had on the very essence of Las Vegas, Nevada. After he left the Sands, he moved to the Sahara, then the Riviera, Caesars Palace, and finally, with the wooing of Steve Wynn, the Golden Nugget.

Chuck Crisafulli wrote an incisive piece entitled "Sin-atra City: The Story of Frank Sinatra and Las Vegas" for *Medium Magazine*

(December 2, 2015). The following extract is being reprinted with his kind permission.

> Sinatra began his long relationship with the Sands in October 1953. From the stage of the Sands' Copa Room, however, Sinatra's star power was resurgent. His swinging takes of standards such as Cole Porter's "I Get A Kick Out Of You" and "I've Got You Under My Skin" and the Gershwins' "They Can't Take That Away From Me" perfectly captured the equally earthy and urbane vibe of Vegas, and the voice of Sinatra quickly became the de facto soundtrack to nights on the Strip. Sinatra soon had a real stake in the city as well — in addition to being a Copa Room headliner, he became a co-owner of the Sands.
>
> Of course, at the same time he was packing the Sands, Sinatra's success extended beyond Las Vegas. He received a Best Actor in a Supporting Role Oscar for his part in the 1953 hit *From Here To Eternity,* and he went on to achieve bona fide movie stardom with leads in such films as *The Man With The Golden Arm, Guys and Dolls, High Society,* and *Pal Joey.* The extraordinary series of concept albums he recorded for Capitol Records through the '50s and '60s, including *In The Wee Small Hours, Songs For Swingin' Lovers!* and the 1959 Album of the Year Grammy winner, *Come Dance With Me!,* were startling artistic breakthroughs and unquestionable commercial triumphs. In collaboration with talented arrangers such as Nelson Riddle and Billy May, Sinatra perfected the bold, innovative, swinging sound he brought to Vegas stages.
>
> Sinatra's friendship with [Sammy] Davis points to an impact Sinatra had on Las Vegas beyond the realm of entertainment. Through the '50s, Las Vegas was a deeply segregated town, with Black performers not allowed to stay at the hotels and casinos in which they performed. Sinatra frequently dined with Davis at the Golden Steer

Steak House rather than eating without him in segre-
gated hotel dining rooms, and when his tremendous
success at the Copa Room gave him enough leverage, he
demanded that Davis be allowed to stay at the Sands.
Sinatra continued to be an advocate for racial equality,
which played a role in the March 1960 agreement among
hotel and casino owners that effectively desegregated
Las Vegas.

Meanwhile, the Chairman's presence in Las Vegas made
the town a top draw not only for his own fans, but for
fellow celebrities. A typical crowd in the intimate Copa
Room might include such stars as Elizabeth Taylor, Lucille
Ball and Gregory Peck. And, on the opening night of
a Rat Pack engagement in December 1965, the audience included a twenty-three-year-old Steve Wynn. The
magnate-to-be was actually there as one of Sinatra's
guests, having just recently met the singer by chance in
Palm Springs, Calif., through a family friend. That evening
marked the beginning of a lifelong friendship between
Wynn and Sinatra, as well as the beginning of Wynn's
impactful career in Las Vegas.

Carl Cohen told the author, "Unfortunately, many have forgotten how much Al Freeman contributed to our success. His crazy
ideas and concepts were important to the growth of the hotel
and Las Vegas. It wasn't just the floating crap tables or stunts like
that. Al brought movies and TV into the mix and made the city as
the ultimate resort destination . . . and he knew how to use Frank
as our secret weapon."

There were other known publicists who worked to put Las
Vegas on the map, as the author discovered while searching the
archives of the University of Las Vegas. Men such as Harvey Died-
rich, Jim Seagrave, Eugene Murphy, and Abe Schiller successfully
promoted Las Vegas. However, it was Al Freeman, who worked
at the Sands from its opening in 1952 until his death twenty years
later, who carefully crafted the blueprint for its success.

Because he had worked with Jack Entratter of the Copaca-bana, Freeman joined Entratter when the latter moved to Las Vegas in 1952 as entertainment director and one of the owners of the new Sands Hotel. From the opening night, Freeman was instrumental in making the hotel the leading entertainment cen-ter and resort along the famed Las Vegas Strip.

What set Freeman apart from the other publicists was his skill-ful promotion of the Sands in movies and on television. While some publicists worked with production companies reluctantly because of the disruption that making movies and television pro-grams caused guests, Freeman embraced the opportunities as long as the program or movie portrayed the Sands and Las Vegas in a positive light. In addition to variety shows like those hosted by Milton Berle and Red Skelton, Freeman worked closely with producers of several television series, including *The Millionaire, I Spy*, and *Julia*. He also helped arrange the filming of major motion pictures like *Meet Me in Las Vegas*. He felt that movies and pro-grams like these, which reached very large audiences, were help-ful in promoting the Sands as an exciting and family-oriented resort. He even arranged for the Post cereal company to shoot eight commercials at the Sands, featuring the television family of Danny Thomas on the first two episodes of CBS's *The Danny Thomas Show*.

By 1958, Sinatra was deeply ensconced at the Sands. Joey Bishop was his regular opening act, and Sammy Davis Jr. and the Will Mastin Trio were frequent performers there. Al Freeman was looking diligently for a film project that would feature Frank with the Sands and Las Vegas as the backdrop—it would be the ultimate travelogue. The other publicists and hotel owners were entwined in one another's businesses one way or another. Since much of the funding had come from Murder, Inc. and their fran-chises from Cleveland, Chicago, Detroit, Kansas City, and even Youngstown, Ohio, there seemed to be a harmony among the thieves, especially since the money was flowing in. As their select "bagmen" brought home the green paper of cotton and linen, in abundance, there was peace among the boys.

However, Freeman needed a centerpiece to finally put Las Vegas directly on the map for everyone in the world. It had to feature the emblem, the symbol of Vegas cool, Frank Sinatra.

Chapter 14
The Rat Pack Blueprint: Part Two
The Making of Ocean's 11

On the set with (left to right): Richard Conte, Buddy Lester, Joey Bishop, Sammy Davis Jr., Frank Sinatra, Dean Martin, Peter Lawford, Akim Tamiroff, Richard Benedict, Henry Silva, Norman Fell, and Clem Harvey.

The germ of the idea behind *Ocean's 11* started in 1955 with a second-rate director named Gilbert Kay. Following his service in World War II, the Chicago-born Kay worked his way up from the Columbia Pictures mailroom to assistant director on B-Westerns and even a Three Stooges short, *Hugs and Mugs* (1950). By 1955 he had directed a couple of awful B-films, including *Three Bad Sisters*, and episodes of such TV series as *Highway Patrol* (with Broderick Crawford) and *Passport to Danger*. In other words, nothing impressive.

Kay had in his possession a story written by a gas station attendant about a group of G.I.s who, after World War II, do some smuggling jobs for the army. That gas station attendant turned out to be George Clayton Thomas, who later found recognition as a science-fiction writer (*The Twilight Zone, Star Trek, Logan's Run*). At this point, however, Thomas was doing an assortment of odd jobs and had no experience as a writer. As he said in an interview for the American Archive of Television in 2003:

> I got a buddy of mine named Jack Golden Russell to
> help me write a screenplay. Kay envisioned Broderick
> Crawford as Danny Ocean, a tough-as-nails ex-army
> sergeant that no one said "no" to. Kay had worked with
> Crawford as a director of several episodes of *Highway
> Patrol*. He said the only problem with Crawford was
> that you had to shoot the scenes before noon, because
> he was always drunk by 2 P.M. We flew to Vegas with Kay
> and shot pictures of the hotels and then concocted
> our schemes as to how to escape. You see, robbing the
> hotels was the easy part—it was getting the money out of
> the town since there was only one road out. So, we sold
> 10% of the script to a Beverly Hills furrier named Charles
> Fuerman for $10,000 and opened up an office. We wrote
> it in longhand and Gilbert had it typed up. And I never
> saw it again. Gilbert then said Peter Lawford was to star
> in it and we'd get $10k to divide up, and 10%. It was my
> story, and it was being stolen.

After trying unsuccessfully to peddle the story with himself attached as director, Kay approached Peter Lawford in 1957 and sold him the story for $10,000 ($5k was from Peter; the other $5k came from his wife, Patricia Kennedy Lawford). Lawford pitched the story to Frank, who joked: "Forget the movie, let's pull the job!"

Frank was under contract for one more film from his Dorchester Productions with Warner Bros. As luck would have it, Jack Warner liked the idea of the caper film. A deal was struck in July of 1958 to move forward with the project. Warner suggested Richard Breen for the script and began talks with Jack Lemmon to co-star with Sinatra.

In April 1956, a *Daily News* item stated that director Gilbert L. Kay and producer Earl Colbert had signed jazz guitarist Barney Kessell (who was married to Mickey Rooney's second wife and was raising his two sons) to score *Ocean's 11*, which was to be the first picture produced by the newly formed Matador Productions. The news item also listed the authors of the original story, George Clayton Thomas (and Jack Golden Russell), co-partnered with Kay and Colbert. According to an item in the *Los Angeles Times* in 1957, Lawford and Sinatra bought the screenplay.

A September 1958 news item which mentioned that Sinatra and Lawford's friendship had "blossomed into a business deal," confirmed their plans to produce the film in the Las Vegas area, at "the famed magnesium plant in Henderson, Nevada," a few miles outside the city, and at the Sands Hotel, of which Sinatra and Martin had part ownership. It further stated that small cottages near the plant would be used in the story to advance the plot, which called for them to be set on fire, so that the story's "gangsters" could hold up six hotels on the Strip while the fire and police departments fought the blaze. The news item also reported that during production, Sinatra, Lawford, Martin, Bishop, and Davis would alternate performances at the Sands each night.

According to an item in *Daily Variety*, the film would be co-produced by Sinatra's Dorchester and Lawford's KenLaw production companies, and that Sinatra and Lawford would star in the film, along with Davis, Martin, and Buddy Lester. According to *The Hollywood Reporter*, that production of the film, which was being written by Richard Breen, was to be postponed until after Sinatra completed the film *All My Tomorrows*, the working title for the 1959 United Artists release *A Hole in the Head*. According to the *Los Angeles Mirror-News* and *Daily Variety*, Lawford and Breen traveled to Las Vegas to work on the script, which they discussed with the Las Vegas police chief, R. K. Sheffer Breen. (There is no mention of the chief in the onscreen credits.) *The Hollywood Reporter*, which erroneously referred to the film as "Oceans of Loving," reported that Sinatra was negotiating with Jackie Gleason, who did not appear in the final film. An unsourced but contemporary article at the AMPAS Library adds that Tony Curtis and Milton Berle had been signed for cameos, and that Daniel Fuchs had worked on the screenplay. According to an August 1960 *Los Angeles Examiner* article, producer-director Lewis Milestone had discarded most of the original melodramatic story, keeping only the basic idea of twelve ex-paratroopers robbing five Las Vegas casinos. January and February 1960 *Hollywood Reporter* items stated that portions of the film were shot at the Sands, the Sahara, and the Riviera, three of the five hotel casinos mentioned in the story, as well as the Warner Bros. soundstages.

Although it was later refuted in a modern book about the Rat Pack, an August 1960 *Los Angeles Examiner* article reported that the cast and crew shot the casino sequences during the establishments' slowest times, between 1:00 and 5:00 A.M. A March 1960 *Los Angeles Mirror-News* article stated that television-style cue cards were used to eliminate the need for the cast to memorize lines. Several autobiographical sources and documentary footage describe the party atmosphere, the pranks, and the drinking during the making of the film, all in the Rat Pack's flamboyant style, which can be summed up by one of their signature phrases: "ring-a-ding-ding."

Sinatra was delighted that Vegas was being used as the backdrop for the film. That way, he could play the Copa Room at night and film during the day. He talked to Jack Entratter and Al Freeman, and they both loved the idea as well. Freeman offered Frank a full run of the hotel to film wherever the crew wanted. Sinatra, being a part-owner of the Sands, liked the idea of making "his" hotel the backdrop. Then Freeman came up with the following concept:

Sinatra, of course, was the keystone act, the backbone of the Sands. Dean Martin had signed a five-year deal with the hotel in 1957, after his heavily reported breakup with Jerry Lewis, with a deal in which he got a cut of the proceeds. Sammy Davis Jr. was also under a five-year agreement with the hotel. Freeman suggested that, during the making of the movie, they alternate nights and have the movie feature Dean, Frank, and Sammy. Frank suggested adding Lawford, since he came up with the script for the film, and use his opening comic, Joey Bishop, as the emcee/ straight man. This was the same time when Bishop was hitting it big with Jack Paar. Then Freeman said, "Why not just all do the act together?" Make it the meeting of the biggest acts in show business— a Summit at the Sands, as Freeman called it (in a memo in the UNLV Archives, donated by Al Freeman in 1972).

The Summit at the Sands. Dean, Sammy, Peter, and Joey jumped at the idea as well. They all agreed that it would be a carefully rehearsed show that would have the appearance of free form.

Frank, along with Sam Weisbord, worked out the deals. Frank, Dean, Sammy, and Joey would get their standard full salaries. Peter sold the script to Dorchester Productions (Frank) and Warner Bros. Lawford was paid $20,000 for the script, $300 a week for the shoot (plus another salary for the nighttime shows, about $8,000 weekly)— the topper was the back-end deal. Lawford got one-sixth of the gross revenue from the film. Thus, Lawford's return on his $10k investment for the script was initially a $500,000 profit. (His estate continues to profit from that film and its later incarnations.) Dean got $150,000 flat for the film, plus his nightly salary during the shoot. Sammy received $125,000 for the film and his nightly salary. Supporting actors Richard Conte took home $8,200 per week, and Cesar Romero made $5,000 per week. Those with cameos—Shirley MacLaine, Red Skelton, George Raft, and seventeen others—received scale. Frank also bought all the celebrities (twenty-two in all) brand new Volkswagen Beetles in the color of their choice. The VW Bug was the hot new car of 1960.

Frank received his nightly salary, $30,000 for the story, $200,000 to appear in the film, and a third of the gross revenues. This did not include his share as a 9% owner of the Sands and the incredible returns there would be during the weeks of filming. Since *Ocean's 11* was being shot during the traditionally slow month of February, it was a windfall profit for all the Sands' owners.

Carl Cohen said, "It was an absolute stroke of genius. A Summit at the Sands. It was a win/win all around. Everyone, from the maître d's to the cocktail waitresses to the shoeshine boys, were profiting. And we spread the good fortune throughout the town. It was February and the town was jumping as it never had. We couldn't handle the tens of thousands of reservations that were called in [they only had two hundred rooms at the time] and the overflow spilled out to Henderson and as far out to Stateline."

Ocean's 11's August 1960 Las Vegas premiere was themed as a New Year's Eve celebration set in the summer, and included the leads performing together at the Sands as part of the festivities. According to the *Los Angeles Examiner,* "The film is one of the few that typifies the de-moralization trend in filmmaking today. There's no punishment for the crime." A critic for *The Los Angeles Times* stated, "If this picture can be parlayed . . . into a great success, then they've gotten away with real murder. If not, and the public ignores one of the truly emptiest displays on record, maybe some of these many talents will have to actually go to work."

Despite the mixed reviews, *Ocean's 11* became the highest-grossing motion picture of Frank Sinatra's career.

Chapter 15
Ocean's 11

Pulling Off the Heist

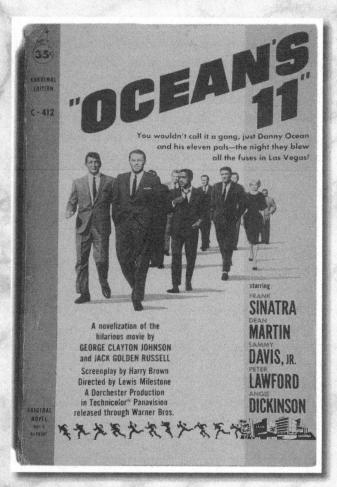

As the twenty-eight days of the Summit began to wind down, the Rat Pack frenzy remained at fever pitch. Sammy, Dean, Frank, and Joey had their own club dates to attend to after wrapping *Ocean's 11* in Burbank at Warner Bros.

Meanwhile, back at the Sands, it was a wild scene. Literally, it was decadence galore. That catchphrase "What happens in Vegas, stays in Vegas" was very much in place in 1960, at least in theory. Everyone from the noted New Orleans district attorney Jim Garrison to attorney Louis Nizer were caught in compromising situations, but they were quickly swept under the rug. Carl Cohen and Jack Entratter were masterful hosts and, whatever the high roller sought, they were given. Their egos were stroked in every way imaginable.

Rocky Kalish was a guest of Jimmy "Blue Eyes" Alo during those twenty-eight days. Rocky had worked for Alo in his college days in New York, transporting bags of money from Grossinger's resort in the Catskills. Alo, who owned a piece of the Sands through Meyer Lansky and the Genovese family, was often seen at the resort. (Alo was the inspiration for the Johnny Ola character in *The Godfather: Part Two*.)

As Rocky recalled, "When Jimmy was in Vegas, he would stay at the apartment owned by Jack Entratter. Alo would treat me like a king. Entratter walked on eggshells around Alo—everybody did. Frank loved him, and he loved Frank. I got ringside seats at a couple of the Summit shows and went to the after-parties too."

Shecky Greene said candidly, "I would not say that the show was the greatest I've seen; it was more of an event. It was the feeling of excitement, even mystery. You just never knew what was going to happen."

Keely Smith was appearing with her then-husband Louis Prima (and Sam Butera) in an amazing lounge act at the Sahara. She recalled, "My gosh, it was swinging. It's like a wave hit the town. Everybody came to our shows. Every star, politician, every mobster, it was a Who's Who. Louis loved it. There was a buzz in Vegas as I never experienced."

Kaye Ballard remembered, "It was a special time. It was just exciting to be part of the business. It was a once-in-a-lifetime event and you wanted to be part of it. To just be present. Every great musician was there, whether they were performing or not. Many would just jam at the lounge shows all over town."

Rose Marie told the author, "My husband [musician Bobby Guy] and I were not working then as it was a slow month. We drove up to Vegas just to be a part of it. Bobby then got a job while we were there, and it was an amazing time. I was there at the beginning [the opening of the Flamingo with Jimmy Durante] and it was a whole different town by then. I knew all the wise guys and they took care of Bobby and me."

Location work on *Ocean's 11* wrapped on February 17, after which the crews returned to Burbank to shoot various take-up shots on the Warner Bros. lot the following day. While the schedules were tight and strictly followed on location, the hope was that it would be easier to focus back on the lot.

However, chaos followed. Frank did not show up for the first few days as he went back to the recording studio to cut some tracks with Nelson Riddle. Dean Martin appeared at the Sands doing his solo act and stayed on to fill in for, surprisingly, his ex-partner Jerry Lewis, who claimed fatigue from shooting *The Bellboy* in Miami. Peter had flown to Israel to film *Exodus* for Otto Preminger. Sammy had club dates in New York. Joey had begun talks with Danny Thomas and producer Louis Edelman about a possible television series that would be spun off from *The Danny Thomas Show* as they had done with Andy Griffith earlier that season. Joey had also flown home to Englewood and then back to Los Angeles to be a guest on *The Dinah Shore Show.*

During the Summit, the boys were preoccupied with their current partner. Frank was involved with a young dancer named Juliet Prowse, and the two were on the verge of tying the knot. In between visits with Prowse, Frank had the "fun" girl Judith Campbell, whom he introduced to JFK while he was in town. Sammy was involved with the Swedish starlet May Britt, whom he later married. This was at a time that Las Vegas was run by racist rules. On one infamous occasion, Sammy was seen swimming in the Sands' pool. A group of Southern high rollers demanded that Carl Cohen drain the pool—which he did. Frank Sinatra volunteered and acted as the "beard" for May Britt when she visited Sammy, because of the prevailing attitudes toward a Black man dating a White woman. (Later, during the Kennedy inaugural, complications arose from that relationship.) Dean was with his wife, Jeannie, and some of his kids during his month in Vegas. Peter had Pat tagging along with him. And Joey was alone much of the time until he flew Sylvia out to visit him.

Jan Murray's son Howard recalls, "Joey was the least social of the group. He never attended a lot of parties with Sylvia when they lived near us in Beverly Hills. He did not drink at all. He played golf and that was the extent of his sociability."

While Dean, Frank, or Sammy might go out for dinner and drinks, Joey stayed home.

As he remarked to the author on more than one occasion, "I didn't drink. *Ever.* I loved my wife. So, I was never one of the boys. Frank respected that. He knew I was my own man and we both came from similar backgrounds and knew the streets. And I was all business. Frank trusted me."

When the filming returned to Burbank, director Lewis Milestone rushed through production to accommodate everyone's schedules. Frank, as is well known to anyone who has studied his acting career, was best on the first or second take, a fact that Frank Capra discovered when he directed him in *A Hole in the Head.* After the success of *Ocean's 11,* Milestone spent two years filming the big-budget remake of *Mutiny on the Bounty* with the difficult Marlon Brando, who tried to take over the directorial duties. While *Ocean's 11* was a great success, *Mutiny* bombed, and Milestone, nearing seventy, walked away from all the aggravation and retired; he died at age eighty-five in 1980. Meanwhile, despite all the *mishegas,* he brought in *Ocean's 11* $100k under budget, at $2.037 million, which pleased Jack Warner immensely. The film wrapped on March 18, 1960, and was sent to post-production to be ready for an August premiere. Warner Bros. wanted to cash in while the Rat Pack was sizzling hot. Everyone involved realized that it wasn't so much a movie as it was a publicity stunt.

The group reunited at the Fontainebleau in Miami for another Summit in March. During that time, they also shot the Frank Sinatra

Timex special, which featured the duet between the Chairman and the King.

The Summit gathered for the grand finale at the opening on August 3, 1960. It was an Al Freeman masterpiece, made in conjunction with the studio. A one-night Summit. Everyone had scattered by then. Frank was working hard campaigning for Jack Kennedy; he had not performed in Vegas since January. Dean was already in Las Vegas doing a stint at the Copa Room. Joey was at his favorite Chicago haunt, the Chez Parée, and flew in from there. Sammy flew in from Canada, where he was appearing in Montreal. Peter had just finished his stint on *Exodus* and was also on the campaign trail for his brother-in-law. Many of the co-stars in the film were invited to the premiere and to the Summit performance. The guest list included Angie Dickinson, Cesar Romero, Richard Conte, Hank Henry, Akim Tamiroff, and Shirley MacLaine. There were a slew of other celebrities, such as Leo "The Lip" Durocher (manager of the L.A. Dodgers), Joe E. Lewis (whom Sinatra portrayed in *The Joker is Wild*), Sophie Tucker, George Raft, Louis Prima and Keely Smith, Diana Dors and Richard Dawson, Tony Curtis and Janet Leigh, and the nefarious Nick the Greek (who had left a lucrative poker game with Benny Binion to attend). It was the epitome of nightlife royalty. Although the film was to be screened at midnight, there were a number of pre-screening events: a cocktail party, then the Rat Pack dinner show in the Copa Room; there was a parade down the strip to a stage set up downtown on Fremont Street where ten thousand fans converged to see an impromptu performance given by the boys. Jack Paar was there, filming the whole event for a special on NBC. Every columnist from the East and West coasts was there on paid junkets to cover the event, along with *Look, Life, Time,* the best-selling magazines of the era. As always, in true Al Freeman style, everything was organized perfectly to allow the maximum coverage and to override any hard feelings by those who had been left out of the hoopla. No detail was overlooked. Even the iconic "Welcome to Las Vegas" sign was covered over with an *Ocean's 11* banner.

And, as always, Joey fully believed he was the keystone, the hub to the success of the group. "I was with Jack Paar telling him what to shoot. I got him to cover me opening onstage and introducing everyone. When it came time for me to introduce Dean, I said, 'And now—direct from the bar!' . . .They forget that I cultivated that image of Dean as the happy drunk . . ."

Chapter 16
The Jack Pack

Washington Becomes Hollywood

Joey with JFK

At no time in United States history had the world of show business been used to affect the outcome of a national election. Image-maker Joseph Kennedy expertly plotted to have the entertainment world's hottest performers—Frank, Dean, Sammy and, yes, Joey—sprinkle their gold dust on his favored son. Their carefully executed embrace in Las Vegas and the countless events held nationwide for the rest of the year put JFK in a position to win the presidency and to christen the Kennedy family as America's royalty.

For the most part, Joey was apolitical. As he said to the author, "Frankly, I didn't give a shit about politics. I was focused on my career, and my world revolved around my family and show business. I was in the army, I had supported FDR, but beyond that, I never got involved. I never discussed politics—I didn't want to step on any toes, if you know what I mean."

Joey told Maria Torre, a columnist for the *New York Herald-Tribune*, that he had received a call from the White House. "Vice-President Nixon's secretary called to invite me to perform at the convention next week in Chicago," he said. "I didn't know what to do. I thanked the secretary and the vice-president for thinking of me, but I was too busy to go. After all, if I'd be out politically, out professionally . . . actually, I'm a Kennedy man. Have been since the nightclub encounter when Kennedy told me he was a fan of mine for years."

Joey had spent his life as a politician. He did whatever was best for his career and it would have been career suicide to appear at a GOP convention for Nixon. He was going to be part of the Democratic convention in Los Angeles from July 11th to the 15th. He made appearances with the rest of the Rat Pack and was present when Sammy was booed by the Southern delegates.

"*Nigger!*" some Neanderthal yelled out.

Sammy looked around and hollered back: "*Where?*"

In 1960, Joey was everywhere. His stint at the Copacabana was standing room only. He had several appearances as a panelist on *What's My Line?* He appeared on *The Jack Paar Show* regularly. He made a second appearance on *The Jack Benny Program*.

On December 1, 1960, the prestigious CBS show *Person to Person* came into Joey's home in Englewood, New Jersey. Correspondent Charles Collingwood, who had replaced Edward R. Murrow as the host, would conduct the interview from CBS's New York studio. As a touch of hominess, Sylvia was asked by the producers to be dusting the television when the show began. Not being accustomed to the spotlight, however, when she heard Collingswood's disembodied voice say, "Hello, Sylvia," she fainted. From that point on, Joey carried the show.

After the convention in late November, Joey was roasted by the Friars Club in Los Angeles. The dais included his hero, Jack Benny, along with George Jessel, Henny Youngman, George Burns, Danny Thomas, Jack Lemmon, Carol Burnett, Milton Berle, and heavyweight champ Rocky Marciano. Although fellow Rat Packers Dean, Frank, and Sammy were not available, Dean Martin's daughter Deana was there for the fun.

"It was hysterical," Deana told the author. "I was only about twelve and I felt so adult."

Jack Benny joked, "For eighteen years, I was his idol . . . Now, to appear on my show, he wants twenty thousand dollars for a short spot . . . Today, this guy is his *own* idol!"

A pre-*Tonight Show* Johnny Carson said, "Joey Bishop's feud with Ed Sullivan is a clash of personalities. Neither has any. Joey looks like an untipped waiter. Sullivan has the sparkle of the back wall of a handball court."

The actual effect that the Rat Pack had on the 1960 election's outcome has, if anything, been underestimated. Factors leading to the Kennedy family finding favor with the American public included Peter Lawford's marriage to Jack Kennedy's sister, Patricia, and later through Sinatra's friendship with U.S. Senator John F. Kennedy. But the Rat Pack's Hollywood and business network in the entertainment world also made it a potent force for fundraising and voter turnout.

After JFK's victory over Richard Nixon in November of 1960, the plans for the 1961 Kennedy inauguration festivities began in earnest. Frank Sinatra and Peter Lawford began planning a big, star-studded gala and party fundraiser to be staged at the National Armory in Washington, D.C., on January 19, 1961, the night before JFK's formal inauguration. Among the performers and notables gathered for this event were Harry Belafonte, Milton Berle, Nat "King" Cole, Tony Curtis, Janet Leigh, Ella Fitzgerald, Gene Kelly, Fredric March, Ethel Merman, Jimmy Durante, Mahalia Jackson, Bette Davis, Laurence Olivier, Leonard Bernstein, Sidney Poitier, Bill Dana, and Kay Thompson. The biggest honor of all went to Bishop. Frank selected him to emcee the Kennedy inaugural gala, with the hearty endorsement of the president-elect.

The inaugural gala had been carefully planned by Joe Kennedy, with Sinatra's help. When it was televised, the world watched as the Rat Pack left its imprint. Frank escorted First Lady Jacqueline Kennedy to her box at the National Guard Armory for a pre-inaugural gala staged by Sinatra to help pay off JFK's campaign debt. Sinatra was personally responsible for recruiting many of the stars, some flying in from filming and performing locations abroad. He and Lawford also convinced several Broadway producers to shut down their shows for one night so that Anthony Quinn, Ethel Merman, and Laurence Olivier could attend. According to one account, Sinatra personally bought out the theater tickets for the performances of the Broadway plays in conflict.

The National Armory in D.C. hosted two inaugural events: The Pre-Inaugural Gala (January 19) and Post-Inaugural Ball (January 20). Several thousand seats at the National Armory would be sold for $100 each, and seventy-two ringside boxes for small groups were sold at $10,000 apiece.

"We've already sold out the seventy-two boxes," Peter Lawford told *Time* magazine in early December. Sinatra added, "This will be the biggest take in show-business history for a one-nighter. We expect to raise $1,700,000 for the one night." In January, Sinatra and Lawford flew to Washington on Kennedy's private Convair plane to begin work on the gala. The Hollywood stars, producers, directors, conductors, and musicians were housed at the Statler-Hilton Hotel in Washington, reportedly taking over the top floor. Sinatra also hired Hollywood photographer Phil Stern to document the events, later giving each of the participants their own photo album.

The one thorn in the side of the Rat Pack was Sammy's relationship with Swedish actress May Britt. Davis had planned to take leave from his engagement at the Latin Casino near Philadelphia in order to perform at the gala. But given his recent (mid-November 1960) mixed-race marriage to Britt, Sammy was still too hot politically for the Kennedys. Reportedly, there had been discussions among Bobby, Jack, and Peter on Sammy's participation in the gala, the concern being that Southern Democrats would object to Sammy and his bride attending. Three days before the gala, after Sammy had bought a new tux and his wife a new gown, he received a call from the White House. It was Evelyn Lincoln, JFK's personal secretary. She told Sammy the president didn't want him at the inauguration, a decision he claimed had been forced upon him by the politics of the moment, circumstances that would be counterproductive to fight. Sammy said he understood. In truth, he was crushed.

On gala day, there was a snowstorm in Washington, dumping eight inches on the city throughout the evening. But the show went on.

Gene Kelly danced, Sydney Poitier read poetry, and Pat Suzuki sang. Kelly sang "The Hat Me Dear Old Father Wore" and did an amazing dance routine. Fredric March did a recitation invoking God's help to "give us zest for new frontiers, and the faith to say unto mountains, whether made of granite or red tape: Remove." Bill Dana, famous at that time for portraying a fictional Chicano character known as José Jiménez, did a well-received comic routine with Milton Berle. Nat "King" Cole sang and so did a young Harry Belafonte, whose 1956 Calypso album had become the first long-playing album in history to sell over a million copies. Jimmy Durante gave a poignant performance of "September Song," a JFK favorite. Sinatra sang twice that evening, once with "You Make Me Feel So Young," and also "That Old Black Magic," putting a few new twists on the old standard with lines like:

> That old Jack magic had them in its spell
> That old Jack magic that he weaves so well . . .

Another song with altered lyrics was "High Hopes,"

Jack and Lyndon B.
Let's follow their lead.
They're the men that our America needs!

Todd Purdum, writing a *Vanity Fair* retrospective on the famous JFK gala for *Vanity Fair* fifty years later, summed it up this way:

It was an only-in-America blend of high culture and low comedy, of schmaltz and camp, and it may have marked the moment when popular entertainment became an indispensable part of modern politics.

Bette Davis, in fact, said as much during the show in a skit she did, reading from a script by radio dramatist Norman Corwin: "The world of entertainment—show-biz, if you please—has become the Sixth Estate."

JFK spent a lot of public time with Frank Sinatra at the pre-inaugural gala. At one point, near the show's end, with an introduction from Sinatra, JFK rose to speak as a single spotlight shone on him. "We saw excellence tonight," the president-elect said, while commending Sinatra and Peter Lawford for their work on the gala. "The happy relationship between the arts and politics which has characterized our long history, I think, reached culmination tonight."

Of Sinatra's role in the gala, Kennedy said, "You cannot imagine the work he has done to make this show a success." Kennedy called Sinatra "a great friend," and added: "Long before he could sing, he used to poll a Democratic precinct back in New Jersey. That precinct has grown to cover a country, but long after he has ceased to sing, he's going to be standing up and speaking for the Democratic Party, and I thank him on behalf of all of you tonight."

The gala would raise millions to help reduce the Democratic campaign debt, and despite the snow and other logistics, Sinatra had pulled off one of the greatest Hollywood-on-the-Potomac fêtes the city had ever witnessed.

"I can say that it was certainly one of my high points," Joey recalled about hosting the event. During one of the author's visits to Joey's Lido Isle home, he pulled out a scrapbook of photos and newspaper clippings about the inaugural. "The president said to me, 'Joey, I have to introduce you. Could you tell me what to say?' So, I reminded him that he promised not to allow his Catholicism to, in any way, affect his political positions. So, I gave him the line he could say to introduce me: 'Wouldn't you know? With my luck, the first speaker I'm introducing is a Bishop.' He hugged me. He kissed me . . . you understand? And he got such a laugh and applause when he said that!"

Incidentally, comedian Don Sherman told the author that it was actually *he* who had written that line for Joey to give to the president-elect to use.

For the main event, Joey was decked out in tux and tails. Larry and Sylvia were seated next to Tony Curtis and Janet Leigh.

Joey was in top form and the crowd roared with every quip. Looking up to Jack and Jackie, Joey said, "I *told* you I'd get a good seat. And you were so worried! Mr. President, now that you've been elected, can you tell me how I get that sticker off my bumper? I don't know where that came from!"

Actress Pat Suzuki, known for her award-winning performance in the play and film *Flower Drum Song*, was the wife of White House photographer Mark Shaw (who was murdered by President Kennedy's doctor, Max Jacobson). Reflecting on her performance at the gala, she told the author, "It was really a high point to sing and read poetry at the event. It was a magical night."

It was nearly 1:30 A.M. when the gala ended. Jackie Kennedy had long since gone home as she was still recovering from the Cesarean birth of John Jr. JFK went to another party that night, one given by his father at Paul Young's restaurant in downtown D.C. JFK didn't get home until 3:30 A.M. The following morning, Inauguration Day, Kennedy was up at eight, reviewing his speech and preparing for a full slate of official and ceremonial meetings with outgoing president Dwight D. Eisenhower, and then on to Capitol Hill for his swearing in and one of the more memorable inaugural speeches in U.S. history.

On the evening of the inauguration, as the president and first lady were making the rounds to the various inaugural balls being held in Washington, Sinatra threw a party at the Statler-Hilton Hotel for all the cast and crew who had been involved in the preceding night's gala. The president, on a visit to the Statler-Hilton for one of the balls that evening, managed to slip away to join Sinatra's party and mingle with the guests there. Frank was very pleased and went home to California feeling pretty good about himself and his friend in the White House.

The world changed after the intervention of the Rat Pack into presidential politics. Entertainers were now in bed with politicians and played a role in how elections were won (or lost). The Rat Pack's interweaving in the campaign of John Fitzgerald Kennedy was that watershed moment.

Chapter 17
The Last Gasp of Misogyny

How a Bullet Changed Popular Culture

Frank and Dean march for women's rights.

It is time to take a step back to note how Joey and the Rat Pack impacted society in two significant ways. First, they influenced the 1960 election and may have elected a president who forever changed our culture. Second, they temporarily swung the pendulum towards a more misogynistic, paternalistic attitude that had been changing since World War II, in what we believe to be the last gasp of misogyny.

The impact that Frank, Dean, Sammy, Peter, and Joey had on the converging worlds of entertainment and politics cannot be overstated. Joseph P. Kennedy was highly cognizant of the effect the Rat Pack could have on his son becoming a blood brother with the early 1960s version of cool, hip, and pop-culture gold. This was the moment Joe Kennedy had waited for his entire life: seeing his Irish Catholic son elected president of the United States. The elder Kennedy's reputation as an audacious image-maker was well established by 1960. He had designed a mysterious image for his mistress, Gloria Swanson, effectively transforming her into an international movie star of the 1920s. He did the same for other actors, including cowboy star Fred Thompson and child actor Mickey Rooney, the latter in the guise of the comic-strip character Mickey McGuire. He controlled FBO, then RKO, studios. And, despite the notoriety he engendered as a bootlegger during Prohibition, he became Ambassador to England, The Court of St. James, under Franklin Delano Roosevelt. He was a brilliant strategist whose finger was always on the pulse of public interest.

Joe Kennedy recognized the appeal of Frank Sinatra. He admired his swagger, his self-confidence bordering on cockiness. When he carefully plotted his son's political career, he saw a weakness in the GOP's potential candidate, Vice-President Richard Milhous Nixon. Despite Eisenhower's popularity, the booming economy, and Nixon's relative youth, there was a definite chink in the armor. Dick Nixon was stodgy, square, and old beyond his years. The image-maker had to sell his son as vibrant, energetic, young, and hip. Joe Kennedy knew he needed to get a huge voter turnout to overtake the popular GOP platform. He needed to get the younger voters to turn out *en masse*.

The late C. David Heymann was the author of several brilliant, best-selling books about the Kennedy family: *A Woman Named Jackie*, *RFK*, *Bobby and Jackie: A Love Story*, and *American Legacy: The Story of John and Caroline Kennedy*. He had known and researched the Kennedy family for decades. As he told the author: "Joe Kennedy was a keen observer of trends and society. He read polls and fully believed that Nixon's feet of clay were his lack of charisma and definite dislike by younger voters. Through his son-in-law Lawford, he attempted to encourage Jack to pursue a friendship with Frank Sinatra. Jack loved the girls, and Frank certainly knew his way around. When Momo [Sam Giancana] told Joe about the Summit, Joe saw his opening. He explained to both Momo and Lansky how having Jack in the White House would protect Vegas from federal scrutiny and laws clamping down on them, gambling and all that. They were intrigued. Joe asked for campaign support, cash, money. They arranged for JFK to be anointed by the Rat Pack. To crown him as their candidate. To make him look cool and hip. They got it and put the plans in place to put Jack in the center of the event."

Heymann's research on this subject is nothing short of amazing. His archive, which he kindly shared with the author, is an incredible collection of documents, recordings, interviews, and more—all supporting his claims. He had used much of this research in an earlier book, *Dr. Feelgood: The Shocking Story of the Doctor Who May Have Changed History by Treating and Drugging JFK, Marilyn, Elvis, and Other Prominent Figures*.

As Heymann observed: "Those two days in Las Vegas [February 7 and 8, 1960] represented a watershed moment in history and had a huge impact on the election of John Kennedy as president. The world had rarely seen an event like that [the Summit], and at the center of it was Jack. Here is the number-one cool dude [Sinatra] praising him and embracing him as part of the Rat Pack. It swung the under-thirty crowd towards him. No question."

As the author points out in the Rat Pack chapters, Kennedy being the focal point of a slew of high-octane celebrities resulted in a cash payday from the mob in helping to finance the election. The Rat Pack was made up of more than just your garden-variety-

womanizers. Instead, they represented a sleazy lifestyle of men who viewed women as disposable and not of any value outside the bedroom or the kitchen. In short, they were misogynists.

In those pre-feminist days, Frank and the Rat Pack were not generally looked down upon for their rampant promiscuity; they simply reflected a healthy male libido. Their Mafia ties and thuggery were deemed macho. They were men's men. Sinatra was respected for the notches on his bedpost, with names like Lana Turner, Ava Gardner, Mia Farrow, Anita Ekberg, Marlene Dietrich, and Marilyn Monroe.

In "John F. Kennedy Was Too Complicated to be Idolized," an editorial for the *Los Angeles Times* (October 25, 2013), senior editor Mary McNamara asked:

> So what was the attraction of the Rat Pack? There's a lot of good to say about him, but Kennedy did have some serious issues with women. There was almost no place for women in his life or in his administration outside of the ones he had sexual relationships with. And he had many sexual affairs. It was also characteristic of a wealthy, powerful family of men to be able to cheat while their wives were not to object to it, which I do think is a sexist double standard. . . . Even after years of sordid revelations—the prostitutes, the mistresses, the Marilyn Monroe affair—he remained "our Jack," the bittersweet touchstone of a moment when it seemed to them that this country could shift, radically and irrevocably, toward an age of social enlightenment. . . . That he made his way through women as if they were sexual Tic Tacs angered and pained them, but it didn't change the way they viewed the man. Hate the sin, love the sinner. . . . I was raised to love the Kennedys just as I was raised to receive weekly Communion and view Yeats as the world's greatest poet. But I came to political consciousness at a time when it seemed there were far more call girls on Capitol Hill than congresswomen, and I wasn't quite as willing to give "our Jack" a pass. Kennedy's use of women showed a lack of respect not just to his office,

his wife and his faith but to women in general. Did his policies of empowerment and liberal equality outweigh personal choices that seemed to directly contradict those values? In many ways, John Kennedy personifies the ongoing and ever intensifying battle between reverence and revelation. Should our feelings about a person's work, whether policy, poem or painting, be changed by the posthumous knowledge that the man or woman who created it was anti-Semitic or misogynist or a terrible parent?

While this book's central focus is to tell the story of Joey Bishop and his connection to the Rat Pack, the author feels it necessary to theorize that the Rat Pack represents the rise in misogyny following the independence women experienced during the four long years of America's involvement in World War II. Was it exacerbated by the election of a president who firmly embraced a playboy lifestyle? The conclusion we have come to is that this unfortunate trend was ended by the bullet that burst through the president's head on November 22, 1963. In an instant, it brought an end to JFK's life and the life of the Rat Pack. Attitudes regarding women as men's equals would change dramatically in the years to come.

Chapter 18
Joey, the Actor
The Face That Couldn't Light Up the Screen

Joey and Dean in Texas Across the River *(1966).*

I was in a film called The Naked and the Dead.
I played both parts. —Joey Bishop.

As Joey started making his presence felt on the small screen, his longtime agent, Norman Brokaw at William Morris, thought it was time for his client to spread his wings.

As Brokaw told the author: "It was a time when many comics were making the crossover to films, and we thought the timing was right for Joey. The problem was that filmmaking took extended periods of time, which took the comics out of the clubs where the income was far more lucrative than the pay they received for appearing in Las Vegas and the other venues."

Buddy Hackett said, "I know I got a lot of exposure from doing a film like *The Music Man*, but that took months to film and paid just thirty grand. Meanwhile, I'm losing hundreds of thousands in bookings."

Shecky Greene can relate: "I was doing a part on the television show *Combat!* for pennies and all I thought about was the fifty grand I lost out on by not playing Vegas!"

Joey could relate as well: "It's great exposure to do a film, but you got to weigh it against what cost it means to your earnings. The reality is that it paid *bupkis*."

Regardless, Joey took the plunge in the hopes of attaining national recognition. He did so by appearing in a trio of World War II–themed films. In each one he was the comic relief, the soldier with an attitude.

The first of those films—the one that marked Joey's cinematic debut—was *The Deep Six*. Shot in the summer of 1957, its opening was held in January of 1958. Rudolph Maté was the director. The story depicts the conflicts of a naval officer with his shipmates and the values instilled in him by his Quaker upbringing. The impressive cast boasted Alan Ladd, William Bendix, James Whitmore, Efrem Zimbalist Jr. and, as the token Jew, Ski Kronkowski, that up-and-coming comic Joey Bishop.

His next film role was in *Onionhead*, a military comedy starring Andy Griffith. Joey plays Sidney Gutsell, a fellow Coast Guard cook. Shot in October and November in 1957 on location in Long Beach, California, with interiors at Warner Bros. in Burbank, Joey was allowed to work weekends at the Sands. The film was helmed by veteran director Norman Taurog. This attempt to capitalize on Griffith's success in *No Time for Sergeants* was a huge flop and became the main reason Griffith turned to television. The *New York Times* review, while harsh, had this to say: "Joey Bishop as a dame-chasing gob . . . adds a few realistic bits to the proceedings."

Next up was an ambitious attempt to bring one of controversial novelist Norman Mailer's works to the cinema. *The Naked and the Dead*, directed by Hollywood veteran Raoul Walsh, is a gripping drama set during World War II at a remote island in the Pacific Rim, where a small platoon of American soldiers is stationed. Most of the plot centers on the infighting and growing tension among the enlisted men and their officers, something that could destroy them. Joey plays Private Roth, the token Jew (what else?) of a platoon led by a psychotic, Jew-baiting sergeant, played by Aldo Ray. Private Roth's untimely demise comes when he sprains his ankle and is climbing a hill in a hail of gunfire.

"I was stuck on location for two months in Panama," Joey said of the shoot. "I kind of realized that, given the realities of doing a film, television was more up my alley."

The *New York Times* review noted that, with the exception of Ray's character, the "other members of the detail are competent, but also appear to have been chosen solely to represent the types that comprised our citizen army. There are, to name a few, Joey Bishop, as the wry, comic Jew . . ."

Joey received some recognition for his small but memorable role as Roth. Reviewer Kevin Sellers at TCM wrote:

> It's not Mailer, but it's close. Actually, except for that
> cloyingly "upbeat" ending, where Cliff Robertson gives
> us a sermon on the nobility of man, it's pretty faithful
> to Mailer's dark, curdled war novel (for my dough, his
> best book). Raoul Walsh's direction is properly somber
> and menacing, as is Bernard Herrmann's score. And

the acting is first rate. With the exception of L.Q. Jones and James Best, who overdo the Southern *schtick*, all cast members are good. Hell, even Joey Bishop is good! I particularly liked Aldo Ray's evil, misogynistic, racist sergeant; Raymond Massey's evil, Fascistic general (as bad as the enemy he's fighting); and Robert Gist's atheistic, eternally complaining foot soldier. And many of the scenes, like a soldier surviving battle only to die at the fangs of a little green snake, and the battle within the war between Massey's power crazed general and Robertson's humanistic lieutenant, manage to stay with you long after the film is over. Let's give it a B-plus instead of an A-minus for flubbing that ending. (Hollywood had to wait until after 'Nam and the advent of "Apocalypse" and "Platoon" to really plumb the depths of anti-war sentiment.)

Joey told a columnist for the *New York Post* that "once you've acted in a picture, people accept you as an actor and you're that as well as a comic." But Joey was already burned out by the movies. As he told Earl Wilson, "TV is the only medium. There is nothing else. If you are a hit in a picture, it doesn't mean anything today. And only a few nightclubs matter. It doesn't mean anything anymore to be a hit in Pittsburgh or Des Moines. Those people can see you on TV."

Joey and his management had a clear vision of his future. He had struck gold on *Keep Talking* and in guest shots with Jack Paar.

"That was Joey's strength," Norman Brokaw told the author. "He was a great host, an emcee, or a panelist. His money was made in the clubs, and television brought him the crowds. Our job was to work to what Joey did best."

As for Joey, he summed up his big-screen career thusly: "I really did not enjoy spending time on location, doing films. I missed my family and my home. And the money you make for a film is nothing like you make in saloons. You get instant response and you are gratified when you get a great response. In films, by the time you finish, you even forgot you were *in* it. Or your best scenes can be edited out."

Nevertheless, Joey continued to say yes when a film role was offered. In early 1966, he took a supporting part in *Texas Across the River*, starring Dean Martin. The film's director, Michael Gordon, got a wake-up call when he attempted to do three or four takes of a given scene. As Dean Martin told him, "Joey and I aren't actors; we are performers." Still, Joey acquitted himself well as Kronk, a rather low-key Indian. A reviewer on the Classic Film Freak website had this to say about his performance:

> Joey Bishop plays the foil to Martin during most of the picture, babbling incoherently in his own mishmash language. Every so often, he will lapse into broken English for a punchline. Though he uses the same gag consistently throughout the film, it strangely never grows tiresome. With lines like, "How come your dad isn't a Comanche?" how could it fail? The answer, of course, according to Kronk, is, "Mom run too fast." High art it definitely isn't.

Along with numerous other celebrities, Joey had a cameo in the "adult" comedy *A Guide for the Married Man* (1967), directed by Gene Kelly and starring Walter Matthau and Robert Morse. Joey's two-minute segment, called "Deny, Deny, Deny," shows him in bed with a young woman. Just then, his wife (played by Ann Morgan Gilbert, who had been Millie on *The Dick Van Dyke Show*) walks into the bedroom. She is shocked by this display of infidelity. Joey and the girl, however, never even make eye contact with her. The girl, in fact, wordlessly dresses and leaves the premises. Meanwhile, Joey, who is wearing only white boxer shorts, slips on his shirt and zips up his pants. He phlegmatically asks his hysterical wife, "*What* girl?" while she goes on accusingly. After efficiently making the bed, Joey settles into his living room easy chair, takes out the paper and lights up his pipe. The poor wife, now doubting her senses, begins to think, *maybe it never happened.* The scene is well paced and is an ideal premise for Joey's deadpan expression, voice, and overall comic attitude.

Joey also guest starred in various character parts in episodic television. One such role was in *Valentine's Day*, a 1964 detective series starring Tony Franciosa. He had a walk-on, as a security guard, on an episode of the Don Adams sitcom *Get Smart* in 1967 ("Viva Smart"). In the camp classic *Valley of the Dolls* (1967), based on Jacqueline Susann's torrid novel, Joey Bishop played . . . Joey Bishop, emceeing a telethon. One of the film's leading characters, Neely O'Hara (Patty Duke), is a singer and, at least according to the script, a good one. So good, in fact, that following her performance, Joey says enthusiastically, "Tell Frank, Dean, and Sammy to wait. Neely's going to sing again!"

Another cameo-laden picture featuring Joey is *Who's Minding the Mint?* produced by comic-book artist Norman Maurer, directed by Howard Morris, and starring Jim Hutton, Walter Brennan, Milton Berle, Bob Denver, and Dorothy Provine. Joey plays Ralph Randazzo, a small-time hood. Howard Morris, who had been one of Sid Caesar's sidekicks on *Your Show of Shows* and had portrayed the lunatic Ernest T. Bass on *The Andy Griffith Show*, became a sought-after comedy director. Speaking to the author about *Who's Minding the Mint?*, Morris said, "Norm [Maurer] had wonderfully sketched out on storyboards the film, which made the setups easy. The performers were all professionals. We tried to tone done Miltie [Berle] a bit. Joey was wonderfully understated as a hood, and we had Jamie Farr do a bit as his cousin who spoke no English. It was quite funny."

Following a long dry spell, Joey once again began popping up unexpectedly in theatrical features, TV movies, and the occasional series. In 1976, for instance, producer James Komack invited him to appear as Charlie on *Chico and the Man*, a popular NBC sitcom starring Jack Albertson and Freddie Prinze. The episode was called, "Too Many Crooks."

Two years later he was "Coach" in his first made-for-TV movie, *Sorority '62* (1978), a coming-of-age comedy produced by *American Bandstand*'s Dick Clark. Also seen in a supporting role was the rising comic Robin Williams.

On *Trapper John, M.D.*, a CBS series set in a San Francisco hospital and based, at least nominally, on a major character from the 1970 film *MASH*, portrayed in this current incarnation by Pernell Roberts. On one episode from 1981 ("The Pagoda Cure"), Joey finally fulfilled his parents' dream by becoming a doctor.

It would be another four years before he made not one but two appearances on TV series. The first was on the episode "What's So Funny?" of Brian Keith's ABC series *Hardcastle and McCormick*, in 1985. He was also one of the long-unseen guest stars on the senior-friendly CBS series *Murder, She Wrote*, starring Angela Lansbury.

The Delta Force, a 1986 action-thriller starring Chuck Norris and Lee Marvin, had Joey as Harry Goldman. This was followed by *Glory Years*, a 1987 made-for-TV movie set in Las Vegas. In that, he was cast as the equally Jewish-sounding Sidney Rosen.

Joey was next seen in *Betsy's Wedding*, a 1990 romantic comedy written by, directed by, and starring Alan Alda. The eponymous Betsy (Molly Ringwald) is engaged to Long Island construction worker Eddie Hopper, Alda's character. Joey plays his father.

In his son Larry's picture *Mad Dog Time*, Joey again played himself—or at least a character with his own real name, Mr. Gottlieb, the owner of Gottlieb's Mortuary. Joey had but one word of dialogue ("Hello") in an eerie scene with a faded Richard Pryor as a gravedigger. Even with such noted actors as Ellen Barkin, Gabriel Byrne, Richard Dreyfuss, Jeff Goldblum, and Diane Lane, the film was summarily slammed as an incoherent mess. Chicago critics Gene Siskel and Roger Ebert both considered *Mad Dog Time* to be the worst film of 1996. Ebert even wrote of the film: "*Mad Dog Time* is the first movie I have ever seen that does not improve on the sight of a blank screen viewed for the same length of time."

And on that dismal note, Joey's film career sputtered out for good.

Chapter 19
The Sitcom

Season One Debacle

Joey and his TV wife, Abby Dalton.

"**F**eh! Feh! Oy! Oy!—that's what I think of Joey Bishop! He almost ruined my career."

These were the first words uttered by actor Warren Berlinger in his reply to our request for an interview.

The author had a lively conversation with the noted character actor who played Larry Barnes, Joey Bishop's brother in the 1961 version of *The Joey Bishop Show*. Although he was only twenty-four when he co-starred with Bishop, Berlinger was a veteran of the stage, having gotten his first big break in 1946 when he was nine years old, in the original Broadway production of *Annie Get Your Gun* with Ethel Merman. He even guest-starred on the *Howdy Doody* television show and was featured on *Kraft Television Theatre* and John Cassavetes's *Johnny Staccato*. Berlinger appeared in both the stage and film productions of *Blue Denim* (winning a Theater World Award for the stage version), *Happy Time*, and *Anniversary Waltz* (later adapted as the movie *Happy Anniversary*). His career in film began with *Teenage Rebel* (1956) and was followed by *Because They're Young* (1960), *The Wackiest Ship in the Army* (1960), and others. In 1961, Warren was winning kudos as Buddy, in Neil Simon's first Broadway play, *Come Blow Your Horn*.

"I was having the time of my life, starring in a Neil Simon play on Broadway," Berlinger recalls. "One night, Danny Thomas and Sheldon Leonard came backstage after the show and asked to talk with me. I was thrilled. In that great Sheldon Leonard voice, he told me he wanted me to co-star with Joey Bishop on a new half-hour comedy they were going to produce. They said 'co-star.' I was thrilled. Leonard and Thomas had an incredible string of big hits they were producing, including *The Danny Thomas Show*, *The Real McCoys*, and *The Andy Griffith Show*. My agent called Leonard, and the salary was incredible. It was more money than I've ever seen. Here I was, twenty-four and starring in a Broadway hit and would co-star on a television show. I'd never met Bishop, but everyone knew him from the Rat Pack.

"The first thing I remember was jetting off to Los Angeles and going on the Desilu lot, where they shot all of the Thomas-Leonard programs. The cast of *The Joey Bishop Show* was amazing:

Marlo Thomas was to play Joey's and my sister; Joe Flynn, who was always great, played our brother-in-law; Madge Blake, a grand old character actress, played our mother—just a great cast. They hired the best writers, including Milt Josefsberg, who was with Jack Benny for years [and later with Lucille Ball], and Marvin Marx, who was one of the creators and head writers of *The Honeymooners*. Just great credentials.

Everybody seemed very tense and nervous. So, we go into a conference room for our first table read. It was the first time we received the scripts and met the cast. I sat down and looked for my character and started circling my name in the script, as I usually did, so I could learn the part. Joey came in, looking angry and never even said hello or introduced himself . . . not a hello . . . he just yelled, '*Do not do that! Do not circle your name!*' And then he walked away. Everybody got quiet, but I laughed. Joey was a comic. He played that kind of character, so I assumed he was kidding, joking to make me feel comfortable. So I went back to circling my name. This time Bishop ran over to me, got in my face and screamed, 'I said do not—*do not*—do that! Do not circle your name or speech! I'm telling you now—if you do it again there will be consequences!' He was deadly serious. I was visibly upset, and everyone tried to calm me down."

It was shocking to Berlinger, a well-trained, award-winning actor who, despite being only twenty-four at the time, had been in theater, television, and films for more than fifteen years. Plus, he was promised he would have a major role on the show. Warren immediately called his agent at William Morris and told him to get him out of this mess and back to *Come Blow Your Horn*. The agent reminded him that he had a seven-year agreement. Nevertheless, he called Louis Edelman, the lead producer with Thomas-Leonard. Edelman had also helped to create *Make Room for Daddy/The Danny Thomas Show*.

"Louis Edelman calls me, and I went to his office. Now Mr. Edelman was an incredible man. Just wonderful. Very trustworthy. He explains to me that it was Joey's first show and he was nervous, but that he would talk to him. He also tried to calm me down—I was very shaken up . . . I had already booked a flight back to New

York. I went back to my hotel room in Beverly Hills and I start-ed getting calls from Mr. Edelman, Danny Thomas, and Sheldon Leonard. My wife, whom I trusted, told me to go back to the play. I still was hemming and hawing . . . Then Danny Thomas and Shel-don Leonard, both of whom I respected and liked, begged me to reconsider and assured me that they would talk to Joey. They said they loved me and that I would become a star in my role. I was going to play Joey's brother Larry, so there had to be some sort of camaraderie. So, then, Joey comes in with Edelman, Thomas, and me. He apologizes and said it will never happen again.

"Joey sits down next to me and said, 'Listen, this is the first time I'm doing a character on a show. I've always been a standup comic and I'm a bit uptight about the process. I just think that when an actor reads a role the first time around, he wants to get the right rhythms and pacing of what the script calls for.' Joey was just charming this time—and maybe the only time—but it was in front of the big bosses [Edelman, Thomas, Leonard, Marx] . . . just a big show . . . The real Joey was a jerk."

Still, Joey was making a good point: he was not an actor, not by a long stretch. Given the type of character he was playing—which was basically an offshoot of his stage persona—that of a dyspeptic cynic, someone who had seen it all and found little of it to be any good—would have been the perfect vehicle for an accomplished stage and screen actor like Tom Ewell. But the part hadn't gone to Ewell, it had gone to Joey Bishop, former Cleveland nightclub comic. As a result, it is apparent in many scenes that Joey is not making eye contact with his fellow actors—he is reading cue cards.

Another fatal flaw for the show was Bishop's insistence that he be the only cast member to elicit laughs. Joey, with his deadpan delivery, was a born straight man, not unlike Jack Benny. Benny, however, had the wisdom to allow his talented group of co-stars (Mary Livingstone, Rochester, Dennis Day, etc.) to get the lion's share of the laughs, which contributed greatly to the classic sta-tus of both his radio and television shows. A more recent example of this approach is the megahit *Seinfeld*, in which standup comic Jerry Seinfeld played straight to Elaine, Kramer, George, and the many eccentric individuals who inhabited their world.

Bishop's insecurity, however, prevented him from giving his own stable of supporting players a chance to shine. It would be his loss.

●

To start at the beginning, Danny Thomas was a longtime admirer of Joey Bishop, the nightclub comic. They had worked many of the same clubs, including the Chez Parée in Chicago. They had also appeared in some of the same mob clubs with out-front owners such as Jules Podell and Lou Walters. And Danny usually listened to advice from his "uncle" Abe Lastfogel, king of the William Morris Agency. Lastfogel took an early interest in Danny and carefully guided his career to stardom. Whatever Uncle Abe suggested, Danny did. It was Lastfogel who set up his hit television show, *Make Room for Daddy*, and had hired Louis Edelman to guide it. Certainly, Lastfogel and the William Morris Agency were making big commissions from the Thomas/Leonard shows and it was certainly a synergistic arrangement. Uncle Abe had never hit an off-key. The last William Morris client that Uncle Abe "recommended" to Thomas was Andy Griffith—and look how *that* worked out.

Through the creation (by Sheldon Leonard) of what he called a "backdoor pilot," Andy was introduced as Sheriff Taylor on ABC's *The Danny Thomas Show* on the February 15, 1960 episode. *The Andy Griffith Show* premiered on CBS on October 3, 1960. Hoping that lightning might strike twice, Uncle Abe was carefully watching the sudden rise of his longtime client, nightclub comic Joey Bishop. With Uncle Abe's (and others') help, Joey had become the opening act for Frank Sinatra and had backed his way into what had become the legendary Rat Pack. Joey, once an obscure comic, was now hot.

However, there was quite a difference between Andy Griffith and Joey Bishop. While Griffith did start off as a comic, he had also been the star of a Broadway hit, *No Time for Sergeants* (as well as a teleplay and feature film version). The year before, he had given an amazing dramatic performance as Lonesome Rhodes in Budd Schulberg's story *A Face in the Crowd*, directed by Elia Kazan. His film career faded, and he had gone back to Broadway in *Destry Rides Again*. Bishop did not have the acting chops of Andy Griffith and lacked his natural charisma. Bishop was strictly a nightclub comic. Unlike many standup comics, such as Don Rickles, who had trained at the American Academy of Dramatic Arts, Bishop was not a skilled thespian. He was interchangeable with other comics of that era, from George Gobel to Alan King.

Shecky Greene said, "Some liked Bishop, as he was bland. He didn't stink. He didn't smell. And he didn't appear to be *that* ethnic. In other words, not too Jewish."

Nonetheless, Lastfogel directed Thomas and Leonard to create a backdoor pilot for his client. The series was conceived by Danny and Louis Edelman in mid-1960 after the Griffith show had been such a huge hit in its first year. At the time, Thomas was starring in his own hit series, which was now airing on CBS. It was then a top-twenty hit.

Joey's backdoor pilot, "Everything Happens to Me," aired on March 27, 1961, during the eighth season of *Make Room for Daddy*. In the pilot, an incompetent Hollywood "public relations man" named Joey Mason (Bishop) forgets to make proper accommodations for an exhausted Danny Williams (Thomas) after he arrives in Los Angeles to perform a show. Joey is then forced to put Danny up in the home he shares with his colorful parents, Mr. and Mrs. Mason (played by the legendary comic Billy Gilbert, and Madge Blake, who later played Aunt Harriet on *Batman*). Joey also had two unmarried sisters, Betty (Virginia Vincent) and Stella (Danny Thomas's daughter Marlo Thomas, who was just starting her career).

Despite the success of *The Danny Thomas Show* and *The Andy Griffith Show*, CBS passed on the program. At that time, Mike Dann was at NBC; two years later, he would become the CBS vice-president in charge of programming. He told the author, "I learned that CBS hated the format and thought Joey was just unlikable. He tested terribly in the Q rating. [Television and film executive] Jim Aubrey lived by the Q rating . . . I believe it was an early version used by Jack Landis. Bishop tested very negatively. CBS absolutely hated the premise, which was overloaded with characters. So it was a tough decision for CBS, because of

Thomas/Leonard and the Morris office, but they foresaw a quick failure and passed."

Dann continues. "At NBC, we were desperate for half-hour comedies, so we quickly bought the show with the hope of getting a foot in the door for future Thomas/Leonard productions. We did ask for changes in the format and tweaked it a bit. Also, Benton & Bowles advertising group, who represented the sponsor, really inundated the producers with memos for changes to the show."

First, Bishop's character's name was changed to Joey Barnes (Bishop had insisted his character and he share the same initials). Second, the character of Joey's father was dropped. Two additional characters were added: a younger brother named Larry (Warren Berlinger), and Frank (Joe Flynn), the husband of Joey's older sister Betty. The premise had Joey as a well-intentioned but hapless and trouble-prone young man (Joey was forty-three at the time), who works for the Hollywood public relations firm Willoughby, Cleary and Jones. The firm is headed by J. P. Willoughby (John Griggs), Joey's demanding boss. Willoughby's secretary, Barbara Simpson (Nancy Hadley), is Joey's girlfriend. Joey lives with and supports his widowed mother, Mrs. Barnes (Madge Blake) and younger sister Stella (Marlo Thomas). His younger brother Larry is a pre-med student (played, of course, by Berlinger, who was almost twenty years Bishop's junior). Joey also supports his older sister Betty (Virginia Vincent) and her proudly unemployed husband, Frank (Joe Flynn).

"It was horribly miswritten," recalled Joey of that first year of the show. "They wanted me to be a victim of fate, a *schnook* . . . I contended that an audience wouldn't listen to a complainer. When I got there, I found some of these writers never saw me or watched me on *Paar* [*The Jack Paar Tonight Show*]. I thought the people I worked with would at least know who I was. They didn't."

Assigned to the show was a top-flight television director, David Lowell Rich, whose brother was John Rich, the director known for *The Dick Van Dyke Show*, which was also owned by Thomas/Leonard and shooting on the same Desilu Cahuenga lot. (John Rich would direct a couple episodes of the Bishop show as well.)

David Rich had directed many dramatic shows such as *77 Sunset Strip* and Westerns, including the show's lead-in *Wagon Train*. The most recent comedy he had directed was the feature film *Have Rocket, Will Travel* (1959), starring the Three Stooges. Unlike his brother, he was not an expert in half-hour situation comedies. Rich was offered an ownership piece of the show to take over as the director. Sheldon Leonard thought that with Joey's inexperience in front of the camera, a veteran leader was needed. By episode eleven, the war between Bishop and Rich had intensified and Joey demanded that he be fired.

Bishop told *TV Guide*, "I found out he wasn't a comedy director. . . . I could have played it safe and not made waves. I wonder if I hadn't created more trouble than I bargained for."

Danny Thomas, when asked about the firing, told *TV Guide*, "I have one great talent: I delegate authority and allow it to function. Let's put it this way: It took some time to find our lead horse's gait." Thomas added that there was a "mild personality clash" between Bishop and Rich.

"A *mild* personality clash?" laughed Joe Flynn. "It was a knock-down, drag-out battle for everyone to watch . . . fireworks."

Rich, like his brother, a no-nonsense, domineering director, agreed with Flynn. "Listen, my reputation was on the line. He bad-mouthed me to everyone. He blamed all of his troubles on me. I admit that after this experience, I needed to do some soul searching. I found I wanted a more diversified material and performer, so I got out." Rich relinquished his shares in the show and came out of the experience unharmed. He went on to have a long career directing countless television shows, films, and made-for-television movies.

Joey later said, "He [David Rich] and his brother bad-mouthed me to everyone. It was very hurtful. I lost out on a lot of projects due to them . . . He knew nothing about comedy, pacing, or rhythm."

The storylines during the first season typically revolve around Joey's misadventures concerning his job. Problems also arise when family members, who often think he has more influence in Hollywood than he actually has, attempt to take advantage of that nonexistent influence. As the series was a spinoff of *The Dan-ny Thomas Show*, they also took advantage of the "crossover," which was another brainchild of Sheldon Leonard. Danny Thom-as, Marjorie Lord, Rusty Hamer, and Sid Melton all appeared as their *Make Room for Daddy* characters in the first season's fourth episode, entitled "This Is Your Life."

Upon its September 1961 premiere, NBC had high expecta-tions for the show. It was scheduled with a great lead-in, *Wagon Train*, a top-rated program, at 7:30 P.M. *The Joey Bishop Show* got the plum spot at 8:30 and would be followed by the popular *Per-ry Como Show*.

"We knew that the Bishop show was a longshot," Dann admit-ted. "All of the indicators that CBS did in its testing we were aware of. Yes, we wanted to succeed and get our foot in the door with Thomas/Leonard. We knew Joey had limitations, so we sched-uled the show in the best timeslot available with a good lead-in and lead-out. I recall that the show held its own that year. The drop for the Como show was insignificant."

The reviews were almost universally negative. Harsh. Brutal.

However, unlike a Broadway play, a television show—a prime example being *The Beverly Hillbillies*—can survive even the most critical critics' wrath. That wrath was on display in the *New York Times*'s noted television columnist Jack Gould's review of Sep-tember 21, 1961, titled, "Television: Joey Bishop Begins a Situation Series; Plays Milquetoastian Aide of Press Agent; Channel 4 Pre-miere is Same Old Fluff."

> Joey Bishop, whose deadpan monologues have justly won him a substantial following, is the latest comedian to risk the perils of a half-hour filmed situation series. The premiere of his show occurred last night on Channel 4, and once again it was the old Hollywood story: Joey was put in the mold....a figure of Milquetoastian overtones who constantly gets in trouble and is buffeted about by people with louder voices . . . the writer completely miss-es the humor of Mr. Bishop, which lies in his unexpected turn of a phrase and mind. Instead, there was substituted

only the canned and predictable artificiality that is the recurrent blight of so [many] filmed TV comedies.

Joey was understandably upset. This was his big break, after all. This television series symbolized his reward for years of hard work. Now, Joey was frightened that this show could destroy his career. He admitted this to us in 1997. At that time his show, which had been basically off the air for three decades, was being rerun on the cable network TV LAND and it was introducing Joey to a new generation of viewers. Since Joey controlled the rights, he demanded that the first season be omitted from the package. The final three seasons were the shows that were finally rerun.

"I just want to burn those shows, that first year . . . It was awful . . . We did not get one favorable review in the country . . . not a solitary good review . . . and I didn't disagree, the show was awful . . . I was embarrassed by it . . . I screamed to Norm Brokaw, 'They're killing me!' to get me out of the deal, out of the show. . . . It wasn't me; the character was so far off . . . Hey, I've had thirty-five years to think about that. We had writers trying to turn me into a *schlemiel* [Yiddish for a stupid, awkward, unlucky person]. They were writing for Gleason and *The Honeymooners* . . . The series struggled in the ratings."

In an effort to improve viewership, NBC decided to "re-adjust" the series. Several characters, including Joey's older sister Betty, brother-in-law Frank, and girlfriend Barbara Simpson, were dropped. Several crew members were also dismissed. The changes helped the series' ratings and NBC renewed it for a second season. At least that was the official word from those who carefully monitored their public relations through Warren Cowan.

According to Warren Berlinger, this was far from the real story. "Joe Flynn was incredible in anything he appeared in," he insists.

Joe Flynn had been an actor for nearly fifteen years when he joined the show. Just after being fired from the Bishop show he landed the plum role of Captain Binghamton in *McHale's Navy*, playing opposite Academy Award-winner Ernest Borgnine and a young Tim Conway. Flynn later became a vice-president of AFTRA and was the son-in-law of director Byron Haskin (*War of the Worlds*, *The Outer Limits*).

In an interview with *TV Guide*, Flynn pulled no punches, calling the Bishop show "one of the most unpleasant experiences of my life."

The problem, according to Flynn, was Joey's inflexibility: "Danny Thomas would come in and beg him, 'Please, Joey, you're not doing *The Jack Paar Show*. Don't play it that way.' It was no use. The first reviews came out. Joey was like a man in shell shock. He was the darling of the press and he'd never been attacked before. I was just thrilled to get a regular gig and for the Danny Thomas company, who had the best writers and producers . . . he took the scripts home to 'fix' them and I think he was having his comedy writer friends punch up his character. . . . Once he was supposed to tell Madge Blake, who played his mother, to 'Shut up!' and he came back the next day and demanded they change the line to 'Mom, please!' He thought people would dislike him for saying shut up. He desperately wanted to be loved. I've spent my career playing unlikable characters . . . I knew I was in trouble when he began giving me a dissertation on what a joke was. . . . Oh, we had a good rating. But anybody could get a good rating in that spot. Joey knew that. So, he made more changes. That meant he had to fire Virginia Vincent, who played my wife. Then he decided he didn't need John Griggs as his boss and made himself boss. Then he decided Nancy Hadley wasn't right as his girlfriend and . . ."

Virginia Vincent remembers, "The writers knew how to write for Joe Flynn, and they wrote better for him than for the star. You knew that spelled doom for Joe."

"It was pure *mishegas* backstage at the show," reveals Berlinger. "Chaos. Always some form of drama was playing out. Everybody was tense. The crew walked on eggshells."

At first, the ratings were decent. As the show progressed through October and November, however, there was definitely an erosion: it was not feeding the audience that *Wagon Train* had delivered to the show that followed, *The Perry Como Show*. This, combined with the turmoil on the set, looked like doomsday for the series. However, assistant director Mike Dann recalls, "We persevered as we thought we could improve the show. The sponsors were not backing out and we wanted to please Danny and Sheldon."

Warren Berlinger remembered, "Writers were leaving the show every week, as were producers and directors. Many directors just refused to work on the show. Joey remembered two young writers from *The Jack Paar Show* named Garry Marshall and Fred Freeman. They were paid ten dollars a joke by Paar, so Joey offered them twenty dollars a joke. He flew them out to Los Angeles to work on the show. I was close in age [to those men] and I became good friends with both Garry and Fred."

Garry Marshall recalled being hired by Sheldon Leonard to write for *The Joey Bishop Show* in his interview with Karen Herman of the American Television Archives in 2000.

> Sheldon [Leonard] hired me and became a great influence on my life and talked just like I did . . . he graduated from college like I did, but we didn't speak well (*laughs*). . . . *The Joey Bishop Show* never made any sense; it was a mixed-up show. Yet it ran for four years. So I stayed and worked on it. It was a messy show backstage with screaming, yelling, and drama. So it reached the point where he fired everybody but me—and only because I stayed out of his way. So I became the de facto producer. I didn't get any credit. I was supposedly the punch-up kid, but I had the duties of a producer. So I was kind of producing the show and became responsible for the script every week. I was under fire every week . . . there was so much fighting, screaming, yelling, and drama that one day, my writing partner Fred Freeman said, "Goodnight. I'm going home." So he went back to New York and I was there, all alone. So I said, "Let's see what happens here." Because I loved it. I really loved it—it was fun. I enjoyed the experience of creating the show. The audience came in on Friday night and you can really hear them laugh. I loved it that we had a live audience like the *Danny Thomas* and *Dick Van Dyke* shows on the lot. And that was very exciting. So I learned, on *The Joey Bishop Show*, how to run a show. I learned to do all the jobs to run a show. Actually, Joey Bishop was a great influence on my career. Even though he would change

things all the time, he kept me around. And I learned from the writers like Phil Foster—who was another mentor of mine—and great old writers like Marvin Marx and Milt Josefsberg. Danny Thomas took a liking to me and, eventually, I paired up with my army buddy's brother, Jerry Belson . . . during my four years on *The Joey Bishop Show* on the Desilu Cahuenga lot, I got to eventually work on *The Dick Van Dyke Show* and others as well . . . So *The Joey Bishop Show* was the start of my career—my first credit that included my name. I still wanted my name on things and the work I was doing on the show was going uncredited. My first credit ever was for the Bishop show as a writer called "Penguins Three." I did get a story credit before that for the great Leonard Stern in a show he did called *I'm Dickens, He's Fenster.* But my first credit as a writer—that was with my first partner, Fred Freeman. Then, when Fred left, an old comedy writer named Harry Crane offered to write with me. I learned off *The Joey Bishop Show.* You can't learn till you do it, make mistakes and get better. I learned a lot. And it helped that I was writing for a comedian [Bishop]. What I learned was to write for the stars. It wasn't like writing for an ensemble like *Friends* or *Cheers.* We wrote for the comedians, which I started for Bishop, then Danny Thomas and Lucy. . . . It was tailored to the person who was paying you. To their talents. I learned to be nice to the person who was paying me, like Joey. We learned to write [for] the stars well. And I was liked for that. I also started off writing for people [like Bishop] who nobody wanted to write for. Carl Reiner really taught me that. He said that they don't want to see the mailman be funny—the viewers want to see the star be funny. That is how we became busy as we wrote for Joey, Danny, Lucy . . . it was actually the opposite of radio. Fred Allen or Jack Benny wanted their side characters funny. On TV, their faces were up there, and *they* had to be funny. That is why I understood what Joey wanted, and he liked me for that.

After being basically a joke writer for comics, Marshall also discussed how he learned to craft funny stories for situation comedies on *The Joey Bishop Show*. He recalled, "There was a big change in the industry. They were having the funny comedy writers do the variety shows and they assigned serious writers to write 'funny' for the situation comedies, which was a mistake. So they decided to teach the comedy writers—who were mostly writing jokes for nightclub comics—to write stories . . . and we didn't know how to write for pleasant shows like *Leave it to Beaver* or *Ozzie and Harriet*. All we knew was how to write BIG, big hard jokes. Before Phil Silvers and *Bilko*, no one wrote stories. Nat Hiken changed that."

Warren Berlinger recalls, "It was a fascinating year. Joey was mercurial. You never knew which Joey you would get. Once I was in the room when Joey got a call that he put on a speakerphone. His agent told him that Frank, Dean, and Sammy were planning to jet off to Japan. And then the agent said, 'They don't want to involve you!' I'm telling you the blood drained out of Joey's face. He threw a huge fit. He was throwing things, screaming. We all ran for cover!"

There seemed to be a morbid curiosity as to what was going on behind the scenes at *The Joey Bishop Show*. It became almost a cause célebrè. Speculation was rampant about what Garry Marshall described as "the fighting, screaming, yelling, and drama."

Rocky Kalish, who was working on *The Danny Thomas Show*, remembered: "We would sneak on to the set during breaks. It was free entertainment. A circus. You'd see producers and writers carrying their bottles of Maalox. No one was immune. Even the owner of the company, Danny Thomas—Joey was yelling at him because he forced him into a *farkakte* [Yiddish for crappy] format and shoved his daughter [Marlo Thomas] down their throats. Lou Edelman, who was the most even-keeled, sweetest man you'd ever meet, was aging before our eyes. Directors were wearing pith helmets to protect themselves. Joey was an *enfant terrible*. I was offered nearly double my salary to turn out a couple episodes and I turned them down. And at that time, I could have used the scratch."

"'Sick, Sick, Sick': All's Not Right with Joey," a rather frank article by Dwight Whitney for *TV Guide*, related that that was how
Joey felt when his new comedy show fell apart.

> Joey Bishop was a deeply troubled man. Nobody liked
> his TV show. The critics didn't like it (they said it was cli-
> ché-ridden; the director didn't like it (he quit); the actors
> didn't like it (four of them were fired); indeed, for a while
> even Bishop himself didn't like it. Privately, what they
> were saying was even more distressing. The show was in
> a "chaotic" state. The star was behaving like a martinet.
> Going on the set, to quote one player, was "like stepping
> into a mortuary to view the remains." Specifically, the
> charges were that 1.) Joey, a tyro in television, had impul-
> sively altered test-film writer Mel Shavelson's original
> story line on the week that shooting was supposed to
> begin; 2.) he had refused to allow director David Lowell
> Rich to direct; 3.) when it turned out that second banana
> Joe Flynn was getting all the big yaks, he had fired Flynn
> along with three other actors; 4.) when this failed to put
> the patient back on its feet, he made changes so fast
> that even his producer could not keep up with him. All in
> all; Joey was sick to death of it... sick...sick!"

The article continues.

> Despite everything, the show still thrived. *The Joey
> Bishop Show*, in format an almost totally undistinguished
> new situation comedy about a press agent, continued
> to thrive. Its Nielsen ratings (thanks in part to follow-
> ing *Wagon Train*, Wednesday night) hovered around a
> respectable 28. Earlier this year, the show's option was
> picked up, thus ensuring it one full season, come what
> may. For the ordinary comedian, this would be cause for
> rejoicing. But Bishop is no ordinary comedian . . .

> "So they say the show is cliché-ridden, "he moaned
> recently. "So they changed it. They holler panic. I go to
> New York and I see a couple of writers (Garry Marshall

and Fred Freeman). Very good one-line joke kids, so I hired them. They holler panic. They tell me the brother-in-law character—that's Joe Flynn—is a cliché. So I replace him. They still holler panic." Joey figured whatever he did, it was wrong. "I was guilty of the cliché," he insists. "I absolutely was. How do I say this and not sound immodest? Mine is a very dangerous kind of comedy. I gotta be Joey Bishop. And Joey Bishop is a very undisciplined guy in a very disciplined situation."

Veteran comedy writer Marvin Marx, who was a producer on the show, said, "Well, it is a shakedown cruise. The final decisions lie with Joey and Lou Edelman."

Edelman remarked, "We all conferred but the final decision is made by Joey. For Joey it was suddenly like being in Tibet and not speaking the language. We knew we weren't getting the greatest value out of Joey."

One of the wildest stories that demonstrates the animosity on the set was told to us by Warren Berlinger. For his birthday, Betty Berlinger gifted her husband with a dartboard that had Joey's picture. As Berlinger told the author: "I took the board and the darts to my dressing room to use to get my frustrations out during breaks. Every morning, Marlo [Thomas] and I would play a round of darts at Joey's head. Joey was coming down hard at Marlo at every instance. During one scene, Marlo, who played an aspiring actress, was supposed to do an imitation of Bette Davis. Her line was that exaggeration of Davis saying, 'Peetah, Peetah, Peetah.' Joey was angry with her delivery, which was just fine. He went ballistic. We did several takes and he was getting angrier. Finally, he said to her, 'Why don't you go to your father and learn comedy. You are the worst, a horrible actress,' and on and on. Then he threw her off the set. It was just brutal. . . . Marlo, who was just wonderful to work with and was, like me, an accomplished actor, was humiliated."

During the series, Berlinger made several attempts to get on Joey's good side and try to gain some rapport and chemistry. "I was just making more money than I had ever seen, so being a kid, I went out and bought a big, beautiful, new Cadillac. I was just itching to use it, and my wife was back in New York. I had heard that Joey was appearing at the Sands Hotel in Las Vegas. I had become close to Garry Marshall and I asked if he and Fred [Freeman], his writing partner, wanted to drive up to Vegas with me and we could show Joey that we support him. It was a gesture. Trying to mend fences, so to speak. So we go to the show and I was surprised. He killed. He was fantastic. And after the show, we go back to Joey's dressing room. Now, we had driven in from Los Angeles and we expected at least a 'thank you.' But he just looks at us and goes, 'So?' So? Like, *why are you here?* Geez, we worked together every day. So while we are there, some thuggish-looking guy comes in with a big paper bag. Joey opens it and it is literally bundles of cash. Joey looks at him and says, 'I'll count it later.' The next morning, Garry, Fred, and I go to check out and Joey grabs Garry and Fred's bill and said, 'It's on me.' He pays their bill and just looks at me, just being his usual asshole self. I'll never forget that."

Joey was determined to make changes to better suit the Joey Bishop he played in clubs. As he told *TV Guide*: "I didn't know anything about TV. I would like to lose the smell of a failing show. They (this time he meant the press) won't let me." Dwight Whitney wrote, "More detached observers agree the specialized comic is likely to find series TV a strange and hostile environment. As for Joey himself, he is determined to show them all. And without help from his friend, Frank Sinatra."

"I wouldn't use our friendship," he says. Then he grows confidential. "You know what I think Frank thinks? I think he thinks I'm nuts."

Berlinger begged his agent to get him out of the seven-year contract at the end of the season. He was offered another Broadway show. And with the upcoming format change, Thomas/Leonard were happy to accommodate him.

Warren had no contact of any kind with Joey for the next thirty years. "I was at a play in Los Angeles with my wife, Betty. From behind me, Joey puts his hands over my eyes and says, 'Guess who.' My wife, who was nicknamed 'No BS Betty,' just looked away. I saw it was Joey. I nodded. So Bishop goes, 'So, are you snubbing me?' I looked at him and all my anger at his almost destroying my career came back into my head. So I said, 'I guess I am.' Joey walked away angry and I never saw him again. It was an experience I would not soon forget. So, when you ask about Joey Bishop that is why I say FEH -OY!"

Chapter 20
The Overhaul
Saving the Sitcom and
Losing Frank's Friendship

Johnny Carson stands in for Joey during a videotaped performance of the Rat Pack in 1965.

The DVD box set of The Joey Bishop Show, Shout! Factory.

Surprisingly, NBC did not cancel *The Joey Bishop Show* after the disastrous 1961–1962 season. The ratings were mediocre and the format of the show, with the countless changes in both cast and structure, made the future look dismal. However, NBC, seriously lacking successful half-hour situation comedies, was desperate. The executives were still trying to court the production team of Sheldon Leonard and Danny Thomas to bring more product to their network. Their shows on CBS, *The Andy Griffith Show*, *The Dick Van Dyke Show*, and *The Danny Thomas Show* and *The Real McCoys* on ABC, were all strong performers and had a stable of some of the best comedy writers under contract.

On August 5, 1962, just prior to the fall television season, Bob Thomas wrote a column titled, "Joey Bishop Show Keeps Name, Rest Is Changed."

> About the only resemblance between last season's Joey Bishop show and the coming season's is the name. It's still "The Joey Bishop Show," NBC having vetoed the comedian's suggestion to call it "The New Joey Bishop Show." Bishop fans may be startled to find their hero is no longer a press agent but a late-night television comic. Furthermore, he has jettisoned his mother, bless her heart, for a curvy wife. And he has acquired a whole new bunch of pals.
>
> That Joey was able to make these changes is one of the minor miracles of television. Just about everyone, Joey especially, agreed that something was wrong with last season's shows. When a series is that flawed, it is usually yanked at the first sign of spring.
>
> But the series had somehow managed to best its competition on ABC and CBS and rack up an impressive rating. So when Joey promised a clean sweep in format for the next season, NBC went along. I found Joey in the midst of his fourth show, and absolutely happy—*for him*. That is, he smiled every fifteen minutes. I asked what went wrong the first season. "I showed up," he replied.

But on a more analytical basis, he continued: "We did many things wrong. We didn't have enough time to prepare. We violated a very basic concept in comedy. When you have a clever comedian—and in all modesty I think I am—you surround him with funny people. When you have a funny comedian, you surround him with clever people. I made the mistake of working with clever people," he said. "Now I am working with funny people—Guy Marks, who is a bright young comedian; Joe Besser, who can get laughs just walking on stage; and Abby Dalton from the 'Hennessy Show,' a brilliant talent."

"Our ace in the hole was Grant Tinker," Sheldon Leonard told the author in a 1992 interview. "Grant worked for the ad agency Benton & Bowles and was instrumental in saving *The Dick Van Dyke Show* with their client, Procter & Gamble, when the ratings were mediocre. Then he moved over to NBC as vice-president of West Coast programming for NBC, for whom he had worked earlier. Grant liked Joey, who still had a high Q rating due to the Rat Pack shit. Grant gave us a go-ahead for a second season, if we revamped the show. He also bumped up production costs and allowed us to film in color.

"We brainstormed with Marvin Marx, Milt Josefsberg, Harry Crane, and Charlie Stewart. And, of course, Joey (God forbid). Garry Marshall was also there; his partner had quit. Joey wanted to do a show like Jack Benny. Milt tried to tell Joey that he was NOT Jack Benny. God bless Milt, but he was a nervous wreck from Joey after the first season. We put Joey in a place that could feature his deadpan look, his dour disposition. Joey hired Frank's buddies Jimmy Van Heusen and Sammy Cahn to write a new theme song—as if *that* was our biggest problem. We had Earle Hagen on staff, who was wonderful, but you pick your fights with Joey."

Leonard's final solution, after much discussion, was to reintroduce Bishop with the same character name, Joey Barnes. No explanation on how he jumped from being a public relations man in Los Angeles to a New York talk-show host with an overbearing manager and a bride from Texas.

Rocky Kalish, then under contract to Thomas/Leonard Productions, was assigned to the show. As he recalled: "Joey wanted the eccentric type of characters that Jack Benny encountered and let him play straight to them. After lots of casting tryouts, we selected Guy Marks, who really had zero experience acting. He was a standup. Bishop liked him because he was from South Philly." Marks's biggest claim to fame was an appearance as an impressionist on *The Ed Sullivan Show*. Joey knew him vaguely as a former roommate of another South Philadelphia homeboy, Eddie Fisher.

"Joey wanted a man-servant, à la Eddie Anderson's Rochester, but we quickly nixed that," recalled Garry Marshall. Joey suggested quirky comic Joe Besser as the building's handyman, Jillson. Besser had memorable turns as the man/child "Stinky" on *The Abbott & Costello Show* in the early 1950s and later with the Three Stooges, replacing the late Shemp Howard as the Third Stooge.

Bishop's admiration for Besser dated back to the 1940s. As he explained, "When I was in the army and I was the head of the entertainment division in Texas, we owned a print of the Besser film, *Hey, Rookie* (1944), which starred Ann Miller and Larry Parks, with Besser as the comic relief. We played that thing for all the servicemen until the sprockets fell off. Finally, I had to order a new print!"

When Besser visited Sammy Davis Jr. on the set of the Rat Pack film *Sergeants 3*, Joey asked for an introduction. Joey offered him a job on his television show. Besser was thrilled. As he recalled in his autobiography, *Once a Stooge, Always a Stooge*:

> I was really scuffling for work after [my stint as one of] the Stooges. Joey got me a small bit as a mailman in his first show [season one]. I did six shows that year in small parts. I was very thankful to Joey.
>
> After my appearances when the Bishop show aired, NBC received thousands of letters from fans who wrote in and said, 'Thank you for finding Besser. We missed him!' Joey heard about the deluge of mail my appearance on

his show created, so after we filmed the last show of the season, James V. Kern, the show's director, came to me and said, "Joe, we're going to do a new series for next season. It's already been set and I've got news for you. You're going to be a regular right from the go."

When Bishop guest-hosted for Johnny Carson in the summer of 1963, before the debut of his new version of the series, he had Besser on as a guest. The applause he received on his entrance so overwhelmed the comedian that he had to fight back the tears.

In his four seasons on the Bishop sitcom, Besser appeared on more than ninety episodes, whereas he only had limited appearances on the first season of *The Abbott and Costello Show* and only shot sixteen shorts with the Stooges (from the spring of 1956 to December of 1957). When the author talked with the veteran comedian in 1978, he made it clear that being a member of the slapstick trio was anything but a career highlight. "It was not my style [of comedy]," he said emphatically. "I was pigeonholed into their act and I didn't fit." Besser's work on the Bishop show garnered him work for the rest of his career in film and television, as well as voice-over work in cartoons and commercials. For this, Besser was unfailingly grateful.

In February of 2019, the author interviewed Abby Dalton, who was cast as Joey Barnes's wife. Dalton had always been reluctant to discuss her work on the show. She has had a prolific television career, beginning as the co-star of the popular 1959–1962 series *Hennessey* with Jackie Cooper. She was also a regular cast member of Jonathan Winters's CBS variety show (1967–1969), playing Jonathan's wife in a series of skits. However, she is likely best remembered for her ongoing role as Julia, the strong-willed daughter of Angela Channing (Jane Wyman), on the prime-time soap opera *Falcon Crest* (1981–1990). The following is our interview with Abby Dalton, which was graciously arranged by Abby's daughter Kathleen.

AUTHOR: *How did you get cast as Joey's wife?*

DALTON: I auditioned for it. And I think he kind of fell in love with me at the time. Sorry, I can't help it (*chuckles*).

I was coming off three years on *Hennessey* with Jackie Cooper.

AUTHOR: *Do you believe you enhanced Joey's performance?*

DALTON: Oh, yes. I led him by the nose. Truly. I don't mean to brag about it, but I *did* inspire him. I wanted to be noted as an accomplished actress and I was happy to be featured in a series, so I made sure he looked good, as well. He had very [few] skills as an actor. You couldn't get close to him. They wanted us to be similar to the relationship Dick [Van Dyke] and Mary [Tyler-Moore] had. It was impossible. Dick was far, far, far more accomplished than Joey and he could convey those feelings. Joey was a comic. Not an actor. Stiff. It shows.

AUTHOR: *How was it working with Guy Marks in the first year, before he was released?*

DALTON: It was a living hell! (*laughs*). It was the first time I felt like I didn't want to go to work. I wanted to get away from it and him because I was in so much pain! My days were awful. Guy Marks would slink around everywhere I was and he would say filthy things to me, off-camera. He would wait right before I was to go to work, then he would say absolutely crude, filthy things to me. Honest to God! When I first heard it, I couldn't believe it. I had never been exposed to someone as awful as him. I could not believe it the first time I heard it. I thought I was imagining things. But it was true. He was so foul, he laughed, and it really stank!

AUTHOR: *Do you know why he was let go?*

DALTON: Because he could not get along with me. I went to Sheldon and Danny and I asked to be released from my contract. I put it clearly. It was him or me. And they kept me. I was more important to the show. He was easily replaceable. There has been a longstanding belief that Joey was integral in getting Marks fired because he felt he was overshadowing him. Being funnier than Joey. And Marks pushed this belief in subsequent interviews. He said he was replaced halfway during the first season with Corbett Monica, as Joey wanted him *out*. That was absolutely not the case. It was the conflict between me and him. Joey stood up for me. He was horrified when he heard what he was doing, as were Sheldon and Danny and Milt [Josefsberg].

AUTHOR: *Any thoughts on Corbett Monica?*

DALTON: Corbett was a darling man. I loved him. What a relief working with him after that horrid man [Marks].

AUTHOR: *How was Mary Treen to work with?*

DALTON: Mary was the maid. She lived her part. You just thought she was the funny maid. Always reliable. Always knew her words. Very professional.

AUTHOR: *How was it working with Joe Besser?*

DALTON: (*big smile and laugh*) Oh, gosh. Everyone loved Joe. He was like a dumpling! A perfect, perfect dumpling! He was the same in his part and off-camera. Just a sweet, darling man. He did whatever you needed him to do. He never caused any trouble. He just wanted to please everyone. He was a professional actor—but not a good one. And to be truthful, I did not like his character that much. Truthfully . . . can I be truthful?

AUTHOR: *Of course.*

DALTON: I did not like wisecracking maids or slapsticky comic handymen or characters like his. I just thought they were demeaning. I liked the people who played those roles [Treen and Besser] and I don't know how they did it, but *Jesus* they did. It's their *characters* I detested.

AUTHOR: *How was the atmosphere on the set?*

DALTON: (*exaggerated eye-roll, head nod, followed by a raucous laugh*) It was . . . uh . . .uh . . .(*laughs again*) I don't know how to say this without being nasty. It was mostly tense. *Very tense.* I've been on sets my whole career, but this was a comedy, so it should have been light. It was not joyful. You had to watch where you stepped—you didn't want to step on a raw egg. I look back on it as a learning experience. I thought I was good, professional, and consistent. But then again, I was happy to be there. I was a co-star on a television series for three years. I was happy for the work, so that was a great experience. I would actually wake up each morning and look forward to the great work. I loved the wardrobe too (*laughs*). I was happy being on the Desilu Cahuenga lot. I was a star and I was treated like a star. I was disappointed that I didn't do any crossovers on the other shows at the time, though. It was great to be on the lot with the other casts from *The Andy Griffith Show* and *The Dick Van Dyke Show* and *The Danny Thomas Show*. Everybody was just happy to be working . . . and treated with honor. It was a great atmosphere. And I was pregnant twice during the show's run, and they catered to me. Very accommodating. They looked out for me. When I told Joey that I was pregnant a second time, he joked, "Hey, we already did that show!" That was his remark in lieu of congratulations! I'll never forget that about him—it was always all about *him*! He hated if you told him anything personal. It's like, don't take your shit to him. He didn't care and didn't want to know. You couldn't get close to him.

AUTHOR: *What did you think of your role as Ellie Barnes?*

DALTON: I thought it was mediocre. I did, really. She was a second banana. I got to say, "Yes, dear." She didn't really have any career goals of her own. Ellie was just a *wife*. I tried to imagine what her life had been like before Joey. *Did* she have a life? She just happened in a bottle. Joey needs a wife. I think I was too tall for his taste. He would have preferred someone shorter than him, I think. He wasn't very tall. They made me wear tennis shoes to appear shorter. Did I change the world with my role? No. But entertainment is creating a bit of escapism. I was constantly being compared to Mary Tyler Moore. We were on the same lot and from the same producers. So I constantly got that comparison, and I hated that. I did not try to be Mary. Ever. In many ways they tried to copy *The Dick Van Dyke Show*. They were both shows about show business. They had a work life with writers [Marks, then Monica] and then a home life. Both showbiz type of shows.

AUTHOR: *You played the wives of Jackie Cooper, Joey Bishop, and Jonathan Winters. What was the difference between those three men?*

DALTON: Jonathan was a darling man. He would set you up beautifully. Then knock you down. Beautifully. He made you look good. He tried hard to. Always helpful. I just absolutely adored Johnny. Just loved him. One of the reasons he stopped the show was that his [real] wife got jealous of me. Silly. Johnny was married to a witch. She really was quite a bitch, actually.

AUTHOR: What was the difference between working with Joey and Jonathan?

DALTON: Oh, no comparison whatsoever! Joey was about Joey. He was *all about Joey*. How *he* looked. Jonathan was giving. Caring. He was like a Jack Benny or Dick Van Dyke. They made *you* look good. Joey had no concept of that. It was a one-way street. But someone like Johnny was special. One of a kind. It was a treat to work with him. Joey could not give a shit about anyone else but Joey."

Gossip columnist Dorothy Kilgallen added fuel to the fire when she wrote, "Joey Bishop's explanation of why Guy Marks is no longer a member of his 'happy' TV family is a hot one—Joey gave out a statement contending that success came too suddenly to Guy and he couldn't take it. . . . It's no secret that the parting between Joey Bishop and Guy Marks was far from friendly, but no one revealed that they were close to the fisticuffs stage."

The *Toledo Blade*'s "Television Tidbits" column (December 30, 1963) had this to add to Kilgallen's item: "No room at the top? The second bananas of one of television's new service comedies were ordered to shed their press agents as they we're getting more press than the star. And Vine Streeters believe that comic Corbett Monica deserves a medal for bravery for stepping into that role in Joey Bishop's show to replace Guy Marks. Joey doesn't seem to like having sidemen around who get too many laughs. Joe Flynn, now a star on *McHale's Navy*, found that out last year, and now Guy Marks."

Joey and his team needed damage control to kill the bad press he was getting with both Joe Flynn and now Guy Marks speaking out against him. Hal Humphrey, television columnist for the Hearst syndicate, wrote on April 26, 1963,

A silly rumor persists that if anyone gets funnier than the boss of "The Joey Bishop Show," they will be summarily fired.

So, Joey did fire two comic foils in the last season and a half. So what? Maybe he forgot to take his Anacin and then blew up when he found their cars parked in his parking space [shades of Danny Dayton during *Keep Talking*].

At any rate, there is now a witness to testify that he's a sweet lovable character whose main mission in life is to help other comics get laughs.

"I don't know what it was with Joe Flynn or Guy Marks, but it's foolish to say they are out because they got too many laughs," attests the newest replacement, comic Corbett Monica.

"Joey is the boss and he is in control. If he did not want those guys to get laughs, he could have taken them out of the scripts before show time, right?

"I get a lot of laughs and I wouldn't if Joey didn't want me to. I don't get all this talk about Joey."

To further prove how Joey gets along with others who make their living being funny, Corbett introduces the following startling fact:

"I've been living at Joey's house. Would I be doing that if Joey couldn't stand other standup comics? This is really a strange town. No one wants to believe that people help people.

"Why, comics always give others a lift when they are in New York. You walk into Lindy's and a friend says, 'Hey, Harry's opening over at the Blue Angel tonight.' The next thing you know, two or three comics are over at Harry's table and saying, 'Hey, Harry, I've got a great opening line for your show tonight!'

"It's like doctors. You call one for an appointment and he says, 'I'm filled up then, but why don't you call Dr. Schmidlap?' Comics are exactly the same way. Believe me!"

In Joey's case, they go back a long way. They both live in Englewood, New Jersey, and for eight years they lived only four blocks from each other.

"Once, when Joey was guest-hosting on *The Tonight Show*, he had me on as a guest twice during the week. It was actually then that Joey thought I'd be perfect for his show."

Does Corbett fret sometimes on being the second banana on his television show?

"Are you kidding? There is no such thing as a second banana anymore. TV changed all that. Look at Art Carney or Carl Reiner and guys like that. Once you are on TV, you become a personality. If you believe you're a second banana, then you are in trouble. You begin pressing to top the other guy. It's sick.

"Now, Joey and I like to ad-lib during rehearsals. Or maybe we chew it around the house the night before, then make a few minor changes the next day.

"You see, everybody on the show looks to make the show a hit. Joey keeps all of us in every episode so we don't lose the character identity with the audience. This way we all make money.

"Just a couple weeks ago, I had a chance to do a big one-nighter in Baltimore with Ethel Merman. It was a big break for me, huh? So what does Joey do? He changes the schedule around so I can make it to Baltimore and back, so I don't miss out in my part on the show. How about that?

"I'm already signed for next season and thirty-two weeks with Joey. It's great. I'm really going to school, because I never have really done anything but standup comedy before. I'm really learning how to do television comedy and Joey made it possible!

"Heck, Damon and Pythias never did it better and they never had a comedy series!"

Hallelujah!

Garry Marshall noted, "The star of any show has to be comfortable with the supporting players and whether Joey felt threatened with Marks—he probably did, but we can't risk having that. Corbett filled in nicely and we had a much smoother path."

Marshall recalled about his partner Fred Freeman's departure from the show: "Joey was always insecure about everything. He kept calling Fred 'college boy.' Possibly, because of the way I speak, he thought I dropped out in the eighth grade (*laughs*). [Garry was a graduate of Northwestern University.] Fred left the show and I stayed. I saw this as an opportunity, and it was. Joey was tough on all the writers. He was merciless with Marvin Marx, who eventually went back to work for Jackie Gleason. He hired Fred for that staff. I saw him get physical with Milt Josefsberg, who was in his sixties by then. Sheldon blew a gasket on that and read Joey the riot act. Joey never started with Sheldon. I decided to tough it out, and I'm glad I did."

As the second season came to an end, it was still not doing great in the ratings. There were rumblings in Dorothy Kilgallen' s column that NBC was considering offering a variety show in place of the situation-comedy. When the second season wrapped in April, Corbett Monica had settled into the role as Joey's writer and Guy Marks was long forgotten. NBC, as it had done during the turbulent first season, had gone into damage control and tried to enhance Joey's image with a slew of positive stories from Monica, Abby Dalton, Milt Josefsberg, and even Danny Thomas. Despite some hard feelings concerning Joey's treatment of his daughter Marlo, Thomas still had a large stake in the series with Leonard. The series failed to crack the top twenty-five in the ratings.

Comedy writer Sam Denoff, who with his partner Bill Persky wrote and produced *The Dick Van Dyke Show* for Carl Reiner and later helped create shows such as *That Girl*, also worked on the Bishop show. Denoff said, "Milt Josefsberg gave us a big break on *The Joey Bishop Show*, which led us to Van Dyke. He [Josefsberg] was such a wonderful man. He was so helpful when we were just beginning. We really got an education and he was so experienced."

Bill Persky told author Scott Lewellen (*Funny You Should Ask: Oral Histories of Classic Sitcom Storytellers*): "Milt was a sweetheart of a guy. He was gentle, gentle. Joey Bishop almost killed him. You couldn't have had a worse person to work for, because Milt took everything personally. He was a real gentleman and very funny. Very kind. He was always supportive and came up with great jokes."

Irma Kalish told the author that her husband, Rocky "never let me venture to the studio on *Joey Bishop*. I wrote at home. He wouldn't let me near Joey. It was like a war zone."

As for Rocky, he recalled, "I had gained the respect of Sheldon [Leonard] by then, so I absolutely ignored Bishop. He would come into where the writers were cloistered and rant and rave. He said he sat in a taping of the Van Dyke show and how smoothly it ran there and how their dialogue was much cleaner and sharper. We never told him that Van Dyke and that group were a thousand times more talented than him. Morey Amsterdam, Rose Marie, and [Richard] Deacon were professionals and could make your words play like gold. Joey had a ragtag group, starting with him, Joe Besser, [Corbett] Monica. The delivery was different. Despite the great writers and producers for Bishop, there was only so much we could do to make him seem funny. It always made me laugh when Bishop would say he was all ad-lib and didn't use writers. He was out of his fucking mind. Every word that came out of his mouth was carefully crafted. Garry [Marshall] and his then-partner [Fred Freeman] wrote all those sparkling *bon mots* he said on the Jack Paar show. As always, Bishop grabbed all the credit."

In his memoirs, Joe Besser recalled how Joey would agonize over every line.

> I always thought of Joey as a perfectionist. If one line of dialogue was off he would work on it until we got it right, many times right up until minutes before we filmed. One time, I vividly recall the day that Joey tried changing a line of dialogue on me before I made my entrance—but it backfired on him. Joey frequently did this to others on the show, but this time he didn't give me fair warning. Joey and I were supposed to make our entrance together through the apartment door. We were standing behind the door when Joey stopped me. His exact words

to me were, "Joey, when you come in don't say this line, say that." When our director, James V. Kern [noted director of *I Love Lucy*], rolled the camera, I walked in and repeated exactly what Joey told me to say. . . . Well, Joey busted up laughing and, in the future, he never changed a line on me at the spur of the moment like that again.

Directors like Kern must have been pulling out their hair as Joey meddled in every aspect of production from writing, directing, and even editing.

Director John Rich told the author, "I understand that a lot of the show was on his shoulders. It reflected upon him and it *was The Joey Bishop Show*. However, you never saw that kind of micromanaging from great stars such as Jack Benny, Andy Griffith, Van Dyke, and others. They trusted their writers, directors, and producers. They hired great talent and relied on them. Not to say they didn't get involved, but they never stepped over the line. The only two that I recall that would were Lucy and Joan Davis. Davis was just a real cunt. I was doing [*The Dick Van Dyke Show*] then and I refused any assignment from Sheldon with Bishop."

Surprisingly, despite his attachment to the Rat Pack during this period, there was no sign of Frank, Dean, Sammy, or Peter on the show. It certainly would have been a boost in the ratings had they appeared on the show. Since both Dean and Frank were under contract to NBC at the time, there would not have been any conflict.

Notably, Joey's unchecked arrogance affected his relationship with his fellow Rat Packers. After filming *Sergeants 3*, in another minor part, Joey was feeling underappreciated for everything he had contributed to the Summit. He quickly forgot that much of his success was due to Frank, who had included him. Dean and Sammy never were particularly close to Joey.

The late film historian and TCM host Robert Osborne shared the following with the author: "Bishop was always distant. Frank was going through a rough period, including the kidnapping of Frank Jr. [on December 8, 1963], which was just a couple of weeks after JFK was assassinated. Frank was already on the outs with Peter after being snubbed by Kennedy in Palm Springs, which he blamed on Peter. So Lawford was out of the group and the film *Robin and the 7 Hoods* [he was replaced by Bing Crosby]. Joey screwed over Frank that summer. He was going to play the plum part of Guy Gisborne, which Peter Falk ended up playing. He had signed a contract for $100,000. Then Frank asked Joey to fill in that summer for him at the Cal-Neva Lodge. Now, Frank and Dean owned a piece of it, so if Frank asked a favor, you did it, no questions asked. Joey, who was feeling his oats, started making demands of Frank. He wanted Frank to fly him out on his private plane, he wanted a top-drawer salary, and a bunch of other shit. Frank just said, 'Fuck him.' And once Frank feels you turned on him, he does not forget. Joey was out. Out of the film and out with Frank. No more Rat Pack for Joey."

Joey, who had burned bridges earlier with Ed Sullivan and had alienated Danny Thomas, was attacking and firing the top writers and directors on his show, angering NBC executives with his prima donna-like behavior. But to bite the hand that fed him—Frank Sinatra—the man who made his entire career possible—*that* was tantamount to career suicide.

Joey attempted to apologize to Frank. When Frank Jr. was kidnapped, Joey called and wired Frank with an offer to help. When Frank nearly drowned in Hawaii in 1965, Joey sent him a telegram, reading, "I thought you could walk on water." This was exactly the kind of joke that amused the Chairman. The result was a 1965 appearance of Frank and Dean on *The Tonight Show* when Joey was subbing for Johnny. And Joey was still under contract to the Sands, of which Frank owned 9%. They made a joint appearance at a mini-Summit in 1966. That was the last time they appeared together. But more on this later.

Robin and the 7 Hoods was shot during November and December in 1963, during Frank's time of turmoil, which included his son's kidnapping. But there was nary a word in the press about Joey and Peter Lawford, the missing-in-action Rat Pack members. To fill the job of de facto comedian for the Rat Pack's dwindling live performances, Jan Murray was drafted into service.

Joey had a welcome break from the backbiting in Hollywood when he flew to New York to be roasted by members of the Friars Club. Despite his reputation on the set of his own show, Joey was named "Entertainer of the Year" for the second time in a decade. The glittering event was held at Manhattan's tony Waldorf-Astoria Hotel. The host of the roast was "Fat" Jack E. Leonard, the famed insult comic. And on the dais that evening were some of Joey's cohorts, including Danny Thomas, Corbett Monica, Buddy Hackett, Sidney Poitier, Sammy Davis Jr., the McGuire Sisters, and his Rat Pack replacement, Jan Murray. Murray, an old hand at such affairs, may have had the best line of the night when he said, "I could talk about Joey and his wonderful accomplishments . . . for a minute or so, easy!"

Chapter 21
It's a Wrap
Joey Ponders His Future

Corbett Monica, Joey, and Abby Dalton.

As the third season began, Joey and Sylvia had made several changes in their home life. After renting a house in Beverly Hills, they decided to make the westward move permanent. Joey explained, "We knew by that point that the business for us was in Los Angeles. Whether the show continued, most of the production was in Los Angeles. My future was in television and what was there to complain about being in L.A.? The weather was great, and I was near Vegas and under contract to the Sands."

It was time to start living large. Joey and Sylvia bought a mansion in Beverly Hills. Their next-door neighbors were Ernest Borgnine and movie mogul Jack Warner.

Norman Brokaw, who eventually became the president of the William Morris Agency, was Joey's agent for nearly fifty years. As he told the author, "Joey had a great contract at the Sands, he had the television show, and the films. He was always very cautious; however, he was now a major star."

Sunday night bagel-and-lox parties became a tradition at the Bishop household. Regular attendees were Jack and Mary Benny and Milton and Ruth Berle. Joey went first class, no Nate-n-Al's for their parties. He had Max Asnas, owner of the New York's Stage Deli on Seventh Avenue, personally fly out the bagels, whitefish, corned beef, chopped liver, and other goodies. Joey and Asnas, who remained close friends, seriously considered opening a West Coast version of The Stage Deli. Max was actually quite astute about the field of comedy. Dick Cavett quotes Asnas as having said, "Some comedians have a fast face and a slow mind. Joey has a slow face and a fast mind."

Meanwhile, Joey and Sylvia's son Larry was enrolled at Beverly Hills High School, where his closest friends were Rob Reiner (son of Carl and Estelle Reiner); Albert Einstein, later known as Albert Brooks (son of the late comic Harry Einstein a.k.a. Parkyakarkas, and brother of the late comedian-writer Bob Einstein a.k.a. Super Dave Osborne). Larry and Rob would later start an improv group together and even toured for a while as a comedy team.

During a television interview in San Francisco in 1967, Rob and Larry were asked whether their famous fathers were supporting their career choice. Rob quickly answered that his dad supported anything that made him happy. Larry said that his father "didn't dig" his choice of careers. Larry said his father would have been happier if he had gone into medicine or law. He also said that comedy was not his future and that he planned to study acting. His goal was to become a serious actor.

Comic Jack Carter said to the author, "There always seemed to be a rift between Larry and Joey. Both Joey and Sylvia doted on their only child. They had higher expectations of Larry, who seemed enamored of show business. Joey was very disappointed. Joey, who was nepotistic in hiring his brother Freddie (and other relatives) to work on his shows, never seemed to include Larry. Whether that was Larry's choice, I'm not sure. But I really believe that there was very little support of Larry by his father, throughout his career. Years later, Joey appeared in a film that Larry produced [the critically panned *Mad Dog Time* (1996)]. I think Joey may have invested in the film. But I never sensed a close relationship between the two. There seemed to be a wedge."

Among Joey's entourage was his brother Freddie, who had been a maître d' in Miami and became the script supervisor on *The Joey Bishop Show*. His former stage partner Mel Bishop had become Joey's personal assistant.

One episode of *The Joey Bishop Show*, filmed on November 15, 1963, has never been seen. Indeed, it has been reported that the negative of the show was destroyed. The episode, known only as "#85," had as its guest star Vaughn Meader, who achieved temporary fame for his uncanny impersonation of President John F. Kennedy on the comedy album *The First Family*.

On November 22, 1963, one week exactly after the episode was filmed, President Kennedy was shot in Dallas, Texas, by Lee Harvey Oswald. Episode #85 was originally planned to air in February 1964, but after the news, it was pulled by NBC.[2] *The Joey*

---

2   Not surprisingly, JFK's assassination put a quick end to Vaughn Meader's career. The album, which was considered a good-natured parody upon its release, was now considered to be in highly questionable taste. All unsold copies were pulled from store shelves and destroyed. Meader, who overnight had become a show-

Bishop Show promptly went on hiatus for a few weeks, returning in early 1964. Apparently, the sitcom could still deliver the goods. Sam Denoff told author Michael Seth Starr, "I'll tell you the ultimate actor's story. Someone had written a script for the show in which Joey Barnes's long-lost brother shows up. It was wonderfully written and was very funny. The producer, Milt Josefsberg, one of the classic great comedy writers, loved the script.

"So now they rehearse it and it's one of those shows that are good. The crew and everybody are laughing because Joey was actually good playing two parts."

"On the morning they are supposed to shoot the show, Joey shows up in Milt's office. He says, 'Milt, I'm not gonna do the show, it's not gonna work, it's wrong. I'm angry at you for not realizing it's not funny.'

"So Milt says, 'What's wrong with it?' And Joey says, 'I'll tell you what's wrong with it: my brother is getting all the laughs!'"

As the 1963–1964 season was ending, *The Joey Bishop Show* looked like it was nearing its end. Leonard-Thomas wanted at least one more year to bring the second version to a total of 100 episodes, which was the magic number needed to get a good release in syndication. Of course, although there were the requisite number of episodes, the first season has a completely different cast and premise.

Garry Marshall recalled, "Jerry Belson and I were also working on *The Dick Van Dyke Show*, so we were not upset. Sheldon, being the brilliant producer, knew he needed an additional year under his belt. The show was not setting any records, but it was moved around to many time slots and never gained a big following. Sheldon even tried stunting with *The Dick Van Dyke Show* [in the final year when it moved to CBS], but Carl refused that. I don't blame him [for not wanting to do a crossover episode]."

Joey's longtime writer Don Sherman told the author, "NBC had asked him [Joey] to do a variety show to replace the comedy, even using the show inside of the variety show like Gleason

business non-entity, returned to his hometown in Maine, where he performed music and managed a pub. Not much was heard of him—or his notorious album— until it was re-released on CD in 1999. Vaughn Meader died on October 29, 2004, at the age of sixty-eight.

did with *The Honeymooners*. Joey asked me to work up a concept. However, it was the end of the season and there was no way he could get a show together by that fall."

Producer Bob Finkel adds, "I was doing *The Andy Williams Show* on NBC when they approached us [his co-producers were Norman Lear and Bud Yorkin] to create a variety show for Joey. Norman hated Joey. Andy was multi-dimensional and could sing. Joey was very limited and we passed on the project."

Finkel—who had produced variety shows for Eddie Fisher, Martin & Lewis (*The Colgate Comedy Hour*), Jerry Lewis (his late 1960s variety hour), Dinah Shore, Perry Como, and many others— was the touch of gold when it came to that form of programming. "We had heard the horror stories from both writers, producers, and executives about Bishop," Finkel said. "I had dealt with him on the Timex/Sinatra special (with Elvis). He was a dead fish. He was like poison and we were not going to get caught with his *mishegas*."

As the 1963–1964 season started coming to a close, Sheldon Leonard, who had pulled off miracles in resuscitating programs from the dead—such as *The Dick Van Dyke Show*, which was canceled after its first season but was saved by Leonard's plea to Procter & Gamble to sponsor it; his moving *The Real McCoys* to CBS and being instrumental in moving *Make Room for Daddy* from ABC to CBS, where it flourished as *The Danny Thomas Show*. It was a Hail Mary Pass, but Leonard went to Mike Dann, who had moved from NBC to CBS as that network's programming executive.

"The show had one huge plus," Dann told the author: "Joey's Q rating was high. He still had that Rat Pack veneer, and Jim Aubrey worshipped the Q. He had just hired Bob Cummings over Bob Crane and Jerry Van Dyke in a Jack Chertok show called *My Living Doll* [with Julie Newmar]. We certainly wanted to appease Sheldon and stay in their good graces. We had an opening on Sunday nights following *My Living Doll* at 9:30 P.M. It had *Sullivan* as the lead-in [followed by *Candid Camera*]. Bishop had somewhat of a following on NBC, so we ordered the series."

The regular players remained. With *The Danny Thomas Show* ending its run on CBS, Thomas insisted that Rusty Hamer, who played Danny's son Rusty Williams, appear as the same character on *The Joey Bishop Show*, only now he was Joey's college student nephew. Hamer, who was precocious and adorable as a child, had morphed into a wooden Indian as a performer. Much like other actors such as Jerry Mathers (*Leave It to Beaver*) and Gary Coleman (*Diff'rent Strokes*), cuteness ended at puberty; after that, genuine acting skills are needed. Hamer had no skills and was more of a distraction than an asset to the show; his guest appearances with Bishop numbered only three.[3]

With the order from CBS, which pleased Thomas/Leonard, there were memos and changes made to the show. Strangely—and this made zero sense—the show was filmed in black-and-white, *after* the last two seasons were shot in color. There had been industry studies that proved the added element of color greatly benefited a show's ratings as many consumers had already made the switch from black-and-white to color television sets. Some of the most popular programs of the time—including the Leonard/Thomas–produced *Andy Griffith* and *Gomer Pyle, U.S.M.C.*—had successfully made the transition. If anything, Sheldon Leonard was acutely aware of the value of color to the syndication package. Color, after all, was the future.

When the author asked Joey about the change, he said, "They were cheap motherfuckers. Save a dime. It killed the package. We were a throw-away and they didn't care."

The first show poked fun at the move, with Joey being fired by his network and being hired by CBS. With the move, Joey and Ellie move into the penthouse apartment. They also saddled Corbett Monica with a new girlfriend. As Joey complained, "We had the show finally going good, and CBS tinkered with it. It became

---

3   Unfortunately, Hamer drifted out of show business after one last try as Rusty on Danny Thomas's hopelessly dated retooling of his earlier sitcom, *Make Room for Granddaddy* in 1970. This was officially the former child star's last job in show business. By his early forties, he was living in a trailer in Louisiana, eking out a precarious existence by delivering newspapers. A victim of untreated depression, he was also in chronic pain due to his back. Finally, on January 18, 1990, forty-two-year-old Rusty Hamer put a .357 Magnum to his head and brought an end to his tragic life.

much more jumbled. They would send countless memos on script changes and other shit."

As it turned out, the better timeslot turned out to be anything but. *My Living Doll* faltered badly in the ratings, squandering its lead-in from *The Ed Sullivan Show*. Viewers, who rarely changed the channel in the days before the common remote control, switched to NBC in droves to watch *Bonanza*. Following this, viewers would switch back to CBS for *Candid Camera* and *What's My Line?*

Garry Marshall said, "Jerry [Belson] and I started focusing on *The Dick Van Dyke Show* and I helped hire Carl Kleinschmitt and Dale McCraven to do most of the writing on that final season. I still was there helping out as a producer and script consultant."

Kleinschmitt hardly considered his experience with the Bishop show a golden opportunity. "Basically, Garry Marshall threw us into that snake pit," he told the author. "Dale and I were just kids—*Who else* would work with Joey? He had chased out all the more mature writers and they let us get our foot in the door." Granted, Kleinschmitt admits, there were some perks to the job: "It was great to work on the Desilu Cahuenga lot on Sunset, where all the great series were being shot, such as *The Dick Van Dyke Show*. In fact, we got to write nine episodes of the Van Dyke show due to our working on Bishop. We also did episodes of *The Bill Dana Show*, *The Danny Thomas Show*, *The Andy Griffith Show*, *Gomer Pyle*, and *That Girl*. I guess you could say that we put up with Joey so we could get other jobs." McCraven and Kleinschmitt wrote a part of the third and most of the fourth season, but the results, he said, "were garbage. There was just no point to the series."

Why, the author asked Kleinschmidt, did Joey seem to so resent his writers?

"Joey resented anyone who knew the English language," he answered succinctly. "Once, Fred Freeman made the mistake of referring to Joey as the show's protagonist. Joey, not knowing the meaning of the word, took it as an insult and punched Freeman in the mouth."

Bishop was similarly out of his depth when he was hosting Jack Paar's show one particular night. His guest was literary giant Carl Sandburg. Kleinschmitt vividly recalls an awkward exchange between the nightclub comic and the distinguished poet. At one point, Sandburg waxed eloquent about his love for the city of Chicago.

"Chicago?" Joey said. "Did you hear the one about the tourist on a bus in Chicago? He goes up to the driver and asks, 'Do you go to the Loop?' The driver answers, 'No, I go *beep beep.*'"

"Sandburg just stared at Joey," Kleinschmitt laughs. "He didn't know what the fuck he was talking about!"

Back at the writers' office, there was little humor to be found.

"On Monday mornings, we would turn in a completed script," Kleinschmitt continues. "Joey would glance at it and then throw it in the trash. 'I'm a comedic genius,' he would say with no trace of humor. 'I couldn't possibly do this material!' We had to go back and rewrite the whole thing, usually staying up all night to do it. He would usually accept the second script, but it wasn't as good as the first one had been.

"Sid Dorfman, an established writer, was hired by the network to back the writing staff up. Sid used to take bets as to what time Joey would have his first blow-up. I remember his being excited once when he put his money on ten thirty-five, and—he won!"

Someone who attempted to impart some perspective to the persecuted writing staff was the legendary TV writer Harry Crane. He told them, "Consider this boot camp. When you graduate, you become a tough Marine. You'll get toughened up and then find that everyone else is better than Joey."

In an attempt to bring some levity to a dire situation, Garry Marshall called the Bishop writing staff—Arnold Margolin, Jim Parker, Jerry Belson, Dale McCraven, Carl Kleinschmitt, and himself—"The Sunset Six."

"Joey cared about nothing but Joey," Carl Kleinschmitt told the author. "One morning he was in an especially foul temper after he heard that his forty-five-year-old accountant had died suddenly the night before. 'That son of a bitch!' Joey railed at no one in particular. 'Here he was making so much money for me and then he just up and dies!'

"Another time, he was bitching about his mother, who lived in a room above his garage in Beverly Hills. 'My mother is never happy,' he said. 'I asked her what she wanted from me. She said she wanted to be *loved*. Can you imagine that? I give her everything and now she wants love!'

"He was so insecure that he would take it out not just on his writers, but everyone. Joey once called Herb Molina at midnight to bring firewood to his house."

This toxic environment brought stress to everyone involved, including his co-star and friend Corbett Monica. "Poor Corbett," Carl said. "He kept thinking that the whole series would fold in a minute. He was nervous all the time."

Even in the worst surroundings, a comical moment occasionally shined through. "One day, Bill Persky showed up to work wearing a loud, flashy coat," Carl said. "It was like something out of *Joseph and the Technicolor Dream Coat*. Joey took one look at it and said straight-faced, 'When your brothers pushed you down the well, were you pissed off?'"

On one rare occasion, Joey invited the writers to join him in Palm Springs, where they could work on some rewrites. They all stayed at Jack Entratter's place, and they were not alone. There were all these racketeer goons sitting around the pool. When each thug was asked what he did, they all gave the same answer: "I'm a businessman."

According to Kleinschmitt, everything just stopped when Joey heard the words: "Mr. Bishop, Frank Sinatra is on line one." Taking the call immediately, Joey was suddenly all charm and compliance. He knew that there would be no television show—no nothing, in fact—without his association with Frank. "So when Sinatra pulled the rug out from under him," Kleinschmitt said, "Joey was in shock."

After the show flopped on Sunday nights, it was moved to Tuesday, where it fared no better. CBS had ordered a full season commitment with a minimum order of twenty-six episodes. Thus, while production was still ongoing, CBS canceled *The Joey*

Bishop Show on January 7. The last episode would be telecast on March 30, 1965.

The reviews of the show continued to be pans. A critic for *Entertainment Weekly*, in its April 2018 issue, had this to say:

> Years after George Burns played a comedian in an eponymous sitcom, and long before *Seinfeld*, there was *The Joey Bishop Show* (TV Land, April 18, 10:30–11 A.M.) Airing from '61 to '65, Bishop's vehicle exuded low-rent swagger. In addition to Marlo Thomas (who got her sitcom start playing his sister), Abby Dalton (as his wife), and ex-Stooge Joe Besser (as his landlord), *Bishop* boasted guests like Leo Durocher and Sheldon Leonard. Tune in for a B-list bonanza.

Noel Murray, of The AV Club, wrote:

> Both *The Dick Van Dyke Show* and *The Joey Bishop Show* launched in the fall of 1961, sharing a production company and a goal: to snazz up the family sitcom by adding the perspective of low-level show-business insiders. Van Dyke thrived playing a comedy writer with a relatively shtick-free home life, while Bishop, known for his sophisticated, self-deprecating style of Borscht Belt wisecracking, foundered in his first season playing a hard-luck publicist living at home with his parents. The people who paid to see Bishop pal around with Frank Sinatra in Vegas couldn't buy him as a suburban schlub bickering with his mother. Luckily for the fastidious Bishop, retooling was common on TV in those days. (How many sons were on *My Three Sons*, anyway?) By its second season, *The Joey Bishop Show* shifted from black-and-white to color, and its star had been recast as a successful variety-show host dealing with life as a newlywed.

> Still, *The Dick Van Dyke Show* went on to become an acknowledged television classic, while *The Joey Bishop Show* is remembered fondly by Rat Pack obsessives, if at

all. That's pretty much as it should be. Yet the second-phase *Joey Bishop Show* still provides plenty of reasons to watch: Abby Dalton brings a surprising level of sexual passion and fashion sense to her role as Bishop's doting wife, while former Stooge Joe Besser, playing Bishop's intrusive building superintendent, remains delightfully weird, more Kramer than Fred Mertz. And even though Danny Thomas (*The Joey Bishop Show*'s executive producer and guardian angel) was mixing standup comedy and domestic trouble as far back as 1953's *Make Room For Daddy*, *The Joey Bishop Show* perfected the blend, presaging the likes of *The Larry Sanders Show* in its star's preoccupation with comic rivals, public image, and the stresses of mounting a nightly coast-to-coast broadcast.

Bishop has always been an undervalued minor celebrity, and this sitcom served as his best vehicle. He glides through routine TV situations like having a baby and dealing with his wife's overspending, waiting for the moment he can pop on his know-it-all smirk and exaggerate the ridiculousness of modern life by trying to live it to perfection.

The reception for the syndication package had been abysmal. After the show ended, it was rarely ever seen. First, Joey nixed having the first season as part of the package of 123 episodes. So, they had a pool of the three seasons of ninety-seven episodes, with one season in black-and-white. Second, with Joey Bishop practically fading from view after 1970, very few even remembered who he was. Except for a short play on the Christian Broadcasting Network and TV Land, the show was in limbo. An attempt at DVD sales, with a restored second season by Shout! Factory, had failed. It faded into obscurity along with other such forgettable shows as *Pete and Gladys*, *December Bride*, and *The Ann Sothern Show*. Joey, however, did not see it that way. As he proudly told an interviewer in 1994, "Whenever I see one of the old episodes, it always surprises me how up-to-date we are." To prove his point, Antenna Television only recently began running all 123 episodes of the show for the first time in decades and received surprisingly decent ratings. Amazon Prime has also bought the package to be seen on their streaming network. Much to everyone's surprise, the series has received new attention.

Chapter 22
Back to the Clubs
Joey Returns to His Roots

Joey subs for Johnny Carson on NBC's The Tonight Show, 1975.

"I was not hurting after the show got canceled," Joey said. "My dance card was filled."

Despite his sense of bravado, he was worried. He no longer had the support of Frank Sinatra to fall back on. He was excluded from the Rat Pack movie, *Robin and the 7 Hoods*, which had a mediocre return at the box office. For all intents and purposes, the Rat Pack had fizzled with the death of JFK. Times and tastes were changing. The Beatles and The Rolling Stones were the new flavors.

By the mid-1960s, many of the legendary nightclubs—from the Copacabana and Latin Quarter in New York City, Ciro's and the Mocambo in Los Angeles, to the Chez Parée in Chicago, clubs that Joey had worked in for nearly thirty years—were quickly becoming extinct. Replacing them were clubs like the Whiskey-a Go-Go and Pandora's Box in Los Angeles. Pandora's Box, on the Sunset Strip, was a popular music venue that featured performances by artists such as the Beach Boys, the Byrds, and Sonny & Cher. As the old nightspots started to vanish, singers such as Eddie Fisher, Vic Damone, Tony Martin, as well as the comics, were losing their venues.

The Las Vegas showrooms and lounges were now among the few outlets for many of the old guard. With the change in musical tastes came a similar movement in comedy. Milton Berle, Alan King, Jackie Vernon, Phil Foster, and even Jerry Lewis seemed outdated. A new breed of standup comedian was developing. This group included Bob Newhart, Woody Allen, George Carlin (who changed from a clean-cut presence to a hipper version of himself), Robert Klein, Dick Gregory, Mort Sahl, David Steinberg, and the Smothers Brothers. Instead of doing tired one-liners about their mothers-in-law, they were doing observational humor, which resonated with this younger generation. They were more likely to discuss the Vietnam War, women's liberation, sexual openness, drugs, public protests, and general turmoil. One could still hear the old-style comedians in the Catskills, but elsewhere that style now seemed prehistoric.

Joey saw his dream of hosting a variety show drifting away. Shows like *The Ed Sullivan Show*, *The Hollywood Palace*, and others had declining ratings. Skit-based variety shows such as *The*

Carol Burnett Show, *The Red Skelton Show*, *The Jonathan Winters Show*, and *The Smothers Brothers Comedy Hour* were the hotter-ticket items.

Meanwhile, Joey was pushing fifty. He had been performing as a comic for nearly four decades. While there are the rare comics who span generations—Bob Hope, George Burns, and Jack Benny—the majority were more like Sid Caesar. He had nearly ten years of solid success on television, from the late 1940s to the late 1950s. He was a household name for a while, and then fatigue set in. Viewers stopped watching and the comic was put into storage, to be brought back occasionally for nostalgic purposes. In essence, except for being seen in short glimpses (such as a guest spot on *The Lucy Show*), Sid Caesar was relatively obscure from his appearance in *It's a Mad, Mad, Mad, Mad World* in 1963 until his death in 2014.

Joey's career paralleled Caesar's. He began hitting national fame in 1958–1959, but now his shelf life was expiring. Joey had one safety net left and that was his noted ability to host a talk show, an ability he adeptly displayed on both Jack Paar's and Johnny Carson's *Tonight Show*.

During the last year of the sitcom, Joey hired one of his fellow Bishop Brothers, Mel Bishop, as his general factotum. As Mel told author Michael Seth Starr, "Joey needs someone he can lean on, someone he can bullshit with, someone he can yell at. He told me what the salary was, and it was more than I was making—and it was a steady job." Joey even had him on an episode during the final season of his sitcom. The other Bishop Brother, Rummy Bishop, was still playing small clubs.

In fact, when Joey played the Sands in the summer of 1965, Mel was standing right next to him, doing part of their old act in which Joey played his mandolin. Joey's contract with the Sands was extended in 1966 and he also became their "go-to" guy when they needed someone to fill in if a performer became ill or couldn't make the date. He had done that for Nat Cole when the singer/pianist was being treated for cancer. Jack Entratter knew he could count on Joey to be the "good soldier" and fill in at the last minute, flying in from Los Angeles to do so.

Joey had a longtime dislike of Jerry Lewis. His reason: "Jerry treated Dean like his stooge. Dean told me all about Jerry. Jerry needed to control everything. There was no give and take with Jerry, just all take. Joe Besser told me he did some scenes in a movie with Jerry that were cut out, because Joe got bigger laughs. You hear that from everybody."

Lewis suffered a life-altering spinal injury when he fell from a piano while performing at the Sands Hotel in Las Vegas in 1965, resulting in partial paralysis and leading to his eventual addiction to the painkiller Percodan. Joey was asked to fill in for him.

"I had other club dates, but Jack [Entratter] called in a panic," Joey recalled. "So I flew in and did a couple nights of shows and I was getting great reviews. Lewis was still in town and heard I was scoring big. So, I'm out on the stage and I hear laughs at the back of the room. It's Lewis upstaging my show. Doing his *schtick* right in the middle of the show. I told Jack, 'I came here to do a guy a favor. I canceled dates to help him out. If he is so fucking paranoid that he needs to interrupt my act, I'm flying home' . . . and I did!"

Joey showed us a handwritten letter from Jerry Lewis, dated March 1949. The original envelope (which Joey had kept as well) read "A sweet and sincere note from one comedy legend to another." On personalized stationery reading "Jerry Lewis, Child Star," was a handwritten note penned by the twenty-three-old comic. It reads, in part,

Dear Joey, . . .

I'm thrilled at your wonderful rise and please forget about the material.

Regards from Dean to you.

Your pal,

Jerry

Joey continued: "I was living in Newport Beach and I was acting as the Goodwill Ambassador for the Newport Beach Yacht Club. I had my boat, *The Son of a Gun I*, docked there, and I was the club president. So I heard Jerry had docked his boat there

and I went over to greet him for the club and to see if he needed anything. He was the biggest fucking asshole to me. When I
knocked on his door, he looked at me like I was trash and said,
'Who told you I was here?'"

Joey's momentum carried into being the host of the 19th Emmy
Awards at the Century Plaza Hotel in Los Angeles on June 4, 1967.
Hugh Downs was the announcer for the show. Joey had hosted
the Emmys in 1961, 1963, 1964, and now 1967.

Bob Finkel, who had been the producer of the show since
1960, told the author, "Joey was the perfect host of the show.
His quips were perfectly timed and he kept the show moving.
He did not infringe on the event and, almost like Bob Hope did
for the Academy Awards, he kept it light. He was easy to work
with. In 1967, Joey had just started his talk show on ABC (April 17),
so naturally ABC, which broadcast the show, wanted him as the
host. There was some infighting by the networks on the elgibil-
ity process and Joey joked about that. He did a decent job and
was funny when he needed to be. Actually, I think he did a pretty
good job."

Meanwhile, the apparent feud between Joey and Sinatra lin-
gered, although it had cooled somewhat when Joey wrote Frank
the telegram (mentioned earlier) after he nearly drowned in
Hawaii. Sinatra, in turn, invited Joey to reunite with the rest of the
Rat Pack (minus the banished Peter Lawford) for a 1965 charity
show to benefit the Dismas House in St. Louis. It was an attempt
to reignite the Rat Pack and was done through a new experiment.
The show would be broadcast from St. Louis to theaters in Los
Angeles around New York through closed-circuit television. Joey,
who at first accepted, had to bow out at the last minute, claiming
that a back issue had left him confined to bed. In that oft-shown
program that gave us a full look at the Rat Pack back in action,
Johnny Carson agreed to sub for Joey. Johnny told the audience
that Bishop would not be attending as he "had a slipped disc by
backing out of Frank's presence."

"He was just being an asshole," Joey said.

Inadvertently pouring gasoline on the fire, the author asked
Joey if he had actually injured his back.

"It doesn't matter!" he yelled.

Clearly in trouble with his host, the author changed the subject to an equally controversial topic. Had there ever been a rift between him and Sinatra?

"Never," he said emphatically. "We got along fine. He was always good to me. Generous to a fault. Frank was one of the good guys."

Joey knew the importance of keeping on Frank's good side and how important it was to his career to continue to appear with him. He agreed to join Frank and Sammy as part of a mini-Summit at the Sands in September of 1966. While the one-week engagement was a highly sought-after ticket, it wasn't the same as those twenty-eight days back in 1960. That era was over. They did the same old bits, such as the rolling booze cart, but it all seemed like "been there, done that."

When asked by reporter Joyce Haber why more such appearances were not on the docket, Joey answered, "We are all busy, so it makes it hard to get together to do these shows. Dean has his television show as does Sammy, and Frank is always making a movie. I have an upcoming show. We can't just drop everything and head off to Vegas. Everyone has a different way of life. It's as if the Rat Pack was something you graduated from."

Joey still remained at Sinatra's beck and call. When Governor Pat Brown (a Democrat) was running for reelection in 1966, he called Frank to help out. Frank, who liked to fashion himself a "kingmaker" as he had with Kennedy, agreed. Brown's opponent was Ronald Reagan, which was ironic since, later, Sinatra became a fundraiser, supporter, and close friend of the Reagans when they occupied the White House. Frank asked Joey to emcee the event, which he gladly did. Joey was in top form and was a big hit. Frank and Dean appeared together at the event as well.

Joey had gained a reputation as a competent host of events such as the Emmy Awards, *The Hollywood Palace*, and his regular appearances as a guest host of *The Tonight Show*. In fact, it seemed the perfect setting for Joey. The next logical step in his career would be as a talk-show host.

Chapter 23
Joey Vs. Comedy Writers
An Ad-lib Isn't Worth the Paper It's Written On

THE GREAT
COMEDIANS
TALK ABOUT
COMEDY

WOODY ALLEN · MILTON BERLE ·
SHELLEY BERMAN · JACK BENNY · JOEY
BISHOP · GEORGE BURNS · JOHNNY
CARSON · MAURICE CHEVALIER ·
PHYLLIS DILLER · JIMMY DURANTE · DICK
GREGORY · BOB HOPE · GEORGE
JESSEL · JERRY LEWIS · DANNY
THOMAS · ED WYNN

by LARRY WILDE

While many great comics such as Jack Benny and Bob Hope kept their writers on staff for decades, Bishop had a hard time keeping them for months—or even weeks. In fact, Joey held his writers in great disdain. This stemmed from his deep-seated insecurity based on his lack of formal education.

Two of the writers for the talk show, David Pollock and Elias Davis, were hired for writing an "off-the-top-of-his-head joke" for the show's premiere (he opened with "So, are the ratings in yet?"). They had a hard time writing all ad-lib type of jokes rather than stories with a punchline. Bishop didn't care.

David Pollock recalled, "We'd write forty jokes by one P.M. He would toss most away, as he wanted 'spontaneous' jokes which are not jokes. He was hard to write for, as he had no set style."

Fred Freeman and Garry Marshall started writing for Joey when he was appearing on the Jack Paar *Tonight Show*. As Marshall recalled for us, "Fred and I were fresh out of college. We gave him the throwaways he wanted. We would learn from the other *Tonight Show* writers, such as Dick Cavett, who the guests were and the topics [that would be covered]. Then we would write throwaways on that subject to make Joey look like The Ad-lib King. Now, Joey could perfectly deliver the material in his deadpan way and it made him seem witty or he would add in a non-sequitur that we carefully crafted."

Joey's vile reputation among writers was well deserved. Among the countless writers the author interviewed, not one remembered him fondly. The most common words they used to describe their former boss were *prick, asshole*, and *son-of-a-bitch* (not *gun*).

"Joey's march to fame followed the path of Sherman's March to the Sea," said Rocky Kalish. "It was a scorched-earth policy and most of us were his burn victims."

Bishop's head writer, Trustin Howard, said that "by the time the talk show ended, we went from a staff of writers to me and maybe Don Sherman. His monologue was unlike Carson's. It hardly touched on the daily news, but mostly on his guests. He had his famous wastebasket where most of the good material ended up."

Another longtime Bishop writer, Don Sherman, concurred, "That is why Joey looked so stiff doing his situation comedy show. He had a hard time with the material. He complained that he was restrained, much like Rickles was on his multiple attempts to do a television show. However, Rickles was a good, well-trained actor. You see him in a film like *Kelly's Heroes* and he is great. Joey could not do that. Joey had a hard time playing a convincing character."

Sheldon Leonard had this to say: "Joey was the product of being associated with Frank and friends. We sold his show based on that. We tried every angle to play upon his strengths. He had the best writers and directors. I remember that many came away very frustrated, including me!"

Writer Elias Davis added: "Joey was hard to wrap yourself around. To get a feel for his comedy. Joey felt he had a style as a wit. He was not a storyteller. Hardly a Fred Allen or a Robert Benchley."

Many comics have also excelled as writers: Woody Allen, Steve Martin, Larry David, to name just a few. Other comics are simply performers and rely heavily on others' material that fit their style. Great monologists such as Jack Benny, Frank Fay, Milton Berle, Bob Hope, and others were fully dependent on their writers. There is a rare breed of comic, such as Don Rickles, who were solely dependent on attitude and could do what is known in the trade as "crowd work." Joey Bishop always stated that he fit in that area of comedy when, in fact, Joey had set jokes. The reason he would not sign on to do ten *Ed Sullivan Shows* was that he did not want to "burn material." Joey *always* had writers, whether he was doing *The Tonight Show, What's My Line?* or *The Match Game*. While Joey did do *some* crowd work, he knew where it would lead.

When a set is consistently bombing, most comedians will communicate directly with audience members to save face; much of crowd work is prewritten, with added improvisation. Some comedians will use small talk that directs audience members to answer a question for which the comedian has a topper. Other comedians will become more intimate with their questions until they get multiple big laughs, before moving on. The result of crowd work is often an inside joke.

A "tight five" is a five-minute standup routine that is well rehearsed and consists of material that reliably gets laughs. It is often used for auditions or delivered when audience response is minimal. That is also the material used for *The Tonight Show* or a variety show such as Ed Sullivan's.

Despite his denials, Joey's shows were mostly a tight twenty-five, as he worked primarily as an opening act for the first twenty years of his career. Whether he opened for Sinatra or others, he needed a structured set. While Joey was accomplished with hecklers or raucous crowds, he was careful not to overstep his boundaries, lest he offend a mobster in the audience. While comics such as Rickles, Buddy Hackett, and Shecky Greene certainly worked the mob-run clubs, they made their bones playing the Las Vegas lounges such as the Sahara, the Riviera, or the Sands, where a wider-open format evolved and they were the sole acts.

Many comics fit into a category of observational humor, a storyteller, a one-line comic, etc. The author asked Joey into which category he believed he fell.

"Attitude," Joey said. "I was a listener. That's why I could do a talk show. I could listen and respond."

"So, would you say you were more like a Groucho?"

"Sure. Except Groucho had great writers. I just instinctively replied."

In 1968, an aspiring comic and interviewer by the name of Larry Wilde released a fascinating book, *The Great Comedians Talk About Comedy*. Containing Wilde's in-depth interviews with a number of noted comedians, some of the classic variety (Benny, Burns, Hope, Durante, Jessel, Berle, and "The Perfect Fool," Ed Wynn) and the more modern (Shelley Berman, Dick Gregory, Woody Allen, Jerry Lewis), the book should be mandatory reading for anyone who aspires to make an audience laugh. Wilde was (and is) a fan of Joey's style of performance. The taped interview (transcribed and reprinted here by courtesy of Mr. Wilde himself)

is astonishing in what it reveals about Joey's self-perception as a comic and wit.

Sitting on the living room sofa of his Beverly Hills home, wearing a brown Paisley bathrobe, face unshaven, hair uncombed, Joey Bishop is the same man audiences throughout America have enjoyed for many years. Serious, pensive, disarming, he chatted with the same charm (despite his costume) and assurance he projects on the television tube.

Bishop spoke authoritatively, completely secure in his views on comedy, as well as in his philosophy of life. He continually removed Kents from a nearby glass cigarette box and smoked while listening to the question being framed. His longtime friend and former partner, Mel, contributed to the relaxed atmosphere by serving coffee throughout the meeting.

WILDE: *While you were with the Bishop Brothers, did you have any idea or plan to one day do an act by yourself?*

BISHOP: No.....no. But then the war came—

WILDE: *You worked with the trio prior to World War II?*

BISHOP: Oh, yeah. 1938 until '41.

WILDE: *And then you went into the service?*

BISHOP: I went in '42. Mel went in before me, and Rummy went in after me.

WILDE: *Did you get your own bookings?*

BISHOP: More or less. In those times, there were local agents, like Pete Iodice in Detroit, Al Norton in Rochester. They used to put you in with a revue. Like, they had the Bishop Brothers and the Eight Cocktail Girls. We would augment the revue.

WILDE: *What did the act consist of?*

BISHOP: A lot of shit. No....it consisted of satires on radio programs. *Lights Out, We the People, Gangbusters.* Rummy did all the commentator impressions—Boake Carter, Westbrook Van Voorhis, the *March of Time* voice. Mel sang and I did all the comedy and dramatic impressions. Actually, it only stayed together about three years, until I went into the service. When I came out, Mel stayed in—he was an officer. Rummy didn't come out until about ten months after. I got discharged at Brook General Hospital, Fort Sam Houston, Texas, but I couldn't leave town because my wife was ill, so I went to work in a place called the Mountain Top Dinner Club—for Captain and Mrs. Talmadge. I stayed there twelve weeks, until my wife was well.

WILDE: *Doing an act?*

BISHOP: Doing a single, yeah. In the meantime, Bob Lee, an orchestra leader who was working the St. Anthony Hotel in San Antone, went up to the Mountain Top Club and he called the Morris Office about me, said, "I saw a kid that would be very good." So they sent me a wire and said, "When you leave San Antone, let us know," and they booked me in the Greenwich Village Inn. I worked there with Joan Barry, then Barry Gray came in for four weeks.

WILDE: *He did a radio show there?*

BISHOP: No, he did a show as a comic.

WILDE: *Barry Gray has always been a successful...*

BISHOP: Yeah, as a matter of fact, he had all the jokes written and he read them, and as each one bombed, he threw it on the floor. When I followed him, I picked them up and said, "You should read the other side," and I pretended to read jokes from there.

WILDE: *Then that was the beginning of an act for you?*

BISHOP: Right. Well, I could always do the impressions. I did Cantor, Jolson, Edward G. Robinson, James Cagney, Fred Allen. I used them as a crutch for my comedy. I originated lines like, "Cagney—five thousand a week and he can't afford a belt."

WILDE: *Did you write your own material?*

BISHOP: I *never* write my stuff. I do what I call "thought humor." If the thought went through my mind, I'd go out and do it without writing it.

WILDE: *And if it worked it became a part of your act.*

BISHOP: Right.

WILDE: *If it didn't, you eliminated it.*

BISHOP: It rarely didn't work, because if it didn't work, I would do something on top of it to salvage it. In other words, if it bombed, it would afford me the opportunity of getting funny about its bombing.

WILDE: *Many people in show business point to you as the classic example of the performer who took twenty years to become a star overnight. As you look back now, why do you feel it took so long to become recognized.*

BISHOP: There are many reasons why someone doesn't become recognized. A new style—until people get used to it—can take a certain amount of time. No exposure, not being known, can take you a long time. In those days, there was no television, so consequently I had to..."Okay, he did good in New York, let's see how he does in Chicago, let's see how he does in Detroit, let's see how he does in Buffalo." And three or four or five years could go by. I don't think it really took me that long. I started working in '46 and in '49, I was the comic with Tony Martin at the Chez Parée—twelve weeks. In '49, I headlined the Latin Quarter in New York for fourteen weeks.

WILDE: *In his autobiography,* Groucho and Me, *Groucho Marx wrote that all comedians arrive by trial and error. During those years, were you consciously experimenting to find your comedic attitude?*

BISHOP: No. No. I don't think you experiment with comedic attitude. You experiment with a routine. Now, there is a difference. A routine can be terribly funny and still have no attitude about it. On the other hand, you can do no routine and still have a certain attitude and be terribly funny.

WILDE: *What is the comedic attitude, then?*

BISHOP: It is not a comedic attitude. It is rather an attitude of life that produces the comedic end of it.

WILDE: *The end result?*

BISHOP: Right. I'm sure you know many friends who are not comedians, who are terribly funny because of an attitude they have towards comedy. My attitude was always one of being overheard rather than heard. The audience thought only they individually heard me. The others did not hear me. So you'd hear people say, "Did you hear what he said?" Of course, if *you* heard, naturally *he* heard. That's why people sometimes were kind of shocked when I said something clever. You know, terribly brilliant. They were shocked, because I didn't say it loud, I said it softly and people would say, "What a chance he took. You got something that clever to say, why don't you say it loud?"

WILDE: *Then in essence, this was a part of your personality you were simply bringing onstage?*

BISHOP: Yes. Well, not so much of a personality but attitude toward life. I don't like loud people who want to be heard. Speak softly and carry a big stick. And the big stick, in my case, was a clever line.

WILDE: *Is there any luck involved in getting ahead in show business, or do you have to make your own breaks?*

BISHOP: I don't know what you mean by luck. We're dealing now with semantics. Only talent can sustain you. Luck can be working in a lounge somewhere and having a big director come in, who has had a few drinks and thinks you're a riot that night, and under the influence of alcohol signs you to a picture—that's luck. But if you have talent, you will then sustain it. And if you don't have talent and it was only luck, then it's all over.

WILDE: *What about making your own breaks? Taking advantage of opportunities?*

BISHOP: That's not my way of life, so I don't know. But that doesn't mean that that's not right. It's just not my way of life. I don't like to start a day fighting. I don't like to start a day organizing that day. I feel *que sera, sera*. If you become that ambitious, you plan every day. Even if you attain the goal, look at how much of life you've lost in the attainment thereof.

WILDE: *To what degree were Jack Paar and Frank Sinatra responsible for your success?*

BISHOP: Well, Frank Sinatra using you as a comic was kind of a stamp of approval, which made it very good, 'cause in show business, the one thing you strive for is acceptance. You would rather walk out and be acknowledged than have to work eight minutes for the recognition.

WILDE: *To prove yourself before they do accept you?*

BISHOP: Right, right. When Frank Sinatra takes you on the show, they say, "He must be good, otherwise Frank wouldn't have him on." So there is a point of acceptance, a stamp of approval, immediately. What Jack Paar did was make it national for me. Remember, in those days, if Jack Paar had you back three or four times, you were a hit.

WILDE: *If you could put a label or name on it, how would you describe the type of comedy you do?*

BISHOP: Its camouflage. Whatever success I've had in comedy is based on the fact that I don't look like I'm gonna say something that's terribly clever. I think I was the first nightclub comic to use the word "folks" to hip audiences. "Now, come on, folks, be fair."

WILDE: *This was disarming...*

BISHOP: Of course, of course.

WILDE: *They didn't expect this, especially in a nightclub atmosphere where they had been used to brash, hit-'em-on-the-head, forcing-them-to-laugh type of comedian. And you came on the complete opposite.*

BISHOP: Exactly. Right. "Folks, I don't want to be a hit; just let me finish!" Then when I worked with Frank, I said, "Look at this crowd. Wait till *his* following shows up." But I did it believing it, rather than a joke, see? Again, we get back to attitude—the attitude with which I did it, not so much that which I said.

WILDE: *Then would you call it "underplaying" comedy?*

BISHOP: Yeah, yeah. But is has to be done with a kind of twinkle.

WILDE: *Is this how you gained recognition as a "dead-pan" comic?*

BISHOP: Well, I think the "deadpan comedian" came from the complaining type of comedy that we all used to do and naturally when you're complaining you can't be full of smiles or laughter. So they all say, "He works deadpan." But if you're complaining, you can't do it from a happy frame of mind.

WILDE: *In a New York Times Magazine article by Gilbert Milstein, you said, "I always use a couple of jokes that don't come off." Did you mean you did that on purpose?*

BISHOP: No. I think what Gilbert was saying was....catching the audience off guard. What the audience *thought* was the punchline was not. They thought that was the finish of the joke, and that I purposely put in a joke that didn't get a laugh. But that was not true. It sounded like the end and then I would build to the punchline, looking like I was saving that particular joke—but I wasn't.

WILDE: *Could you give me an example?*

BISHOP: "We were very poor when I was a kid. I remember one winter, it snowed, and I didn't have a sled." Now that kind gets a laugh, but it sounds like the end of a joke, but not a good joke, 'cause the next line is "I used to slide down the hill on my cousin. And she wasn't bad." They're thinking of it as three jokes and they're not. It's one joke.

WILDE: *"Sliding down the hill on my cousin" is the joke.*

BISHOP: It's not. The joke is "She wasn't bad."

WILDE: *Isn't that the "topper"?*

BISHOP: But that's what a joke is—it is a finish, the final punch of the joke. It's not a topper. That's the line I'm going for, so consequently that's the end of the joke. If the end of the joke is the topper, that's the topper.

WILDE: *In that same article, you said, "An audience always feels inferior. When you make them feel equal, you are actually making them feel superior." Would you explain that?*

BISHOP: Yeah. Too many guys put down audiences. Sometimes there are some who have a right to, but they have to have shortcomings themselves. Jack E. Leonard has his obesity. Don Rickles with his anger. You can't go out there, a nice-looking fellow, and put down the audience, because the audience wants to know what the hell are you complaining about, unless you complain about some shortcoming in your life. But you cannot blame them. A handsome comedian has no right to go out there and be angry or complain, because the audience will say, "You're a good-looking guy, you dress well, you make a good living, what the hell are you complaining about?" The only way you can balance it is letting the audience know that everything isn't rosy with you in spite of the fact that you're wearing a three-hundred-dollar tuxedo and you're making thousands of dollars.

WILDE: *Are you saying that when you make them feel on the same level with you, actually they become superior because...*

BISHOP: Not superior. If an audience feels superior to you, then you're in trouble. I did not say superior. No. They don't feel superior. If you can *pretend* they are superior. There's a difference there. If an audience feels superior to you, they can be rude. They won't even turn around to watch you. If they feel equal to you, then you're in good shape.

WILDE: *What makes a supper club audience react differently each night to the same joke or piece of material?*

BISHOP: The attitude of the performer.

WILDE: *It's his fault?*

BISHOP: Absolutely. Sometimes a guy will take something that works for him, and instead of working for it, like he did in the beginning, he now says it mechanically and the audience senses it, so they kind of turn off.

WILDE: *Some comedians believe that weather conditions can affect an audience's reaction. Has this ever been your experience?*

BISHOP: That would seem like a very poor excuse, simply because you can take adversity and speak about it. Let's suppose I'm working in Chicago and there's thirty-seven people there because there's fourteen inches of snow, right? If I can convey to them I had a tougher time getting here than they did—if I say, "I *have* to be here, but *you!*"—you can break down the barrier that quickly, so I can't see where weather conditions would have any influence at all.

WILDE: *Joe E. Brown, in his autobiography,* Laughter is a Wonderful Thing, *said, "No comedian ever got a big enough reaction to suit him." After a performance are you ever dissatisfied with the audience's reception?*

BISHOP: I don't think so, because it is so spontaneous that whatever reward you are getting, you are getting sincerely.

WILDE: *Even though some nights the response may be bigger than other nights?*

BISHOP: There are many extenuating circumstances. You can sometimes get a group of seventy people who have never been to a club who are a great audience, and the next night you can get a whole roomful of couples, so...what makes the difference?

WILDE: *Then the rule is: Never compare tonight's reaction to last night's, because this is a completely different group.*

BISHOP: When you start to do that, there is a form of deterioration taking place right away. Because then you don't believe in yourself. If an audience's reaction is all you base your performance on, then you're in a lot of trouble.

WILDE: *What about the nights you have to change your material and your attitude to please that particular audience?*

BISHOP: You can't do that. Sammy Davis once had a sign in his dressing room. It said, "I don't know the meaning of success, but I do know the meaning of failure—trying to please everybody."

WILDE: *What happens when you play to a specific audience—like in the Catskills—you often have to do material to fit that ethnic group?*

BISHOP: If you do that, you'll never be big in show business.

WILDE: *You have to decide which audience you want to please?*

BISHOP: No, you have to decide what you want to do, not which audiences you want to please. Based on what you are saying, if we moved from comedy and went to music, everybody would still be playing "Auld Lang Syne" because it pleases everybody—or "God Bless America." That's why you have guys who will divorce themselves from commercialism and strike out on their own. That's why you have an Elvis Presley. That's why you have the Beatles. Now I'm sure in the beginning they did not meet with success, but if you believe it firmly enough—Dean Martin is your best example. It was like the kiss of death when he broke up with Jerry Lewis. Now he could have tried to please audiences, but he decided to remain Dean Martin...and he even carried it over into television, where they wanted to rehearse a whole week, and he said, "That's not me. I'll rehearse one day."

WILDE: *It's doing what you believe is right—win, lose or draw.*

BISHOP: If you really believe it. Some of us have only a façade, some of us pretend to believe in it. Don Rickles must have endured an awful lot of punishment, but he believed in it. The Smothers Brothers believe in it. Jonathan Winters believes in it. You can pretend you believe in it, but you really *have* to believe in it. I'm sure great artists many centuries ago felt the same way. Van Gogh was scoffed and laughed at, but he really believed it.

WILDE: *Do you have a strategy or a device to control an audience?*

BISHOP: Yeah, complete honesty. That's my strategy. Don't bullshit an audience. You can never be a star until you can take an audience by the hand. That's very important to remember—an audience must trust you implicitly. They know in five minutes whether you are just doing what you are doing to go over that night or whether you are doing it to entertain them.

WILDE: *Does that hold true for all audiences—no matter what intellectual or social level...?*

BISHOP: Yes. It also depends on whether you're known or unknown. If you are unknown, then you are in a lot of trouble. If you are known, they come in knowing what to expect. As the unknown, you've got to make a compromise and the compromise is in the first few minutes—to get their attention. You are just a salesman then. Once you've got their attention, you can then do your type of comedy.

WILDE: *Must you also establish a laugh climate?*

BISHOP: Not even that. A respect and recognition. You've seen people where they would mumble after they've seen an unknown comic, "Hey, he's pretty good." That's what I mean.

WILDE: *Many psychologists feel most comedians are shy, introverted people who clown and joke primarily to cover their own insecurity. What is your—?*

BISHOP: To cover up their own insecurity? Then what makes them different from all other people from all walks of life? Who in life doesn't pretend if he's going to the dentist that he's not frightened? What layman doesn't joke when he's about to undergo an operation— even a feeble joke? So he, too, looks to cover up his own shortcomings. What guy jilted in love doesn't pretend for the first day or two "Who needs her?" So what makes him different from the comedian?

WILDE: *They're merely expressing themselves.*

BISHOP: That's all.

WILDE: *I think perhaps the public has an image of the comedian—.*

BISHOP: No, it depends upon the comedian. If he is a "tumult" comedian they expect him to tumult. If he's what I call the "verbal" comedian, they expect him, once in a while, to drop a little bomb during the conversation. Naturally, we're serious people. I know of no one who devotes themselves more to charity than do comedians. That's a form of seriousness. Danny Thomas with his St. Jude Hospital, Bob Hope entertaining the troops in Vietnam, me with Cystic Fibrosis, Jack Benny with the philharmonics of every city, Jerry Lewis with Muscular Dystrophy. When we meet to decide how to raise money for these charities, it's not in the form of a joke. Is that serious? Then we're serious! If one of our children is having trouble in school, or if he's been hurt in a bicycle fall, yeah, we're serious then, too. If we lose a parent, no one expects us to do humor instead of saying Kaddish.[4]

WILDE: *The Greek philosopher Aristotle said, "Melancholy men are, among all others, the most witty." Why is that?*

BISHOP: It's an outlook on life. They take that which is adversity and juxtapose it. But that's not only true of comedians. You go to any battlefront, and if there is a near-hit, somebody there will inevitably do some joke to relieve the tension. He doesn't have to be a comedian.

WILDE: *Does it have to be someone with a sense of humor?*

BISHOP: How do we define sense of humor? You could have a sense of humor if you receive good fortune, and not have a sense of humor any other time. Is that a sense of humor? You can be a miserable guy who apparently has no sense of humor and say some of the funniest things in the world. And yet you're not funny—you have no apparent sense of humor. Again, you get back to a way of life.

WILDE: *And the individual's approach to it?*

BISHOP: Absolutely. Comedy is a form of religion.

WILDE: *Why do you say that?*

BISHOP: Because it's how you live a life.

WILDE: *And your approach to it is total and complete honesty toward the audience, toward your work. It is an honest approach toward your religion.*

4   A prayer for the dead.

BISHOP: Right. Years ago, you could fool an audience, because you were in that town for one week and you may not come back for two years. With the advent of television, you can't fool an audience anymore. Now, if they see you five nights a week you are going to run the gamut of your emotions. They're gonna see you angry; they're gonna see you happy; they're gonna see you melancholy one night, super-charged the next. So unless you have the ingredient of honesty, unless you let them know there is nothing wrong with your being angry...

WILDE: *That's a human emotion.*

BISHOP: Right

WILDE: *It appears that many comedians come from poor families or had unhappy childhoods. Do you think these emotional and psychological scars were the reasons they became comedians?*

BISHOP: Again, comedy, humor is a way of overcoming adversity. I think some of the funniest things to come out of the Israeli-Arab conflict were things that Moshe Dayan may have said. It is comedy that gets you out of adversity.

WILDE: *Do loneliness and being a comedian generally go hand in hand?*

BISHOP: I think preoccupation and being a comedian go hand in hand. Not loneliness. Preoccupation is misconstrued as loneliness. I can be sitting here, preoccupied with some thought I may be going to use, and people will say, "He's sitting there all by himself. He's not talking to anybody. He wants to be alone."

During my show rehearsal from six-thirty to seven-thirty, I sit there and... the script girl, when she first started, would talk to me and I said to her, "Don't get the impression because I'm not doing anything, that I'm not doing anything." She thought that I'm just sitting at the desk. It's not loneliness when you are involved with something—it's preoccupation.

Last night, for example, I had to dance with Jose Greco and I had to make a change. During the course of the show, I was looking for minutes where I could make that change and I found those minutes when Don Ho sang his song, and then his "discovery" sang, and then they did a song together... which ran four minutes, which was all the time I needed to change.

WILDE: *Can the discipline and training of a comedian be compared to any other professional?*

BISHOP: Well, I'm an undisciplined comedian, only because I work better that way. See, a disciplined comedian would get a thought, write it down, rehearse it, work it over and make it a routine. I am an undisciplined man—get a thought, will go out on the floor and do it... only because I have no fear. I say, "What's the worst that can happen?" If it bombs, I tell the audience, "Folks, it's the last time I get a thought like this and not work it out!" See, I can overcome it with honesty.

WILDE: *A doctor has to put in at least ten years before he learns his trade and can hang out the shingle—Is it possible to compare his training to that of a comedian?*

BISHOP: I don't think so. I think we are dealing now with a) God-given talent, and b) academic talent.

WILDE: *The doctor learned his skill by formal education and—.*

BISHOP: Right! Right! That is where we get great doctors from. That's where you get great comedians—You have the dedication and the desire. We've often sat and talked—"Whatever happened to so-and-so? He was great." He didn't have the dedication. He was at the track or he boozed it up a lot...

WILDE: *Lost along the way.*

BISHOP: Right.

WILDE: *Are the requirements to become a recognized comedian the same as they would be in any other business?*

BISHOP: No, no, because there are so many different forms of what makes people laugh. You can be the greatest comedian, and there are still some people who think you are not funny. But if you are the greatest doctor, everybody accepts you as the greatest doctor. Unless it's another colleague, who thinks *he's* greater.

WILDE: *Because we are dealing with individual opinion, personal taste...*

BISHOP: You are dealing with many things. I never saw anybody if you said, "He's a professor," dislike him personally.

WILDE: *He's got the respect.*

BISHOP: Right. But I've heard people say, "He's a great comedian—I still don't like him. He couldn't make *me* laugh." Naturally, you couldn't make someone laugh if he didn't want to...and the audience must trust you and you have to be able to lead them by the hand. Once you can lead them by the hand, you can take them through any avenue of comedy. You can take them on a very serious subject and they will go with you. All of a sudden, you hit them with a blockbusting punchline...but they must trust you.

There are some comedians that don't have that trust. I've seen in Vegas, sometimes a guy wants to do a community-sing number with the audience, and the audience will not sing with him for fear that he is going to embarrass them. So they don't trust him. Now an audience trusts Dean Martin implicitly.

WILDE: *What are the necessary requirements to become a comedian?*

BISHOP: Curiosity is the primary requisite. That's the only way to get material. There's no other way to develop thought waves. If your wife buys a gift for the house, you look at the gift and you dismiss it, you may be blowing a six-minute routine. But if you are curious about it, if you say, "My wife came home with a gadget and I defy any-one to tell me what the gadget is. You put it in a socket, you turn on a switch and nothing happens," you've started a routine.

You look at all good comedians...they will walk into a house and pick up articles and look at them. It's curiosity. It's curiosity about the news, about science, it's curiosity about anything that develops material. Unless you have a curious mind, you cannot be a comedian.

WILDE: *What else?*

BISHOP: I would say honesty, the biggest opening thing I ever did was...I worked a neighborhood spot in Chicago for forty-nine weeks...and for the first time in the history of the Chez Parée, someone went from a neighborhood spot to the Chez [the top club in Chicago]. Even Danny Thomas, as successful as he was, had to leave the 5100 Club and go to Martinique [New York] and then come back to the Chez. It was a policy they had. Now I'll show you the ingredients. First, I became curious as to how I would open, 'cause I had just come from a neighborhood post and now I'm going to the Chez Parée, so curiosity started my wheels going. Then I dealt with honesty. And the routine I came up with was:

"Ladies and Gentlemen, I am here through the generosity of you people. For forty-nine weeks, I worked
at the Vine Gardens and every night one of the nice
people would come and say, 'What are you doing here,
why aren't you at the Chez Parée?' I feel after tonight's
appearance, a lot of you are going to say, 'What are you
doing here, why aren't you at the Vine Gardens?'"

A thought went through my mind, see? But it had those
ingredients...it had honesty, it had humility, it had humor...

WILDE: *It was also spontaneous.*

BISHOP: It *appeared* spontaneous. The thought went
through my mind, you see, not the night I opened.

WILDE: *You worked on it before you opened?*

BISHOP: Right. Just the thought.

WILDE: *It seems that many comedians who became
successful have been fortunate enough to have worked
in one spot for longer than the two- or four-week booking
that is available today. Danny Thomas spent three years
at the 5100 Club. George Gobel...*

BISHOP: At Helsings Vaudeville Lounge.

WILDE: *For a long time. Bob Hope spent something like
six months at a theater in...*

BISHOP: Even Don Rickles' fame only came to the front
from working the Sahara Lounge. Shecky Greene, from
being in one place...

WILDE: *Working that one place, does that allow you to
develop confidence and to relax and...*

BISHOP: No. What it allows you is the thought pattern
that I'm discussing. When you're a hit in a place, you can

go out and do something that you thought about this morning.

WILDE: *And not be afraid?*

BISHOP: Exactly. Exactly.

WILDE: *Then it does build confidence.*

BISHOP: Well, then you go back to attitude again. Those people are now waiting for you to perform. So instead of going out and trying to overcome them or overwhelm them, you take your time, 'cause they are waiting to hear what you've got to say. This is the secret of great comedy. If you can put the audience in a position to wait to hear what you've got to say—and nobody does it better than [Jack] Benny—They are waiting to hear what he's got to say. You can defeat yourself by doing so much comedy that they accept it and don't wait to hear what you've got to say.

WILDE: *Then the mistake the inexperienced comedian makes, in his anxiety and his desire to—.*

BISHOP: Not the inexperienced comedian, the compromising comedian. There is a difference. See, even the inexperienced comedian, if he's not compromising, will come off well. The guy who wants to be a hit that show, that's the compromising comedian.

WILDE: *Instead of looking for a career.*

BISHOP: Longevity. I once said to a comedian, "Why are you developing such a terribly funny, dirty story. You will never use it anywhere else. Why spend years developing a story you can't use on television?" He can't use it at the White House. Where is he going to use it? That's why I say the [Catskill] Mountains are a fallacy. You spend years there killing the people, but what have you developed?

WILDE: *What other requirements are needed to become a comedian? How about a good memory?*

BISHOP: It depends upon the type of comedian you are. Now a good memory would be a shortcoming to me, because it would prevent me from creating. Others are mechanics. A memory is very important for them, to go into a file thing in their minds and yank it out.

WILDE: *Is it important to be well educated?*

BISHOP: Again, we are getting back to curiosity. Well educated could certainly never be detrimental. It can't possibly hurt you, because you have more knowledge. I think what's most important is to never stop learning. Whether you have an education or not, you must continue to learn.

WILDE: *It appears that an emotional rapport with the audience is stronger and longer than an intellectual appeal. Why is that?*

BISHOP: Well, an emotional appeal can act well as a reminder and everybody shares in it. You'd have to be an intellect to share in an intellectual approach.

Let's talk about poverty. You're gonna remind 95% of your audience of either some relative who was poor or that *they* were poor. If you speak about intellect, you may not remind them of anything. It is kind of an affair that you have with the audience.

Many times, if you say, "I know you married men out there..." well, you've already gotten a group. That's why mother-in-law jokes are so strong. Each guy knows exactly what you are experiencing. If you were to speak about your dean at college, you would have a very small percentage who would remember that they also had that kind of dean.

WILDE: *Performers who do comedy are known by various titles: "comic," "mimic," "humorist," "storyteller" "impressionist." Is there a difference?*

BISHOP: Yeah, there's a vast difference. A comic and mimic are not necessarily both in the field of comedy. A mimic does not have to be funny. He can be brilliant as a mimic but not funny. Frank Gorshin, I'd consider a brilliant mimic. As a matter of fact, you will find that most of the mimics do terrible monologues. I've never heard Rich Little do a funny line. Never. The exception, of course, would be Sammy Davis.

A humorist is more of a Sam Levenson. I think the humorist takes the audience and reminds it of things that we take for granted. Will Rogers did it with politics. Sam Levenson did it with large families. Herb Shriner did it with rural type of people. They are what you call reminders. You have Pat Buttram, Minnie Pearl, Homer and Jethro, who are excellent musicians and humorists.

WILDE: *What is the difference between a "comic" and a "comedian"?*

BISHOP: Well, the old cliché that a comic says funny things and the comedian says things funny.[5] I think of a comic as being more physical than a comedian. Red Skelton, for example, is more physical than Jack Benny.

WILDE: *Isn't Skelton referred to as a "clown"?*

BISHOP: He's referred to as a "buffoon," a "clown," right. But it's because of the physical, see. The physical comic resorts to moves, à la Jonathan Winters.

WILDE: *Would you call Winters a "physical comic"?*

BISHOP: Yeah, sure...

WILDE: *Rather than a "satirist" or a "wit"?*

5   An epigram attributed to Ed Wynn.

BISHOP: No. He can be witty, too, don't misunderstand. That's what makes Winters so great. He can do anything. And if what he says doesn't get a laugh, there is a physical gesture or physical move that will salvage it for him.

WILDE: *What is the difference between a "standup" comedian and one who "sits down" and is funny?*

BISHOP: I don't know. I guess the budget for upholstery. It's the same difference between a standup singer and a sit-down singer. It's purely attitude. If one's monologue is such that it's very laconic and is enhanced by laconic attitude, then he's a sit-down comic. If one is more forceful and finds he must move, he's a standup comic.

WILDE: *Is it possible that someone like Jack Carter could do a routine sitting down?*

BISHOP: Yes, he could. He's done it on panels. And he's very brilliant when he does it, but the irony is that Jack Carter sitting down looks like he's standing. Jack Benny standing up looks like he's sitting down.

WILDE: *Is it an informality—a conversational delivery?*

BISHOP: I don't know. I really don't know. I don't know why someone would want to sit down and do a routine, unless they think that perhaps it is the epitome of success.

WILDE: *On the TV talk shows today, including your own, after the comedian does a standup spot, he will sit down on the "panel" and continue to do material or lines that he would normally do in his standup act.*

BISHOP: But now you're not dealing so much with the comedian as with the quantity of whether he's known or not. See, to take someone who's completely unknown and have them join you at the panel without having been funny can be the kiss of death.

WILDE: *He's got to establish himself?*

BISHOP: Right. Taking someone who's already known and sitting them at your panel, there's no problem.

WILDE: *When Alan King sits down, he can do any one of his routines.*

BISHOP: Yeah, but don't kid yourself into thinking that if you do a routine sitting down and it is a routine, if that audience doesn't believe you...if they think it's a routine, you're in a lot of trouble. You better make it look like it's not a routine. It's better not to have the polish. I warn comics that do standup spots, "When you come and sit down, talk at half the tempo you just did in your act in." See, one is overpowering, and one is overheard. That's the difference.

WILDE: *How does working in a nightclub differ from working on television?*

BISHOP: In my case, there is none. I'm just being myself. Whether in the environment of a nightclub or a temple, or church, or television—I don't change myself. There is very little difference between my sitting here on this couch and being on my show in my attitude. I'm dressed, that'd be the only difference, and if we had three or four performers here, I'd be the same as I am tonight.

WILDE: *Is this image of a friendly attitude and unforced, honest delivery a technique that you plan?*

BISHOP: No. You can't plan a technique, 'cause you can't fool people for so long. It's something you have to feel. It's as if I were to ask you, "Can you plan to be pleasant coming over here?" You could plan to make a pleasant entrance, but somewhere during the course of this interview, if you're not a pleasant guy, it's going to come out. It has to.

WILDE: *You're considered one of the sharpest ad-lib comedians in the world. Is this a talent you were born with?*

BISHOP: I don't know if I was born with it, but I remember always having an answer when I was a kid. I think it's a defense mechanism, which is very true in all comedy. For example, if I was going to fight with a guy—if it came to a fistfight—if I could get myself to do it with humor, I did. There was no questions that if this guy could knock my brains out, I would say, "I just want to warn you, if I hit you, I'm gonna go down."

WILDE: *Then this ability can be developed?*

BISHOP: Any way of life can be developed and it's purely a way of life. For example, if my wife walked in here now and said, "I had two flats"—the average guy wouldn't do humor; the comedy mind would try to appease her. We would find some kind of humor in the incident. Maybe, "So that's the way we live, and when they come and take the house away, it'll be fine." Whereas the serious person, who doesn't delve in comedy, would say, "Well, let's call somebody and find out what we can do," it becomes a catastrophe. We try to avoid catastrophes—It's a way of life that's accepted as comedy.

WILDE: *Is it possible to actually create a spontaneous joke or are all ad-libs jokes plots that have been consciously or unconsciously switched?*

BISHOP: You can suck a guy in. It's like boxing. You can feint the guy and the guy will lead, and you'll counterpunch him. It's the same with ad-libbing. When you're ad-libbing you're really, strangely enough, fighting for time...if your mind isn't right there. You can take anything and use words to give you that time. It still sounds like an ad-lib, although you're not doing a stock joke.[6] Once

---

6   A joke that has been done many times by most comedians.

they are waiting to hear what you've got to say, when you come to a period, they'll laugh...

WILDE: *What is it that allows you to ad-lib as well as you do?*

BISHOP: Peace of mind. Yeah, a complete vacuum up here. A freedom. Nothing clogged up, nothing cluttered. And I know how to unclutter it.

WILDE: *Is it the power of positive thinking?*

BISHOP: No. I think the power of positive thinking is when you are looking for a kind of security. The power of positive thinking comes from negative thinking. You convert that which is negative to positive. But if I'm not negative to begin with, what am I converting?

WILDE: *Is this a God-given gift?*

BISHOP: If it's a way of life, then I guess it's a gift from God. I see guys who are failures who are writing stuff... their writers are writing stuff. I go there with nothing. I stole a show one night with two words. They were honoring Sam Goldwyn and they did jokes about him and everything. I stood up and said, "Thank you very much, Mr. Goldman..." and I was the end of the night. How the hell can you honor a guy like Sam Goldwyn and not even know his name?

WILDE: *Did you come prepared with that line?*

BISHOP: I knew about five minutes before. There were twenty-seven comics—Danny Kaye, Groucho, Berle, everybody. I was the twenty-seventh, so I had to leave my mind uncluttered. There were times when I got a thought pattern and somebody else had something like it. But I said, "What will make me different?" Who is the only guy here who has no right to know Samuel Goldwyn?" Me. That's my thought...and from that I went to Mr. Goldman.

WILDE: *You have to trust yourself.*

BISHOP: Right. You don't think, "If I go there, will there be rust, will there be hot water? Will there be cold water?" You go to the spigot, you turn the spigot on, and you get water. That's kind of a reservoir up here. I've a mind that is channeled that way and I know that when I hear my name, they've turned a spigot on, and something is going to come out. Whether it's the introduction that the host gave me where I might say, "I want to thank you for that introduction. If I'm a hit tonight, I owe you nothing!"

WILDE: *Can you ad-lib better today than you did twenty years ago?*

BISHOP: No. I think that they're waiting more to hear the ad-lib today. Because twenty years ago, who could distinguish whether it was an ad-lib or not? Who knew that it was not a "stock"? It is over a period of years...you get to a point where you can do a stock and they say, "He ad-libbed it," because they are tuned that way.

WILDE: *Is it important for the comedian to know all the "stock jokes"?*

BISHOP: No. No. I think knowing stock jokes is a lack of development. It'll get you by an audience, but it won't get you by some guy who's coming in to catch you. The guy will say, "What'd you send me there for? I've heard fifteen jokes he's done before. Is he supposed to be original, clever or what?"

WILDE: *You're credited with helping the careers of Buddy Hackett, Phil Foster, Corbett Monica...*

BISHOP: I know, but I didn't help them. I feel what's wrong with our business today is that no one takes the time to use talent correctly. It's a big curse in our business. Whether you have to make it before somebody gets interested, or you can bomb and it's all over. If a person has talent, there has to be some niche, some place he can fit.

WILDE: *If your son or a close relative decided to become a comedian, what advice would you give him?*

BISHOP: I wouldn't give him any advice. I think he'd have to find his own way. If he wants to be a comedian, he'll find a way. I would just say, "Don't do anything in bad taste."

Chapter 24
Pal Joey
The Talk Show

Joey and his late-night sidekick, Regis Philbin, c. 1968.

While there were mixed reviews for Joey as a film actor, a television situation-comedy star, and a participant in skits on sundry variety shows, his skills as a talk-show host were rarely, if ever, in question. Despite his strained personal relationship with Johnny Carson, he had served as guest host for Johnny on *The Tonight Show* a record 177 times during Johnny's tenure. (In all, Joey would guest host 207 times; Jay Leno holds the record for the most times, 300, prior to his becoming the permanent host in 1992.) Joey's low-key manner and ability to seemingly ad-lib with the guests made him a natural choice as a host of his own program. However, the question remained: Was Joey best in small doses or could he hold a television audience as an ongoing presence?

The first producer of *The Tonight Show* with Johnny Carson was Perry Cross. Cross had also been the producer following Jack Paar's departure, when the interim hosts included everyone from Groucho Marx to Merv Griffin to Art Linkletter. At that time, Joey was hoping to be the Chosen One when a permanent new host was announced.

"Joey did an excellent job," Perry Cross told the author. "I thought he handled the job and didn't cause any waves. However, the most successful hosts over the years have had that Midwest, low-key charm that was easy to watch just before bedtime. Johnny Carson, Dick Cavett, David Letterman, and even Merv had that manner that went down easy at 11:30 P.M. There was always a question with Joey. He was a streetwise, Jewish nightclub comic who, despite his non-confrontational manner, always had that hard edge that might not play so well in Fort Wayne, Indiana. Times have changed now, but the network programmers were very cognizant of that factor. To do ninety minutes, five days a week, the life span of a brash personality was very short term before viewers tired of it. Groucho was fun for a week. Joan Rivers could be funny in small doses. The same with later guest hosts such as David Brenner or even Garry Shandling."

Cross eventually left *The Tonight Show* to produce the disastrous Jerry Lewis talk show on ABC, broadcast live on Saturday nights. Perry recalled, "I was never convinced that Joey was good for the long term. He had that charm on a small window of time.

But there was an edge to Joey that could wear on viewers. There was a quality to Johnny that had a broader appeal. Joey was an excellent comic, but his appeal was limited."

Fortunately for Joey, Norman Brokaw, his brilliant agent, assembled a great team of advisors. One member of that team was a young, aggressive attorney named Ed Hookstratten. Eventually, Hookstratten would represent powerful celebrities and sports stars, including Elvis Presley, Johnny Carson, Tom Brokaw, and football coach George Allen. He was known as "the Hook," and he was always brutally direct, regardless of the situation. Joey liked that toughness and trusted him completely. They would remain connected until Joey's death (Hookstratten died, at eighty-three, in January 2014). The Hook led Joey into some lucrative real-estate investments and, by 1965, Joey had accumulated a fortune. Norm Brokaw had worked out some extraordinary deals, including half-ownership of *The Joey Bishop Show*. Going into syndication proved to be a windfall to him. And with that, the nightclub comic started adding all the accoutrements of a star.

"Joey drove a Silver Cloud Rolls Royce, he lived in a huge mansion in Beverly Hills, moved his parents out of Philadelphia into a condo in Miami Beach, and took care of his brothers and their families," recalls Don Herman. "His brother Mel was working for him. Joey struck gold. He even got a hair transplant. His hair was receding back to Philadelphia."

For the hair transplant, Joey went to a specialist, Dr. Samuel Ayres. Said Shecky Greene, "Joey was the guinea pig and it worked, so Frank was next in line."

Time magazine (June 8, 1970) notes,

> Man's real crowning glory is hair transplanting, a technique that has the benefit of covering the client's head with his own hair. It was pioneered by Dr. Samuel Ayres III, a Beverly Hills dermatologist who has transplanted hair on Frank Sinatra, Joey Bishop, the Smothers Brothers, and many other show business personalities. In a long series of operations, strips or plugs of hair—a plug contains from 15 to 20 hairs complete with roots and

skin—are removed from the back or side of the head and then transplanted into a similar-sized hole cut from the bald spot. Then follows a months-long cycle of scabs, scars, falling out of the old hair, and, finally, the growing in of the new. The process is both physically and financially painful; a complete job may run from several hundred to several thousand dollars.

Meanwhile, ABC was carefully following the ratings of NBC's *The Tonight Show*. Joey maintained the high level of Carson's viewership during his frequent gigs as guest host. *The Tonight Show* was a gold mine for the peacock network. With earnings in excess of $30 million, (according to Perry Cross), the other networks were looking to make clearances to set up their own late-night programming and cash in on that lucrative market. ABC struck first by moving a local New York talk show called *Night Line* with host Les Crane on a trial run in August of 1964. Crane's show, which was similar in format to *The Phil Donahue Show* in that it included audience participation and tackled some contro-versial subjects, then moved to a "lighter" format and a new title, *Nightlife*. It lasted only until 1965, when many of the ABC affiliates were demanding back the time for more lucrative local revenue, since Crane barely made a dent in *The Tonight Show*'s ratings.

ABC was aware that if it wanted to venture back into a late-night show and attract the affiliates, it needed a "name" celebrity to host the show. Joey Bishop perfectly fit that category since he was all but the regular guest host for Johnny. But Joey was reluctant. He was raking in huge sacks of cash from sold-out club dates, and his guest-hosting duties on *The Tonight Show* allowed him the needed exposure to keep his name out there. He was able to push his club dates when he was the guest host, and he did not want to step on Carson's toes. He had the best of both worlds. Also, if he hosted a daily talk show, he would not be able to do the club dates, which paid far more than a television show—without the pressure and anxiety of ratings.

Norman Brokaw remembers, "Joey said he would need time to do the show; he wasn't going in half-assed. And, of course, the money had to be great to lure him."

With millions of dollars in late-night revenue the network was destined to make, the top brass was more than willing to pay Bishop and his team what they were seeking. Other comedians were starting to make noises about joining the late-night fracas via syndication and the local affiliates. Comic Bill Dana was briefly the host of a syndicated talk show, taped in Las Vegas for the new United Network (it had a very short run). After the demise of *The Les Crane Show* in 1966, ABC attempted to work out a deal with Joey.

Norm Brokaw knew he had an upper hand in negotiations. For 1966 dollars, it was a great deal for Joey and put him in range of the salary Johnny Carson was then receiving. Joey was to be paid $2 million in deferred revenue (for the tax savings). If the show was canceled, he would do other programs for the network. The talk show would receive a thirty-nine-week guarantee for one season—with thirteen weeks of replays. Joey would receive $569,000 for thirty-nine weeks, with an option for twenty-four months.

The agreement was finalized in late 1966. Joey would spend the next few months schmoozing the affiliates and convincing them to provide the time access for his show. As ABC was a newer network, *The Joey Bishop Show* faced an uphill battle from the beginning. ABC was created from the NBC Blue network in 1948. It had fewer affiliates (144) than NBC (210) and, at that time, covered only 75% of the nation. Thus, with fewer affiliates and less coverage, he would naturally have a difficult time beating *The Tonight Show* in the ratings, despite his popularity. Also, many of the affiliates were making far more money selling advertising time for that 11:30 P.M.–1:00 A.M. period locally than they would have received from the network. So many affiliates were reluctant to vacate the time slot that, if they agreed to carry the program, it would be relegated to a later time or in the early-morning hours, an option wholly unacceptable to ABC's sponsors.

To sell the show, Joey would spend lots of his time visiting powerful affiliates, doing a closed-circuit conference, filming promotional ads, and attending network meetings in New York and Los Angeles.

Unlike *The Tonight Show*, which was broadcast out of New York City, *The Joey Bishop Show* would be broadcast live from Los Angeles (at 8:30 P.M. Pacific time, so it would be live on the East Coast). ABC bought the old Vine Street Theater from CBS and spent an additional $2 million installing new lighting and equipment to bring it up to then-current color broadcasting standards. Ironically, the theater had once been the home to two of Johnny Carson's earliest television shows, *Carson's Cellar* and a variety show, both in the mid-fifties.[7] Paul Orr hired Hal Gurnee as the show's director. Gurnee had helmed *The Jack Paar Show* and would later become David Letterman's first director for both his NBC show and *Late Night* on CBS. Thus, the Bishop show had two of the best battery men (as in pitcher and catcher) in producer Orr and director Gurnee.

Another challenge would involve booking A-level guests. In many cases, the shows are booked months in advance to accommodate schedules, movie premieres, and other events celebrities are promoting. Joey had hoped to have Frank Sinatra and his bride, Mia Farrow, as his guests on the show's debut. However, *The Tonight Show* issued a veiled threat to comics, actors, and singers that if they appear on *The Joey Bishop Show*, they could expect to be blackballed from Johnny's program.

Joey later grumbled, "We were dead to start. We got the second-rate talent since the top tier, especially comics, needed *The Tonight Show* to push their dates."

Paul Orr began the process of assembling a writing staff. With a daily ninety-minute slot to fill, they needed writers for both monologues and continuity. Joey, however, was being very difficult regarding the type of writers he wanted working for him. As a result, a total unknown, who had never written anything beyond his own comedy act, became the show's head writer. Born Howard Trustin Slavin on the south side of Chicago, he attended high school with both Steve Allen and Mel Tormé. He became a small-time comic, using the moniker Slick Slavin, and hung out with Lenny Bruce. He never played the major clubs, although he did appear for a while at Billy Gray's Bandbox in Los Angeles. With

---

7   The former theater is currently the home of The Pickford Center for Motion Picture Study.

the dissolution of small clubs by the mid-sixties, Slavin was desperate for work. To distance himself from his stage persona, he again changed his name, this time to Trustin Howard.

Howard told the author, "When Joey hosted *The Tonight Show* around 1965 or '66, he had Sinatra, Dean, Sammy, and Peter on during his week of guest hosting and the ratings went through the roof. Joey told me that ABC approached him at that point. So ABC brought out Paul Orr and his team to Los Angeles to plot a course for Joey. Paul was the executive producer of *The Jack Paar Tonight Show* and, of course, knew Joey well. I had never written, but like 99% of the comics then, I was out of work and desperate. I figured it would take a nightclub comic to write for a nightclub comic.

"Orr had offices at the William Morris offices in Beverly Hills. Everything was being packaged by Norm Brokaw and others at William Morris. Orr was a very soft-spoken, gentle man. If he had been a Hollywood producer, he would have tossed me. I had no track record. I played him my comedy album and tried lots of double-talk, as I had never written for anyone. He said to send in some material and that Joey would take a look at it. Well, I figured my chances were a million to one, since William Morris was packaging this. I figured they'd use one of the many writers they represented. I didn't even have an agent. I knew it was a long shot, but I just kept sending Paul material. Constantly. And then I got a call from Paul that Joey wanted to see me. I was shocked.

"So, I went to Joey's office and, as I soon learned, he never smiled. So, he sat me down and went over the material, gag by gag, and rating them. Good! Fair! Ah...*nothing*! Now *that* line is brilliant! He then asked me if I could do fresh gags five nights a week. Then he tests me. He says, 'Give me a line about different subjects.' Well, I was a nightclub comic, so I can think on my feet, so I think I did alright. Afterward, he gave me a long look. Then I figured he'd tell me, as most do, that he'd be in touch or let me know. But he was instinctual and told me to go down the hall and have Elliott set me up with a contract. I was shocked. He was going to give me my shot! I had heard he had done this with Garry Marshall when *he* started. I am sure that William Morris and others tried to talk them away from me, but he stuck to his guns, trusted his instincts, and I got hired.

"My next step was to meet the rest of the writing team. First, there was a team of two young guys, Elias Davis and Dave Pollack, who had been writing comedy on radio. There was Jim Critchfield, who was writing for Jay Ward on the cartoon series, *The Bullwinkle Show*. And then there was Don Sherman, another comic who had been writing for Joey for many years. I found out quickly that Joey did not like or respect writers. I was told later that many of the comics—like Gleason, Skelton, and others—thought it was an affront to their comedy 'manhood' to have writers, but since television would eat up their material, they had no other choice but to use them. Writers would slip their material under the door and run for cover. Comics hated being just 'readers.' Carson was different—he was an ex-radio guy and a professional broadcaster, so he knew he needed writers. Jim Critchfield was let go early, after the first thirteen weeks, and Don Sherman was also let go (although he would drift back occasionally). The staff was down to Pollack, Davis, and me. So, on a late-night show comedy staff, a five-nights-a-week show, we had *three* writers for nearly the whole first year. Carson had ten or twelve writers on staff. We lived by thirteen-week renewal options and held our breath every renewal.

"Eventually, they would try to bring in more writers, some with great credits, but they left faster than guys at a Nevada bunny ranch. So, we didn't write as a team; we sent our material separately to Joey. Well, Pollack and Davis got out as soon as they were offered to write for a variety show for Pat Boone. Now Joey tells me I'm the head writer. For a bit, I was the *only* writer. So, the Morris office sent over a lot of good writers who had done sitcoms and variety shows, but none of them worked out. They didn't know how to write for Joey's style, which was hard. He was a nightclub comic. I was getting drained."

Kliph Nesteroff, who wrote the exceptional book, *The Comedians: Drunks, Thieves, Scoundrels, and the History of American Comedy* (Grove Atlantic, 2017), noted in his WFMU: Beware of the Blog what other comics thought of Joey at that time.

By the mid-1960s, Joey's act was beginning to wear thin, as fellow comics have noted:

"He was a bullshit act," says comedian Jack Carter. "He fought with his writers constantly. Joey was a quick wit and great at ad-libbing, perfect for the Rat Pack because he could keep it moving, but there was no longevity, no warmth. He was a tough little man."

"I never took Joey Bishop seriously," says Shecky Greene. "Joey Bishop was a strange man. There are certain people in our business that have very little talent, but they're good politicians. Joey was a politician. I saw Joey *kill* audiences and I don't know why. Joey Bishop got so far without any fucking talent, it's unbelievable."

Rich Little says, "He was difficult. Very pompous. Hard to get to know. Not friendly at all. Never was. I think he was very bitter that he was a member of the Rat Pack, yet nobody seemed to know who *he* was."

Comedian Slick Slavin had the unenviable job of head writer on Bishop's talk show. "Joey was tough," Slavin said, "very, very tough," Slavin said. "I used to hide when he was around. I never tried to be friends with him. He hated every writer. *Hated* them." If nothing else, Joey Bishop gave the world Regis Philbin. Philbin was Bishop's sidekick for two and a half seasons when Bishop had a late-night talk show. However, Regis came to a national audience in an unlikely way. "Regis took over from Steve Allen," says Pete Barbutti. "How that happened? Steve left in disgrace."

In the early 1960s, Steve Allen conceived a segment for his syndicated program called *Meeting of Minds*, a pretentious labor of love that made the sponsor wince. Buck Henry was writing for Allen at the time and groans at the thought, "Oh, God, the horrible *Meeting of Minds*!" Contrary to the general tone of *The Steve Allen Show*, *Meeting of Minds* was non-comedic in tone. It was a showcase for the philosophy of famed thinkers—Jesus, Aristotle, Darwin—debating one another's beliefs as actors played the parts. "I was there for the taping of the first one and he did it without an audience," says Barbutti. "He would get six character actors. 'We are taping in one month—and you will be Sigmund Freud. The subject is crime and punishment.' Next guy would be Aristotle, and so on. When the segment went on, they were dressed in period [garb] and Steve would just be in his suit. He'd say, 'How do you feel about this?' [Alfred North] Whitehead would say, 'No one should ever be punished for a crime.' Westinghouse produced this show and Westinghouse is real white bread. Westinghouse came to Steve Allen and said, 'Steve, you can't have them say these things on the air.'"

Westinghouse searched for a way to kill *Meeting of Minds*, but Steve Allen's contract gave him creative control. Finally, Westinghouse found a way. Comic Jackie Curtiss, a regular on *The Steve Allen Show*, says, "Steve was kind of a philanderer and fooling around. Jayne Meadows caught him. That was *it*."

"Steve Allen had an affair with a girl singer named Jennie Smith," says Barbutti. "She was an absolutely gorgeous girl. Jayne got wind of the affair and it became more overt than it should have been. Steve was going to break it off, so Jennie attacked him backstage with a pair of scissors and tried to stab him. Westinghouse went to Steve Allen and said, 'Look, either take out *Meeting of Minds* or we're going to invoke the morals clause.' He said, 'Forget it,' and walked away."

Westinghouse had an empty time slot. They grabbed obscure San Diego television personality Regis Philbin and had him fill in. He was initially presented as the guest host of *The Steve Allen Show*, but after a couple weeks Westinghouse changed the title to *That Regis Philbin Show*. Totie Fields, Jack E. Leonard, and Don Rickles were regulars, but Philbin's show vanished in less than three months, a victim of low ratings. Comic Dick Curtis says the comedians felt sorry for him. "We used to always say, 'Poor Regis. He can't *do* anything.'"

Regis told interviewer Scott Rogowski on his YouTube show, *Running Late* (January 18, 2014):

> After I started out replacing Steve Allen...I couldn't sleep at night, as I loved Steve and I couldn't see [myself] replacing him. However, I did for a few months...So, I

went back and did local shows in San Diego and Los Angeles, and a couple of years later, Joey Bishop was starting up a talk show on ABC to compete with Johnny Carson and he needed a sidekick, sort of an Ed McMahon type. So, he called me up and said he wanted to talk to me. At that time, I was kind of down in the dumps, because I was now struggling locally and, after doing a national show after Steve, it was a letdown...So, I meet him at William Morris in Beverly Hills, and I see Joey. He goes, "Hey, I saw you last night; you got talent!" So, I said, "Now really, Joey, *what* is my talent?" Now all these guys loved to be asked a question, so Bishop stood up and I sat down. He looked like he couldn't think what my talent was, but then finally exclaimed, "YOU! YOU! You are a great listener!" Honest to God! So, we got along well and then he said, "Why don't you go over to the Beverly Wilshire around the corner? They have a drugstore there...Go have a cup of coffee and give us a little time, then come back in an hour." So, I came back in an hour. So, in the meantime, all the big shots at William Morris, like Norm Brokaw, started telling him, "Are you crazy, Joey? He had his *own show*. He wants to be the host. He's going to interrupt you...he's going to drive you crazy...he's going to try to steal the show." So, by the time I got back, you could see that Joey was fuming. Steaming. And he was a tough guy, Joey Bishop. So, he screams to me, "How do I know you're going to sit there and keep your mouth shut? How do I know you're not going to want to take over the show? How do I know you're going to be quiet and not interrupt me?" So, I fed him back his line, "I said, 'You know why, Joey, because I am a GREAT listener!'" He didn't know what the hell I was talking about. He forgot he said that!

"So, I made the transition from the star of my own show to sidekick. The first day of the show, he is very nervous. I mean, he had guest-hosted for Johnny like a hundred times. But when it came to doing his own show *against* Johnny Carson, he was very nervous. So, Paul Orr and others told me to go over to Joey and calm him down. Our theater was at Vine Street and Fountain. So, I went to Joey and I said, "Let's take a walk." He screamed, "I got a show to do, how can I walk?" But then, about ten minutes later he said, "Let's take a walk!" So, we walked. And walked. For the next three years, before every show, we walked. And I always had to do all the talking. Once I got around to asking him, "What did you want to be when you were a kid?" He said, "I wanted to be a comedian since I was a ten-year-old kid on the street corners of Philadelphia!"

Joey's writer Don Sherman recalled, "Well, we were destroyed that first night by Johnny Carson. I'll never forget that. I wrote a joke about it: 'I don't want to say we did too bad last night, but we were beat out by a Canadian training film.' And this got Joey so mad. He screamed at me, 'Don't preach failure!' I said, 'This isn't a nightclub; people find it funny if you kid about yourself. I mean, everybody knows the ratings and it was all over the newspapers. You aren't going to hide this.'"

The Joey Bishop Show debuted on April 17, 1967. Luckily for Joey, Johnny had walked off *The Tonight Show* about two weeks prior in a contract dispute with NBC concerning his salary and payment to him over rerun fees (he was making about $15k per week compared to Joey's deal at almost the identical amount). So, when Joey premiered, Jimmy Dean was the guest host of *The Tonight Show*. Joey's opening guest was not Frank Sinatra, as he had hoped. However, he had his old boss, Danny Thomas, along with Debbie Reynolds, Gov. Ronald Reagan (to welcome the show to California), and Ray Charles. Joey joked with Regis as he introduced his agent Norm Brokaw's son Joel as Regis Philbin.

Entertainment historian Mark Steiner observed: "Joey's initial approach as the host was later parodied by SCTV. While much of it comes from the *Sammy & Company* talk show in the mid-1970s, I heard Eugene Levy claim that much came from the Bishop show. That smarmy, fake show-bizzy attitude. *The Sammy Maudlin Show* is based on it. John Candy plays the sidekick, who happens to have the same name as Sammy Davis Jr.'s sidekick from *Sammy and Company*, William B. Williams. Paul Schaffer was a huge fan of this show and it's where he got a lot of his smarmy show biz *schtick* from."

Trustin Howard confirmed Joey's placating nature: "He did not like to ruffle feathers. It was the late 1960s and the attitudes were changing. What passed in the early 1960s or before, many viewers were looking for something edgier. ABC tried to book some rock groups and controversial guests, but Joey did not want to do that. He wasn't exceptionally well read and did not like to tackle 'heavy' subjects."

Rocky Kalish had this to say about Joey's talk show: "It was kind of old hat. Johnny rarely tackled social issues, but if he had an author or commentator, he could hold his own. Joey's world was telling jokes and show business. Johnny could do a monologue that teased both parties, [whereas] Joey wanted nothing to do with politics. Johnny was far more adept at interviews and more comfortable in his skin. Joey seemed to be forced. His material was far inferior to that of Carson. And his guests were, in most instances, from the 'B' list."

While his early ratings were decent, they soon declined. On some nights, *The CBS Late Movie* was attracting more viewers. Several ABC affiliates started to play the show in a later time slot, filling the vaunted 11:30 P.M. period with local shows or reruns and playing Joey at 12:30 or 1:00 A.M. By 1969, CBS, which had beaten *The Joey Bishop Show* in the ratings much of the time (they also had over two hundred affiliates), decided to hire Merv Griffin to host a late-night show starting on August 18. This was a nail in Joey's coffin, as Merv regularly beat Bishop's show in the ratings. Before that, *The Tonight Show* was beating it by three-to-one.

Comedian Don Sherman said, "Joey was always angry, and I believe it showed in his performance. There was almost a bitterness that I had not seen before from him. He had me over to his house once to watch the show and critique it with him. He genuinely wanted to know what he could do better. I had already been released from his staff, but I still wrote for him for his club dates. He would literally yell at the screen."

Actor Jack Riley, who had been a morning radio talk-show host in his native Cleveland, came to Los Angeles to find fame and fortune. He later gained national recognition as Mr. Carlin, one of Dr. Bob Hartley's patients on *The Bob Newhart Show*. Riley and comedy writer Pat McCormick were hired in 1968 to be "roving reporters" on the show, prefiguring a segment on Comedy Central's *The Daily Show*. Bishop said he had seen them perform as a team on the local talk show hosted by satirist Mort Sahl. Riley told the author, "I was friends of Pat McCormick, who was also from Cleveland and he knew Joey in some way. So, we did about ten or twelve shows, doing skits as roving reporters. We spoofed different events that were going on. I had done it on radio with Mark London. I had done *Occasional Wife* [a situation comedy] before that. Joey got angry about something we did and that ended that gig. Joey was never pleasant to be around."

Joey also introduced the "Son of a Gun Players" (not unlike the Mighty Carson Art Players) to perform skits. One of the players in 1967 and 1968 was his old pal from the sitcom, Joe Besser. Besser did skits with two newcomers who played a big part of the forthcoming TV comedy hit *Rowan & Martin's Laugh-In*, Joanne Worley and Ann Elder. They would also joke around with Joey, allowing him to "ad-lib." Besser wrote in his book, "I remember that Dean Martin and Frank Sinatra considered our act their favorite part of the show."

It was at this time that Joey Bishop did a ten-day USO tour of Vietnam with Tippi Hedren, George Jessel, Ann B. Davis, and the Frankel Twins.

Ann B. Davis told the author, "We went there to entertain the soldiers. All Joey did was complain and bitch. I think that he expected luxury accommodations, but that was hardly our mission. I tried to avoid him like the plague."

Terrie Frankel, of the singing Frankel Twins, recalled that trip with Joey: "He would spend his time with his assistant, Mel Bishop. We got to know Joey on that tour. It was kind of a tough time, and we moved all over. Joey had a film crew that was following him to shoot footage to use on his talk show on ABC. We later met him again in Las Vegas, where he was appearing. He was meeting with a comic he knew at The Comedy Store named Alan Bursky. He said he was looking for someone to write material for his *Tonight Show* appearances. We recommended our friend, a new young comic/writer named David Letterman. Joey ended up hiring Dave, who wrote for him for a while."

As expected, Joey used the footage from his tour on the show. ABC was still attempting to make Joey seem more relevant during that turbulent time. As the public's taste in entertainment was changing drastically in the late sixties, ABC was desperate to attract more advertising dollars. Such programming decisions are based on what market they reached. At the end of the 1970–1971 season, CBS instigated a "rural purge," pulling the plug on such longtime family favorites as *Mayberry R.F.D.*, *Green Acres*, *Petticoat Junction*, *Hee-Haw*, and *The Beverly Hillbillies*. As comic Pat Buttram (Mr. Haney on *Green Acres*) famously described it, "They canceled everything with a tree...including Lassie." In addition to these rustic comedies, CBS put an end to variety shows that dated back to television's earliest days, including *The Red Skelton Show*. CBS saw a dramatic change in direction with the shift, moving away from shows with rural themes and toward more urban and suburban audiences. While the ratings were still strong for those shows, the advertising revenue was declining since the market they reached was older viewers. The desired advertising 25–34 and 35–44 were the desired demographic markets. Thus, despite the rating, the age factor played an important element in programming. While Lawrence Welk was still popular on ABC in 1971, his show, too, was canceled. It lasted another eleven years in syndication, but it was not the desired product for a network to reach its full potential earnings.

The Joey Bishop Show, despite its steady rating by 1969, appealed primarily to an older audience. Joey and his brand of show business were no longer relevant. ABC's executives, like their competitors at the other networks, were very conscious of age demographics. An attempt was made to make fifty-plus-year-old Joey Bishop seem cutting-edge in a society where youngsters were warned not to trust anyone over thirty. They brought on Marlon Brando to talk about the murder of a Black Panther activist; Bing's son Gary Crosby discussed his battle with alcoholism; Richard Nixon debated noted Democrats Hubert Humphrey and Eugene McCarthy; and Joan Baez spoke candidly about the atrocities being committed in Vietnam.

Joey had a rather odd story about Nixon that he would tell occasionally. Following the show's taping, Nixon excused himself to use the bathroom. Joey had a line up his sleeve. "I knocked on the men's room door and asked Nixon, 'Can I please come pee with you?' He said, 'What?' I said, 'Well, years from now people will ask me how well I got to know you. And I'll say, "How well? We peed together!"' But he wouldn't let me in! He thought I was serious!"

Interviewing presidential candidates and political activists was well outside Joey's comfort zone. He was a nightclub comic; he could hardly compete with a William F. Buckley or a David Susskind. ABC's attempts to lure in younger viewers were decidedly unsuccessful. They believed they had the "wrong horse in the race." *The Tonight Show* reached all levels of the demographics and, with fewer affiliates to level the playing field, ABC believed that they had their young lion in thirty-three-year-old Dick Cavett, whom they had carefully groomed with a morning show and then a thrice-weekly prime-time talk show. Cavett had all the intangibles that Joey lacked. A Yale graduate, Cavett had that Midwestern, Gentile charm that matched his youthful appearance. His Q rating was rapidly climbing, while Joey's was sinking faster than the *Titanic*. Cavett could mix young and old guests, from Groucho Marx and Salvador Dali to John Lennon and Janis Joplin. He was a former writer for Paar, Carson, and Merv Griffin. He was a favorite of Woody Allen.

The writing was on the wall and Joey was only too aware of it.

Joey's show racked up a surprising 640 episodes, buoyed only by the occasional appearances of Dean Martin, Sammy Davis Jr., Peter Lawford, Don Rickles, or Buddy Hackett. Frank Sinatra never appeared on the show. Jack Paar made an appearance on one of the early episodes.

Most episodes were light and featured mostly show-business types. One major exception was on June 7, 1968, the day after Bobby Kennedy was assassinated. Joey's main guest that night was a reporter who had witnessed the attack at the Ambassador Hotel in Los Angeles. The tragic incident was recorded on audio-tape by that reporter and played on the show.

It is unfortunate that these time capsules were not preserved. The author talked to Retro Video, which has the only surviving tapes left of the Bishop show. They remarked that the vast majority were erased by ABC, with only thirty-five episodes known to exist. The Kennedy episode was, unfortunately, one of the casualties.

Another memorable episode was originally aired on October 10, 1968. Bishop and Philbin had taped *Funny Girl*'s premiere the previous night at the Egyptian Theater on Hollywood Boulevard, interviewing the celebrities on the red carpet. The guest list included the film's leads, Barbra Streisand, Omar Sharif, and producer Ray Stark.

In reviewing files of the show (and Joey's career), "The Joey Bishop Papers," archived at UCLA, the author reviewed guest research files and other records of the program along with materials collected by Joey throughout his career. The only aspect of his career missing records and contracts is from his work with the Rat Pack.

Opinions as to the talk show's quality varied among both critics and those who actually worked on the program.

Arye "Leslie" Michael Bender, the series editor, wrote in a discussion on IMDb:

> I was the series editor for *The Joey Bishop* (talk) *Show*, on ABC late night, as I had been on its equally short run predecessor, *The Les Crane Show*. The Crane show originated in New York as a genuine alternative to the other late-night talk shows, like *Tonight*. ABC got cold feet, decided to make the show more conventional, and moved it to Hollywood. With nothing to distinguish it from the competition, the toned-down *Les Crane Show* met a swift death. ABC needed someone new to front the Crane show and hit upon Joey Bishop. The suits

were hoping that some of the Rat Pack heat would rub off. It didn't. In fact, Joey was cold, not cool.

The casting of Regis and Joey made for an odd, and not very humorous, pairing.

Joey always seemed uncomfortable as ringmaster. His deadpan act was designed to react to outrageous actions. The show had little in the way of outrageousness about it, leaving Joey with little to react to.

Regis had yet to find the style he would develop a decade later as a morning talk host in Los Angeles, first on KHJ, and then on KABC. The KABC show was moved to New York and syndicated, where it still runs today. The idea of Regis playing second banana to Joey, a second banana himself, made for a weak relationship in an even weaker show.

The somewhat brittle but always interesting Dick Cavett took over the time slot, the show was moved to New York, and the guests became much more interesting. *The Dick Cavett Show*, in its prime, was infinitely more interesting than Joey's mercifully short run.

Television critic Sam Kohn told the author, "I always enjoyed this talk show, and it was fun to see Regis become *numero uno* several decades later with his own hit show. The episode I recall in vivid detail was when Robert Culp was a guest; I had been a fan of his as well from the *I Spy* series. This was in 1969, and Culp was going on a mile a minute about Sam Peckinpah—He had just seen a screening of *The Wild Bunch* and was quite accurate in prognosticating its soon-to-be-historic place in film history. What was most interesting to me was Culp's outspoken politics on this segment—He was perhaps the first person to take the tack that *The Wild Bunch* was about the Vietnam War and how important it was for filmmakers to take a stand. This really impressed me, because ordinarily Bishop and most of the other entertainment/talk shows of the day were rather frivolous. Culp's segments were more like watching a guest on Irv Kupcinet, Lou Gordon, or Alan Douglas, among the serious talkers of that time period."

Television historian Marv Leonard noted, "Joey Bishop had a very good talk show. There was a great variety of guests and some very surprising walk-ons by some of Joey's friends. It was also the springboard for Regis Philbin. It's pretty safe to say that Regis wouldn't be where he is today without Joey. Memorable nights include visits by the Three Stooges with real pie fights, walk-ons by Dean Martin or Sammy Davis Jr., Joey's wonderful monologues every night. Great music from Johnny Mann and His Merry Men. Of course, who could forget Regis Philbin's much-publicized walk-off after having trouble with ABC executives? All in all, Joey put out a very entertaining show that was just as good, if not better, than Johnny Carson's at the time. I just wish we could get some of these shows on DVD."

As the show was approaching its third year, ABC, through Joey's attorney Ed Hookstratten, offered an eighteen-month extension, which he quickly accepted. That would have taken the show to the fourth year. ABC was biding its time to allow Dick Cavett to gain more recognition and credibility as a host. Trustin Howard, by that point, was the only writer on Joey's staff. Carson's staff remained at twelve writers, despite doing a similar show, and both ran for ninety minutes, five days a week.

Howard believed that the show would have continued until its fourth year, as it had settled into a regular audience, regardless of the guests.

"Then, late in the second year, we got picked up for eighteen more months. And Joey hired this giant of a comedy writer named Pat McCormick, who had written a television show for Don Rickles. By giant, I mean giant *nothing*. Joey started to listen to McCormick. They decided to change the format and McCormick started replacing Regis in bits. Regis was relegated to just doing the straight announcing. I warned Joey that we had been doing well and to stick to the format we had succeeded with. As it turned out, Rickles had lasted only six weeks on the show McCormick wrote. Joey faced a similar fate. I think the viewers get into a comfort zone with a show after a while, like with Johnny and

Ed. If it is succeeding, just don't change it. Because I told Joey my thoughts, my option was not picked up and forty-two days later, the show was canceled. The ABC brass had tried to talk Joey out of fooling with the format, but he was stubborn. And once he made up his mind, the show was a goner."

Howard said he pleaded with Ed Hookstratten and Norman Brokaw to talk to Joey and convince him that the show was headed into trouble with McCormick's ideas.

It was at this point that McCormick suggested ratings stunts such as had been done on *The Jack Paar Show*. However, when Paar walked off *The Tonight Show* after the NBC censors removed a joke about a "water closet," Paar acted instinctually and left the show. Joey and Pat's plan was to have Regis walk off and create some publicity. As Joey explained to Regis, there would undoubtedly be letters asking for him to return and he would come back with great fanfare. Regis felt that it would hurt him as a broadcaster, as walking off a show is a cardinal sin and could damage a career. However, he followed orders.

Regis came out at the beginning of the show, said he felt he was holding Joey back and was leaving the show. Joey feigned surprise and Regis left. There was some publicity, it temporarily boosted ratings, and the next week Regis *did* return. Howard said that Regis told him it was an "experiment in terror."

Howard was Nostradamus-like in predicting the show's demise, due to the change of format and the meddling of Pat McCormick.

"If I seem angry about *The Joey Bishop Show* being canceled due to a non-talent maneuvering his way into the show, you're right," Howard said. "I hate the fact that non-talents have all the guts and nerve, because that's *all* they have. And true talents just lie back thinking their talent will out, and they are constantly slaughtered. The sad part is that seventeen musicians, musical arrangers, copyists, cameramen and women, sound people, stagehands, about a hundred people went down the tubes and it didn't have to happen. You're damn right I'm angry."

ABC knew it was time to pull the plug on the show by November. It was running a distant third to Johnny and Merv. On November 24, 1969, ABC informed Ed Hookstratten and Norm Brokaw that it was cancelling *The Joey Bishop Show* at the end of December, possibly later. Hookstratten and Brokaw had negotiated a $1.2 million exit deal with a possibility for Joey to do a pilot for a variety series in the future.

"I am a realist," Joey said. "I saw the writing on the wall. I read the ratings. Ed and Norm got me out with a sweetheart deal, so I didn't have a lot to cry about. I thought we had a lot more in the tank and were just hitting our stride. I knew they wanted Cavett for a while. They wanted that *goyim* appeal. I wanted to go out like a pro."

On November 25, Bishop told the viewers that he was being canceled. He quipped, "I asked ABC for a little time off, but this is ridiculous! It was one hell of a good battle...I'm proud of all the talent, the co-workers, and staff that worked terribly hard to make it a success for two and a half years...They gave it everything they had. If I want to say more, I'll get Johnny or Merv to let me on to say it. Right now, I'm going home to have dinner with my wife. Take care, Regis."

And with that brief oratory, Joey was gone. Regis took over the show, with his guest Vic Damone and the entire audience in shock.

ABC was not surprised. They had already been retrofitting their studio theater in New York to broadcast *The Dick Cavett Show*. Two days later, the network announced Dick Cavett as the new host.

Cavett has a distinct memory of how he first learned he was replacing Bishop on the air. As he told Kliph Nesteroff: "I learned about his cancelation while sitting in a theater in London with the curtain about to raise. An American woman slapped me on the shoulder from the row behind and said, 'Congratulations!' I said, 'For what?' She said, 'You're replacing Joey Bishop!' I thought the woman was drunk. It was true, but I didn't know." Nesteroff then asked Cavett if he knew the reason Bishop was going off the air. "I don't really know," he said. "I know he was broadly disliked by his employees, but that can still happen and a person stays on. I don't know. I hope you can find out. Joey's appearances with Jack Paar before that were stunningly good. Just great."

With Regis remaining as the announcer, they brought on Joey's friends Jan Murray, Norm Crosby, Jack Carter, and others to guest host until they could roll out the Cavett show from New York.

Howard Murray, noted television director and son of the late comic Jan Murray, told the author, "My dad liked Joey and played lots of golf with him. They had known each other for decades. Both Norm, my dad, and others called Joey to tell him what ABC had offered, and he gave them his blessing."

Only Buddy Hackett refused to guest host. He told them to go fuck themselves.

Joey admitted, "We had just signed an extension at ABC for eighteen months. I did not expect it *after* the extension. No one ever suspected this. I'm guessing that it was pushed by Cavett. ABC was angry that I had refused to do lead-ins for cigarette ads. But I had quit and I wasn't going to sell that poison to kids. It's just surprising that they extended me, then dropped me like a bomb."

They wanted Joey to carry on through the November sweeps and possibly through December, while they were already assembling a staff in New York, where they would move Dick Cavett into the spot.

"We did our best with Joey," Norm Brokaw said. "Understanding that he was hurt, but he acted emotionally, which hurt his later chances with the network. He took the cancellation personally and retreated at that time."

The Joey Bishop Show—minus Joey Bishop—ended on Friday, December 26, 1969.

That following Monday, December 29, from New York, with Joey's show still warm, *The Dick Cavett Show* debuted, with guests Woody Allen and actor Robert Shaw. Bobby Rosengarden was the musical conductor; Fred Foy, the announcer. ABC had only one studio in New York, TV 15 (the former Elysée Theater at 202 West 58th Street), which had the only color cameras as well. The network rushed to build a set, although ABC must have been at least somewhat prepared.

"We did the show without a technical rundown or anything," Cavett recalled. "We were not planning to be on the air that soon."

Musical conductor Bobby Rosengarden, who also acted as Dick's sidekick during the opening monologue, remarked that, "We were not prepared at all. We had very little rehearsal."

Cavett discussed the hurry up to do the show on the second episode, December 30, 1969, with guests Henry Fonda and Isaac Stern.

"ABC executives made up most of the audience and sat there nervously," Cavett remarked. "They were smiling later at our debut party at The Four Seasons." He looked relatively calm for being rushed into taking over the show.

And, thus, within seventy-two hours, ABC had erased all vestiges of Joey Bishop. Bishop made no comment about the Cavett show at that time. However, Cavett was at the top of his enemies list, a list that was rapidly growing.

Cavett, for his part, has nothing but good things to say about Joey. As he told Kliph Nesteroff, his brief time of writing for Bishop was not especially unpleasant.

"There must be something wrong with me, because I got along with [him]," he said. "A guy named Fred Freeman...was Garry Marshall's partner in comedy writing. Freeman and Marshall. Joey Bishop was in a bad mood or something, throwing away their material. Fred walked into Joey's office with his material one day—and then just put it into the wastebasket himself."

Trustin Howard had this to say about Joey: "By hiring me, he gave me a chance for a new career. The chance of a lifetime. He allowed me to become a professional writer. When all the doors had closed on me, he gave a busted-out comic three years of learning and a whole new life. For that, I owe it to Joey. I'll always be grateful."

As for Joey, his abrupt departure from his second eponymous show spelled the end of his career. He would have thirty-eight years to reflect on his decision, which he did, quite bitterly. And meanwhile, the entertainment industry continued to change and flourish. Joey, however, sank inexorably into oblivion—and he knew it.

In December 1994, *Philadelphia Magazine* ran an article about Joey, who was seventy-six at the time. Joey was upset that, in a recent issue of *Time* magazine, a writer claimed that the comedi-an had an unsuccessful, short-lived talk show. He wrote an angry letter to the author of the piece, reminding him that *The Joey Bishop Show* lasted two and a half years. Then he looked at his interviewer and asked rhetorically: "Why would *Time* pick on a guy whose career was finished in 1969?"

Chapter 25
The Catastrophe of Success:
Joey Hits Bottom

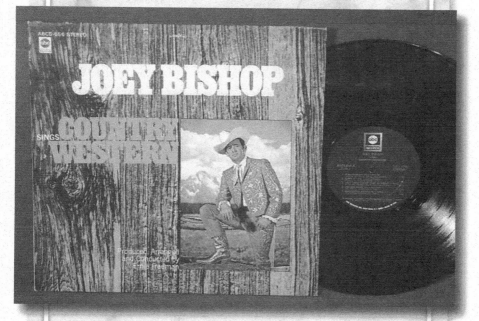

Joey's ill-fated attempt to become a country-western recording star.

The Catastrophe of Success. This phrase is unique to those who have hit the pinnacle of success. How does one top that? As Andreas Kluth wrote in *The Harvard Business Review* (February 17, 2012):

> Something odd and interesting happens to a lot of people who become very successful. Once the initial thrill wears off, they come to perceive their success as "a catastrophe" and even as "a kind of death," as the playwright Tennessee Williams famously put it, after *The Glass Menagerie* became a smash hit in 1944. Athletes, scientists, generals, entrepreneurs, executives, performers, and politicians have expressed this paradox in different words. Paul Samuelson, an economist who won the Nobel Prize in 1970, later concluded that, "After winners receive the award and adulation, they wither away into vainglorious sterility, inspired by a famous line in a Rudyard Kipling poem: 'Meet with Triumph and Disaster, and treat those two Impostors just the same.'" The idea that disaster, or failure, can be an impostor is in some ways more intuitive...triumph, or success—can be the more sinister and cunning of the pair. Success adjusts its weapon to its victim. Some people succumb to hubris, the arrogant overconfidence that often follows success (think Tiger Woods or Eliot Spitzer). Others fall prey to less spectacular but more insidious manifestations of the impostor, such as distraction or paranoia.

Upon the cancellation of *The Joey Bishop Show* on December 26, 1969, Joey Bishop faced this dilemma. He was fifty-one years old and had climbed to the top of his profession. He had become a nationally recognized comic and a wealthy man through shrewd investments. He lived in a mansion in Beverly Hills, drove a Silver Cloud Rolls Royce, had a loving wife and son, two successful television programs, appeared in films and had achieved every goal he had set for himself. How do you top that? With the cancellation of his talk show, it was as if he had been pricked by a pin and began to deflate.

Joey Bishop was on a march to oblivion. For the first decade following his show's demise, he would make infrequent appearances, filling in for Johnny, doing a guest shot on a variety or game show, before all but completely fading from view. The vast majority of his 640 talk-show episodes were erased by ABC. His situation comedy was not distributed for decades due to Joey's reluctance to include the dreadful first season. He had stopped doing club dates in 1967 and no longer had the lucrative contract with the Sands or Riviera in Las Vegas. He was no longer a part of Frank Sinatra's inner circle.

Joey tried to repeat what he had done successfully for over thirty years, but it was now old hat. A new breed of comedians such as David Steinberg, David Brenner, Robert Klein, George Carlin had taken his place. Sure, there were comics of his generation who were still scoring in clubs—Buddy Hackett, Don Rickles, Shecky Greene. However, those performers continued to play the game and appeared with Johnny, Merv, Mike, or Dinah on their shows. They were seen in public, appeared at events, did the celebrity roasts and kept up public relations. Joey became more of a recluse. Frank Sinatra had always known how to reinvent himself. Frank never faced the Catastrophe of Success—he would simply keep moving forward. His sheer talent was unquestionable. Without the aura and mystique of the Rat Pack, Joey became a mere mortal. Instead of enjoying his success and resting on his achievements, bitterness and anger began to gnaw at his core. It is much like the phrase used by General MacArthur when he was stripped of his duties by President Truman: "Old soldiers never die; they just fade away."

When the author met with Joey several times, starting in the 1990s, he was just that—an old, faded-away soldier. While glimpses of the old Joey could peek through, it was apparent that he was a defeated man. He lived a quiet, sedentary life in his gated community, occasionally leafing through his old scrapbooks and mementos of the past. He almost never ventured out.

When the talk show ended on December 26, 1969, Joey had already retreated to his Beverly Hills home. His agent, Norm Brokaw, who had outlined a path for his aging client, stated, "Joey was physically and mentally drained. He needed to take a step back and take a breath. While he had planned to be hosting the talk show in 1970, he had very few club dates and other work, as the show had dominated his schedule. He was definitely well set [financially] and had no worries in that corner."

Joey dabbled in some charity work with Sylvia as the new decade dawned. His charity of choice was helping children with disabilities, a noble cause indeed. But as one of his writers, Don Sherman, said, "Joey was simply crushed when they canceled the talk show. I just remember that he took it hard."

Larry Bishop continued to work at his acting career. His close high school friends—Richard Dreyfuss, Albert Brooks, and former comedy partner Rob Reiner—followed in their famous fathers' footsteps. By 1970, they were starting to become recognizable presences on the small screen. Rob Reiner had written for both the Smothers Brothers' and Glen Campbell's variety shows, acted in several television series, and, beginning in 1971, achieved TV immortality as Michael "Meathead" Stivic on the groundbreaking Norman Lear series *All in the Family*. Richard Dreyfuss had acted in several television shows as well as two major films, *Catch-22* (1970) and *American Graffiti* (1973); in 1978 he won the Best Actor Academy Award for his animated portrayal of Elliot Garfield in Neil Simon's *The Goodbye Girl* (1977). Albert Brooks was a rising standup comic who had appeared on several variety television shows and was a semi-regular on ABC's *The Odd Couple*. Larry Bishop lagged far behind his buddies. He had a couple of small parts on shows like *Love, American Style* and was cast as "the grocery boy" on an episode of Desi Arnaz's groovy sitcom *The Mothers-in-Law*. It was an uphill climb. We can only speculate that Joey's negative reputation harmed Larry's opportunities; certainly, it could have played a part.

Albert Brooks told producer/director Judd Apatow in a magazine article he wrote for *Vanity Fair* (December 17, 2012):

> *Brooks*: Well, we all go to the area of strength in school, so we can be liked by girls. And if you're not going to be a quarterback and you're not going to be a biology honors student...so I was funny. At Beverly High, there was

a parent-student talent show. A big event once a year. Now, Beverly High, a lot of the parents were famous. So, you had Tony Curtis, Joey Bishop, you had Carl Reiner...

Apatow: You had competition.

Brooks: That's right. Rod Serling. So I was the host of the evening—and I was this kid. I wrote jokes and made comments. I still remember a joke that I told. One of the kids, for their talent portion, did those batons—you twirl them around and around—and I still remember, because it was an ad-lib. I was like, "Wasn't she wonderful? Do you know, in practice, a 707 accidentally landed on the football field." People roared.

Apatow: So you weren't like the class clown that couldn't get a girlfriend. You were confident.

Apatow: Humor-wise, I was confident. I mean, my two best friends were Larry Bishop, who's Joey Bishop's son, and Rob Reiner, who is Carl Reiner's son.

While the author's attempts to elicit Larry Bishop's cooperation in this book were not successful, Albert Brooks sent us the following reply:

Mr. Lertzman,

Thanks for writing. Mr. Brooks was friends with Larry Bishop almost 50 years ago and doesn't have any insight into what you are writing about. He knew Joey Bishop as Larry's dad and he is too young to have any memories of the Rat Pack so he is going to pass on the request. Good luck with the book, I will look for it when it comes out.

Herb Nanas,

Manager to Albert Brooks

According to Norm Brokaw, it would take several months to start setting up club dates for Joey. For the first time in ten years, his dance card was empty. No upcoming television shows, no movies, no personal appearances.

"Frankly, Joey was out of steam," recalled Brokaw.

By March, William Morris had set up some dates. Bishop was technically rusty, as he had not worked a club since 1966, except for those annual, three-week dates at the Sands.

A March 1970 issue of *Variety* announced Joey's forthcoming nightclub tour with some old friends, the Philadelphia comedy team of Al Fisher and Lou Marks. Fisher & Marks still played the area clubs, such Palumbo's. Fisher & Marks were Philadelphia's answer to Abbott and Costello, with Al as the straight man, and Lou the manic clown.

Joey warmed up by playing a small club called the Log Cabin, in Philadelphia. Then Joey made a big splash to kick off his tour with a week at the Sands. His opening-night audience included Johnny Carson, Sammy Davis Jr., George Burns, and others. He had decent reviews, with *The Las Vegas Sun* saying, "It's what you'd expect of Bishop..."

Joey, by 1970, was essentially doing the same act that he had done since 1938, with modifications. Unlike the younger comics, his approach seemed quite dated. Las Vegas was still a safe zone for aging comics. Jack Benny, George Burns, and Milton Berle still played well in Las Vegas. Comics such as Don Rickles did crowd play, which was not affected by the material. Bob Newhart was more of an observational comic, adapting his material to keep it fresh. Joey stubbornly refused—or perhaps he was simply unable—to adapt, adjust, or modernize his act in any way. His material was not the stuff of headlining comics such as Buddy Hackett, Shecky Greene, Bob Newhart, or Don Rickles. They each brought a uniqueness that went beyond joke telling. Shecky could sing and schmooze. Buddy was obnoxious and shocking, and you felt a sense of danger with him. Rickles was in your face with insults. Joey was the comic in the Catskills who told the same tired stories.

Joey attempted to kick off his comedy tour with Fisher & Marks back in his hometown of Philadelphia at the Latin Casino, located in suburban Cherry Hill, New Jersey. Don Sherman, who had supplied Joey with much of his material, vividly recalls that opening:

"Joey went back to his old haunts in Philadelphia and thought he would be hailed the conquering hero of Philly," Sherman said. "It was a two-week stint. The crowds were sparse. I mean, the Latin Casino was a big venue and for the rates they were probably paying Joey, they expected big crowds. I heard it was way less than half-filled. He brought along his old cronies, like Mel, and had a girl singer to open. He was really angry at the shitty reception he got and he took it out on the crowd. The crowds were feeling cheated, too, as a ticket to see Joey was not cheap. Joey worked saloons his whole life and knew how to handle hecklers and drunks. So he is into the first week and his anger is showing through. When the hecklers started in on him, he got pissed and walked off the stage until the hecklers were removed. He goes backstage and throws a fit. Now, the owners of the club are not too pleased at this bullshit. I mean, Joey knew how to handle this shit and not to pull this stunt. Joey leaves and goes back to his hotel in the city. And they have to give refunds. So it goes into the paper [*Philadelphia Inquirer*] about what happened. Now there is talk that Joey did this to sell more tickets, but that's pure shit as he was pissed off. So he calls up his agent and cancels the rest of the gig at the Latin Casino. In his hometown. He is absolutely embarrassed. It goes all over the news and the whole business. It is a small community, this business, and word travels fast."

Sherman then made a startling revelation. "Joey literally has a breakdown. He was hospitalized in Philly. I don't think it was a ruse to get him out of his contract or such. He literally had a nervous breakdown. While I don't know for sure, I do believe he was a depressive, as he would have periods of depression in the many years I knew him. He was a real mess when I saw him after that in Los Angeles."

Rocky Kalish corroborated Joey's emotional state: "Bishop, without a doubt, suffered from depression. He was like that when we did the show. He would be wacky at times, such as when he was at Sid Caesar's house and asked Sid to box with him. Sid had a bag he worked out on in his garage and Joey put on gloves and asked Sid to box. Well, Sid was tall and built like a horse; Joey was half his size. Sid was a mule. He nearly tore Joey's head off and then, suddenly, Joey got very sullen."

According to the *Philadelphia Inquirer*, after the aborted two-week stand at the Latin Casino, Joey entered the city's St. Luke's Hospital to be treated for "exhaustion." His attending physician, Dr. Giuffre, was quoted as saying, "We don't expect to find anything serious... . Joey needs a break in his routine. The fact that he consented to go into the hospital is an indication that he really feels rotten...I think he will snap back in two or three days...Joey kept going because he felt an obligation to his public...He has not been eating properly and has dropped too much weight."

The rest of Joey's return tour to nightclubs was dead before it got out of the starting gate. The remainder of the dates were canceled, which included The Music Carnival in Cleveland; The Doral in Hollywood, Florida; the Drury Lane in Chicago, and other dinner theaters. Many of Joey's old haunts, such as Chez Parée in Chicago or The Copacabana, were closed by 1970 or had become discos. Joey's attempt to return to the places where he had found success was short-circuited by time in more ways than one.

Joey returned to his home in Beverly Hills, a rather shaken man. On the plus side, due to the careful investments overseen by Ed Hookstratten and excellent advice by Norm Brokaw at William Morris, Bishop was worth a sizeable fortune of about $8 million dollars in 1970, which in 2020 dollars would be worth $53 million. Joey never had to work again. He was just fifty-two years old and, like many comedians, he enjoyed his profession. He liked the adulation and the applause. Many comics slow down after reaching their biggest successes. Current comedians such as Jerry Seinfeld (who had a massive hit with *Seinfeld*, his classic nine-season NBC sitcom) and Jay Leno (who was at the helm of *The Tonight Show* for more than twenty years) took a step back after they reached their zenith. Yet, in both cases, they yearned for the audience feedback and have returned to doing standup to satisfy that itch. Neither has tried to repeat his earlier success. Joey, initially, made that attempt.

Joey and Sylvia, based on the advice of their counsel Ed Hook-stratten (whom Joey adored and trusted completely, according to Norm Brokaw), decided it was time to sell their mansion and downsize. Their son Larry was an adult and, as empty nesters, the Bishops felt the house was too big for just the two of them. Joey, who now had nothing but time, fell in love with boating. He had bought a boat, that he christened—what else?—*The Son of a Gun*, which he moored at The Newport Yacht Club. Joey and Sylvia, as members of the club, became socially active there. Joey took a great interest in boating and became a member of the Coast Guard Auxiliary. His boating skills were publicized in the media in 1972 when he rescued, on two different occasions, within three weeks, stranded boaters up the coast in Marina Del Rey.

"I loved the water and boating," Joey said. "I found a great passion for it."

With his new love of boating, it was only natural that he should live near the water. "But I had no desire for Malibu or Santa Monica and that. Too crowded. I loved the marina at Newport Beach."

Being built nearby on a man-made island in the harbor of Newport Beach was the Lido Isle gated community, with its luxury houses and condominiums. With a population of only 1800 and a Mediterranean theme (evident by the street names and the architecture being redolent of the Mediterranean Revival style), it was one of the early master-planned developments that included underground utilities.

Joey and Sylvia bought a condo unit that was rather compact (especially compared to their mansion) and had a dock for Joey's boat. In 1972, they sold their Chevy Chase Drive home in Beverly Hills and moved to "the house with the bay window where they can view the setting sun on the harbor," down the coast in Newport Beach in Orange County. Joey described that view rather poetically when he compared it to a "postcard that God sends me each day."

As another sign of his career coming to an end, Joey let go of his personal assistants. His longtime friend, valet/assistant and former stage partner Mel Bishop, was no longer needed. Mel found work for the next fifteen years as an assistant to Rich Little.

Joey and his longtime secretary also parted ways. Joey maintained his management team of Norm Brokaw (who, by that time, was head of William Morris and had delegated Joey to an associate) and attorney Ed Hookstratten.

Despite the abject failure of the Cherry Hill club, Joey still felt welcome in Las Vegas at the Sands, then the Sahara, and the Riviera, where he could earn a weekly salary of about $75,000. As far as television was concerned, he still had a well-known name and recognizable face, making him a perfect guest star on the variety shows of that period. He appeared a couple times on *Rowan & Martin's Laugh-in*, starting in December of 1970, *The Bob Goulet Special* in 1970; *Music Country U.S.A.*, and then *The Glen Campbell Goodtime Hour* on February 23, 1971, *The Jimmy Durante Presents the Lennon Sisters*, Johnny Mann's (his former bandleader on his talk show) *Stand Up and Cheer*, The Danny Thomas special *City Versus Country* in 1971; *The Sonny & Cher Show* in 1971; *The Dean Martin Show* (on which he made fifteen appearances); *Tony Orlando & Dawn*; *The Jacksons*; a Della Reese special; *A Salute to Milton Berle*; and the sitcom *Chico and the Man*. Starting in 1970, he made several appearances on both the daytime and nighttime versions of *The Hollywood Squares*, hosted by his old pal Peter Marshall.

"I had known Joey since the late 1940s," the ageless Peter Marshall recalled. "I crossed paths with him when I was partners with Tommy Noonan and when I did a single. Joey was always great on the *Squares*. Dependable, and he fit the format perfectly with a quick quip."

Joey, who was an ideal panelist on game shows, also did *Celebrity Sweepstakes*, *The Match Game* (both the daytime and nighttime versions), *The Liars Club*, and *Break the Bank*.

And, of course, Joey was a guest on talk shows hosted by Merv Griffin, Mike Douglas (for whom he also substituted), Dinah Shore, Sammy Davis Jr. (*Sammy & Company*), Hugh Hefner (*Playboy After Dark*), Tom Snyder (*Tomorrow*), David Frost, and others. Interestingly, he never appeared on any of the numerous talk shows hosted by Regis Philbin. For his part, Joey had branded Philbin "an ingrate" for walking off their late-night talk show during a salary dispute and then later bad-mouthing Bishop in a book. "In the Hebrew religion, ingrate is the worst," he says. "I once told an interviewer that Regis is terrific. He gives lots of hope to people who have no talent."

He participated in several of the Dean Martin roasts, including those for George Burns (another of his comedic idols), Michael Landon, Sammy Davis Jr., Angie Dickinson, Jack Klugman, and Dean himself. Strangely, the Dean Martin roast for Sinatra included Ruth Buzzi, LaWanda Page, Redd Foxx—but no sign of Joey.

Joey also made a highly publicized return to late night. Johnny held no ill will towards Joey (although Joey still nursed his hurt feelings about Johnny's remark at the Rat Pack Show in 1965) and requested he fill in as a guest host in April of 1971. However, Joey was pressed into service early when Johnny became ill with hepatitis in March. Joey filled in for two weeks and enjoyed good ratings.

Joey remarked to *New York Post* columnist Earl Wilson at that time, "I did it for two years and eight months night after night on ABC. I don't think I could do it again. I faced it with the wrong attitude. You just have to laugh at it. Johnny can do it. I always say I'm constantly helping Johnny. I helped him when I had my own show."

In 1976 and '77, Joey toured with the play, *Mind with the Dirty Man*, by Jules Tasca. This two-act comedy (with roles for three men and two women) made its debut in 1971, with Joey's former co-star Joe Flynn (known by this time as Captain Binghamton on ABC's *McHale's Navy*). The play focuses on a producer of X-rated movies (played by Larry Bishop), whose ulcer-ridden father (Joey, of course) is the president of a morality group fighting for movie censorship. The father-son team played such dinner theaters such as Drury Lane in Chicago, Valley Forge Music Fair, and Resorts International in Atlantic City. His son Larry had a role in that production. Dinner theaters and plays were then exploding in popularity, providing an outlet for veteran comedians and actors, including Phyllis Diller, Donald O'Connor, Don Knotts, Mickey Rooney, Eddie Bracken, Alan Young, Bob Denver, Huntz Hall, Forrest Tucker, Bob Crane, Dorothy Lamour, Bob Cummings, Eddie Albert, and Tom Poston.

Joey followed *Mind with the Dirty Man* with the old warhorse *The Seven Year Itch*, George Axelrod's hit three-act Broadway play starring Tom Ewell. The title reflects the psychological finding that most married men are driven to have an extramarital affair in the seventh year of marriage. Joey was taking his turn as Richard Sherman, who has been described as a "nerdy, faithful, middle-aged publishing executive with an overactive imagination." While Sherman chooses to stay behind in their New York City apartment, his wife and son are spending the summer in Maine. Temptation to the seven-year-married Sherman arrives in the form of a voluptuous commercial actress and former model who has moved into the apartment above his. The play was made famous by its 1955 big-screen adaptation starring Ewell and Marilyn Monroe. The play died in the Granny's Dinner Theatre presentation starring Joey Bishop and Cybill Shepherd.

Chapter 26
Seltzer Down His Pants:

Broadway Conquers Joey

By the time the eighties dawned, Joey was slowing down appreciably. He rarely appeared in Las Vegas, and when he did, for a last time in 1981 at the old Aladdin with Lola Falana, he had been demoted to the opening act. He had no contracts and no offers after that. Slowly but surely, he was being forgotten. The Rat Pack was clearly a relic of the past. Dean Martin had cut back his work in television and only ventured to Las Vegas at the MGM Grand to do occasional shows. Frank was Frank and still toured. Sammy, after his short-lived talk show, *Sammy & Company* in 1976, was rarely seen on television, but his live performances continued. He remained, as ever, the consummate entertainer.

The rare gigs Joey *did* play were at one of the clubs where he started in 1938, Palumbo's in Philadelphia. He played dates there starting in 1975 and 1976 and seems to have played there until the early 1980s.

Palumbo's burned down in a suspicious fire in 1994.

Sylvia and Joey enjoyed their life in Newport Beach and their boat. Their son Larry married and gave them a granddaughter in 1975. In 1978, Joey appeared in a few venues including The Valley Forge Music Fair near Philadelphia with his old boss, Danny Thomas. Joey was the opening act. By the time Danny had moved on to places like The Front Row in Cleveland, he had replaced Joey with Florence Henderson.

Joey would also be paid to speak at private events, sales conventions, or testimonial dinners. For a fee that ranged between $5,000 to $10,000, he would do his act. As lucrative as that may seem, it is a steep decline from the $75,000 a week he was pulling down in the 1970s.

In 1980, Joey attempted to produce a television show in the manner of *Star Search*; its title was to be *The Joey Bishop Talent Scouts*. The concept failed to get financing. In 1981, Joey announced his newest concept, *Joey Bishop's Super TV Bingo*. The published article stated that it was being financed by Group W at KYW in Philadelphia, the former home of *The Mike Douglas Show*. It was set to debut on five Group W stations in January of 1981. Joey was quoted as saying that the show would have a 200-station group of affiliates, which he said was fifty more than he had with his ABC *The Joey Bishop Show*. The show never materialized.

Meanwhile, another old-time comedian was finding success on Broadway. *Sugar Babies*, a musical-comedy stage revue, starring Mickey Rooney and Ann Miller. After touring for six months, *Sugar Babies* opened on October 9, 1979, to unanimously favorable reviews. For Miss Miller, a star of MGM musicals in the 1940s and '50s, the show was a welcome opportunity to find a new public. For Mr. Rooney, it represented more than that—the resurrection of a career that had been all but lost in alcohol and domestic entanglements. To play the role of a burlesque comic, Mickey channeled his father, a one-time top banana named Joe Yule. Mickey, a multitalented performer, could sing, dance, and "get seltzer down his pants." It was the perfect part for him. Financed and produced by Terry Allen Kramer with Harry Rigby, *Sugar Babies* became a monster hit. It revived the career of Mickey Rooney, who was earning nearly $70,000 a week. When Mickey needed a break in February of 1981 to shoot a TV-movie called *Leave 'em Laughing*, he offered a few suggestions for replacements, including Joey Bishop. Mick had seen Joey perform at a dinner theater in Chicago in *Mind with the Dirty Man*, a play he was doing with his son, Larry. Joey, who could not sing (despite having put out a country and western album in 1968), nor could he dance. So, his being cast in lead of a musical revue seemed a questionable move at best.

A *New York Times* article, dated January 30, 1981, announced Joey Bishop's Broadway debut. The article, "'Sugar Babies,' as Seen Through the Eyes of Joey Bishop," was written by Albin Krebs and Robert Mcg. Thomas. It reads:

> When Joey Bishop replaces Mickey Rooney on Monday night for a four-week engagement in Broadway's "Sugar Babies," he won't just be taking the Rooney part in the nostalgic recreation of burlesque. The whole show is being reworked in the Bishop image.
>
> Where Mickey sings, for example, Joey will play the mandolin, a switch Mr. Bishop explained the other day during a rehearsal break at the Mark Hellinger Theater: "Mickey

sings rather well," he said, "but I don't." Some changes are more subtle. Like Mr. Rooney, Mr. Bishop will have a drag scene. But instead of portraying the Francine character developed by Mr. Rooney, Mr. Bishop's character will be Hortense.

Mr. Bishop explained that the self-confident Francine was an ideal vehicle for Mr. Rooney's sassy one-liners, while his own Hortense, designed to exploit his talent for monologue, was something of a loser.

"During the Civil War," he confided, "her family fought for the West."

When Joey debuted in the role, he received great fanfare in the media. Tom Buckley, in the *New York Daily News* of February 2, 1981, wrote:

After Saturday's matinee of "Sugar Babies," Joey Bishop sat in his dressing room at the Mark Hellinger Theater, nibbling at a bowl of chili and applying an icepack to a strained left knee.

"I got this trying to keep up with Ann Miller," he said glumly. "She's incredible." Mr. Bishop is filling in as the co-star of the burlesque musical for four weeks for Mickey Rooney, who is making a movie, and although he has been performing since he was a youngster, he hasn't found it easy to make his Broadway debut at the age of 63.

"I wouldn't have done it if Mickey hadn't asked me," he said. "We've been friends for 35 years. I told him, 'You've got to be kidding. I'm a monologist, and standup comic. I don't sing. I don't dance. I don't do physical comedy.' The Mick said, 'Don't worry about it. You'll be terrific.'"

For that matter, Mr. Bishop continued, he had appeared only once before in a legitimate theater, and, as near as he could recall, hadn't performed in New York since an engagement in the old Copacabana in 1954, with Frank Sinatra.

"That was the show that made me," he said. "Since then, it has been a lot of television, nightclubs and regular appearances in Las Vegas. In fact, I go into the Aladdin with Lola Falana after I finish up here."

Mr. Bishop moved his leg, groaned a little, and recalled again his only appearance in a legitimate theater. "The funny thing is that Mickey saw me in that play. That was about four years ago, in Chicago. 'Mind with the Dirty Man' it was called. My son Larry was in it with me, and it wasn't a hit. Mickey was in Chicago at the same time, appearing in 'Ladies Night in a Turkish Bath,' or something like that. Things weren't going good for him at all, and he was really despondent.

It was only a year or so after that, Mr. Bishop said, that he was approached by Harry Rigby, the co-producer of "Sugar Babies," which was then in the planning stage, to appear with Mr. Rooney and Miss Miller.

"The funny thing was that when I was just starting out in Philadelphia in the late 1930s, I was part of a vaudeville act called the Bishop Boys, which is where I got my name," he said. "We were booked into the old Trocadero, which was a burlesque house, and I had a chance to see the world of striptease and baggy-pants comics at close range. I'll tell you something else. Maxie Furman, who's in 'Sugar Babies,' was the top banana on the bill. Anyhow, I was tempted by the offer, but I didn't think I could stand doing the same thing for a year or two, so I finally turned Rigby down."

"Last December Mickey called me," Mr. Bishop said. "He told me he wanted to do a movie, 'Leave 'em Laughing,' and asked me if I'd step in for him for four weeks. As I said, I didn't think it would work, but I decided to at least see the show. Afterwards, I told him, 'It's crazy.' When they told me I'd have only ten days of rehearsal, I said, 'It's crazier.'

"Finally, I said to myself, 'What the hell, what's the worst that can happen to you? It'll be fun.' So, I said O.K., and Ernie Flatt, the director and choreographer, worked with me, teaching me a few steps.

"I went on in a special matinee on Jan. 31 and I stepped into the cast on Monday, Feb. 2. When I went on that night, I told the audience, 'Ladies and gentlemen, on an opening night there's a tendency to be nervous. Please don't be.' They broke up, and I was on my way."

Mr. Bishop's recital was interrupted by his dresser, bearing a note from Miss Miller. In it were several observations on his performance that day, beginning, "In the schoolroom sketch, come on faster and much louder."

Mr. Bishop shook his head in rueful wonderment. "She does this after every performance," he said. "The way she's still putting out after all this time—I can't believe it."

That was Joey's version of events. This is the harsh reality. He flopped. Big time.

The author wrote about *Sugar Babies* in his comprehensive biography *The Life and Times of Mickey Rooney*. He was able to interview many of those involved in the show, including the play's financer and producer, Terry Allen Kramer, who later produced *La Cage Aux Folles*, *Kinky Boots*, the *Hello, Dolly!* revival with Bette Midler, and *The Goodbye Girl*.

"Bishop was my biggest nightmare," Kramer said. "In a production like *Sugar Babies*, Mickey was irreplaceable. The show is based on his talent. One of the reasons we never attempted a revival was that there really was no one who could replace Mick. We thought of many names, from Robert Alda [Alan's father], who was not in the shape to do it. I never knew much about Bishop, who had been suggested by Harry Rigby. We tried to adapt the part to him, but it was a disaster. We went from SRO and being the hottest ticket on Broadway to half-to-quarter full—and Annie [Ann Miller] was still there. This Bishop didn't have any stage presence. Awful! We bought him out in two weeks."

Joey was to have played the month, but they rushed in comic Rip Taylor to fill the role until Mickey returned.

"AWWWWWWWWWFUL!!!" exclaimed the flamboyant Taylor to the author. "It was a train wreck. Annie was having a nervous breakdown. I watched the night before I was to start. They would have been better off with a rock!"

"I got back just in time," Mickey said. "The ship was sinking."

When the author visited with Joey in the mid-1990s, he spoke of his brief tenure with *Sugar Babies* as a triumph, never mentioning that he had been fired halfway through his run.

After the debacle on the Great White Way, Joey was essentially kaput as a performer. Like over-the-hill boxers, performers always believe they have one more fight left in them. Joey was only sixty-three at the time he did *Sugar Babies*, which is not especially old, particularly compared to some of the veteran actors working today. Case in point: Clint Eastwood, who is still directing films at age eighty-nine. Jane Fonda, eighty-two, and Lily Tomlin, eighty, co-star in the Netflix series *Grace and Frankie*, currently in its sixth season. Harrison Ford is still offered roles as an action star at age seventy-seven, And Sylvester Stallone recently played his vigilante character Rambo at seventy-three. In Joey's time, George Burns was active into his nineties, as were Bob Hope and Milton Berle. Sinatra was active until his late seventies. Tony Bennett, currently ninety-three, is still singing well and selling out engagements. Joey Bishop, on the other hand, was basically past his prime at age fifty-one when his talk show was canceled in December of 1969.

With that, we refer to the previous chapter on the catastrophe of success. While many of the above entertainers who played well into old age and, relying, to a large degree, on their past successes, they nevertheless lived in the present. Joey seemed trapped in his past, specifically the decade from 1959 to 1969, a time when his success seemed endless. He had, shall we say, reached beyond his "Peter Principle." His paucity of talent had simply caught up with him, particularly now that he was no longer associated with the Rat Pack.

For a time, Joey was basically a greeter at the Claridge Hotel. As the tourists were getting off the bus, Joey would be there, offering anyone a dollar who had a joke to share.[8] In the afternoons, he ran a daily game show for the tourists in the Claridge Theater as well. It was certainly a sad comedown for Joey, who had headlined on Broadway just three years earlier, and had commanded $75,000 a week in Las Vegas in 1974.

By 1984, sixty-six-year-old Joey was all but hiding from the public. He seemed to be making good on a statement he made to a reporter regarding his early days when he spent time in burlesque theaters: "I would walk past the old comics backstage and thought to myself, 'The poor bastards. Look at them in their clownish pants and false noses.'" Joey told himself then and there that if he ever achieved fame in show business, he would know when to quit. He promised never to allow himself to become old-fashioned or do projects in which he did not believe. Apparently, he liked the Sunday night show on CBS, *Murder, She Wrote*, starring Broadway legend Angela Lansbury as mystery writer (and ace crime solver) Jessica Fletcher in the small (but apparently deadly) town of Cabot Cove. The show was a haven for veteran actors who turned up week after week in guest roles. Playing a character named Buster Bailey, Joey provided the comic relief from the more deadly aspects of the episode, "Murder at the Oasis."

To help fill up the hours of his days, he did a week on *The New Hollywood Squares*, hosted by John Davidson, in 1988. He was Jay Leno's on-air guest for what would be Joey's final *Tonight Show* appearance. He turned up on the short-lived *Pat Sajak Show* on CBS in 1989. Bob Costas interviewed him on his one-on-one (no studio audience) show, NBC's *Later*. That same year (1993), he also did a few radio interviews. Periodically, he would appear at

---

8 He was later replaced by the affable Larry Storch, who had played Corporal Randolph Agarn on ABC's *F Troop*.

local banquets, corporate conventions, and charitable events, particularly those benefitting handicapped children.

Chapter 27
And Now the End is Near...

The Final Days of the Rat Pack

The official program for Frank Sinatra's funeral.

In the wake of Kitty Kelley's salacious book on Frank Sinatra, *His Way* (Bantam, 1986), Joey was a member of a panel discussing the bestseller on the syndicated daytime talk show hosted by Phil Donahue. Sinatra was reportedly made ill by the contents of the unauthorized biography, and his many loyal friends and fans were up in arms about it. One of the not-too-surprising revelations made in the book was that Frank liked the ladies. Joey made the rather bold statement that he was actually *glad* that Ms. Kelly had written the book, prompting an outcry of "JOEY?" from the predominantly female audience. He quickly added, "All this time, I thought Frank was gay!" There was a roar from the crowd as Phil went to a commercial break.

Joey had apparently been offered a multi-million-dollar deal to write his own tell-all book about the Rat Pack, but he refused to even consider the offer. "I just couldn't do it," he said. "Those guys are my friends."

Perhaps it was not just loyalty that was preventing Joey from writing his book, tentatively titled, "I Was a Mouse in The Rat Pack"—it's possible that he didn't have enough material to justify a fat book contract. "The raunchiest story I could come up with was when I saw Frank and Sammy in the nude in a steam room," he said. "When I saw Frank, he became my idol. When I saw Sammy, *I* became *his* idol."

In 1988, there was an ill-advised attempt to reunite Frank, Dean, and Sammy for a twenty-nine-city tour. Eschewing the name Rat Pack ("that stupid phrase," as Sinatra referred to it), it was billed as "Together Again." Reportedly, Frank wanted to do this to help Dean cope with the grief he was experiencing from the loss of his son Dean Paul, who had perished in a plane crash a year earlier. But Dean simply wasn't up to the task. He felt lost performing in the large venues Sinatra had insisted on playing. Before the tour had truly commenced, Dean walked away, much to Sinatra's chagrin. He was replaced by Liza Minelli in March 1988, and the tour was rechristened "The Ultimate Event."

Dean's final years were sad ones. Depressed, ailing, and drinking hard, he could often be seen, dining alone, his false teeth in a glass (to ward off well-meaning intruders) at La Famiglia, an Italian restaurant on Canon Drive in Beverly Hills. On Christmas Day 1995, he died. He was seventy-eight.

Peter Lawford, who struggled through years of drug dependency, passed away in 1984, alone and forgotten. Eliot Weisman, Sinatra's manager during his final years as a performer, wrote a telling account of a conversation he had with the Chairman while seated at a bar following one of his shows. Although Sinatra was not given to talk about his former Rat Pack cronies, he did share with Weisman just how angry he had been when Lawford phoned him to relay JFK's last-minute refusal to stay at the Sinatra compound following the election. Frank, deeply hurt by this betrayal, particularly after he had worked so hard to put a Kennedy in the White House, asked Peter if he was listening closely. Lawford said he was. Sinatra slammed down the receiver.

Perhaps encouraged by his client's sharing this memory with him, Weisman mentioned Joey Bishop. What happened to end that relationship? Sinatra locked those intense blue eyes on Weisman's and said simply, "Don't ever ask me that question again." Weisman did not.

Sammy Davis Jr., who was fighting the IRS and was swamped with debt, was diagnosed with lung cancer and passed away in 1990. *The Salute to Sammy*, broadcast on network television when the entertainer was gravely ill and unable to speak, had Frank but no Joey. Had he been invited he might have told the following classic anecdote from the 1960s:

"Sammy was doing a benefit for the NAACP in Atlantic City. And he had a team called Stump and Stumpy. They were great dancers and very good comedians, but they couldn't make it that night, and Sammy called me. There were six thousand Black people there. I looked out at the crowd, then I looked back at him and I said, 'Jewish crowd, my ass.' You never heard Black people laugh that hard."

Or this one:

"Sammy and I were in a Rolls Royce doing ninety miles per hour when a cop pulled us over. The cop says, 'Jesus, Sammy, Joey, you were doing ninety!' I said, 'Officer, the man has one eye. Where do you want it, on the road or on the speedometer?'"

Frank Sinatra continued to perform even when he could no longer remember the lyrics to the songs he had been singing for forty years. He gave a final performance at a private event in February 1995, after which he was whisked into a limousine and taken home, where he would remain for the final few years of his remarkable life. Before long, dementia overtook him completely, and he was suffering from cancer as well. With the poignant last words, "I'm losing," the eighty-two-year-old icon finally faced that final curtain on May 14, 1998. The night following his death, the Empire State Building in New York City honored his memory turning their lights blue, a sly reference to those ol' blue eyes. On the Las Vegas strip, the lights were dimmed and, for one minute, the casinos stopped spinning.

Joey gave an interview to *New York Post* columnist Steve Dunleavy just after Sinatra's death. He confided that he had dreamt about Frank on the night he passed away. He recalled, "I fell asleep with the TV on. They must have announced on the news that he'd died, but I thought that I was dreaming. In my dream, I got dressed and I went over to Frank's house, where I found him alive. I said, 'So, another of your practical jokes, Frank?'"

At 7:30 the following morning, Bishop went outside in his pajamas to get the morning paper. He saw about thirty-five media people there, camped out, waiting for him. Then he knew Frank's death was no dream.

"In your mind, guys like Frank never die," Joey said. "I went cold remembering my dream."

Bishop didn't attend the funerals of either Martin or Davis. "Funerals are too phony," he said in a previous interview. "I hate phoniness." But he made an exception for Sinatra.

"They had a thousand gardenias on the casket," he told a reporter. "*One thousand gardenias on the casket!* And I visualized him being in there and couldn't believe that he was dead. And yet I was grateful that he wasn't suffering anymore. If anybody liked to live, it was Frank. And to deprive him of living—that's not living for him, being in a bed. You understand?"

Chapter 28
And Then There Was One:
Joey Fights a Losing Battle Against Myth

An elderly, bereved Joey attends Frank Sinatra's funeral in May 1998.

The title of this chapter is the one used by Bruce Handy in his excellent article in *Time* magazine, dated June 6, 1998.

> Joey Bishop, 80 years old now, is not at all sentimental about the Rat Pack's renewed cultural currency. Nor is he pleased. On the phone from Newport Beach, Calif., where he lives with his wife of 57 years, Sylvia, he says he doesn't much like giving interviews (while graciously agreeing to this one). So, I ask, to what does he attribute the ongoing obsession with his early '60s apotheosis, the nights in Vegas clowning around on stage and off with Frank Sinatra, Dean Martin, Sammy Davis Jr. and Peter Lawford? "Could it be anything else but money?" he snaps, resenting all.

> "I don't understand this searching for things that aren't there. It's like hunger.... Everything you are hearing now is hearsay. Let me give you an example. Are we being remembered as being drunks and chasing broads? I never saw Frank, Dean, Sammy or Peter drunk during those performances. That was only a gag! And do you believe these guys had to chase broads? They had to chase 'em away.... I have been married for fifty-seven years. I never had a drink of liquor in my life except wine at Passover services, I never saw Frank drunk, I never saw Dean drunk, I never saw Sammy drunk!"

During the author's visits with Joey at his home, covering a total of twelve years, it became a part of the ritual—Joey's warning that he didn't want to talk about anything having to do with the Rat Pack. He was painfully aware that he was the last man standing from the Summit. Still, it was obviously important to him to cement his place in that history.

> "All I'm doing is either defending the Rat Pack or puncturing lies," he told writer Ed Bark. "You know what I mean? It's terrible! Would you like for me to name you—I won't, but I could—name you male singers—you hear?— who had more broads than Frank and Dean and Sammy

put together! I could throw in Tom Jones there. Nat King
Cole. You understand? I don't hear anything about them!
You mean they didn't drink either? They didn't have
broads? Who were their best friends? *Nuns*?"

Joey was actually hitting upon some truths that are asserted in
this book. The Rat Pack was a myth. The camaraderie and cavort-
ing were part of the PR plan, the imaging. The five entertainers
were businessmen with a commodity to sell. They carefully culti-
vated images that were cemented in the public's consciousness.
And it followed the *Liberty Valance* dictum "Print the legend."
And the legend is—Frank was the fearless leader. Dean was the
happy-go-lucky drunk. Sammy was the carefree underdog. Peter
was the suave playboy. And Joey was the Frown Prince.

Meanwhile, *real* life continued to pound down on Joey.

On July 22, 1998, Corbett Monica passed away at the age of
sixty-eight. Monica, who had been a longtime friend and neighbor
in Englewood and a co-star on *The Joey Bishop Show*, had stayed
close.

"Corbett was a dear friend," Joey said softly. "He never forgot
that I set him up with Frank as his opening act. He was set for life
after that. I never forgot my friends, and they knew it."

And the bad news kept on coming. Joey was crushed in 1998
when Sylvia was diagnosed with lung cancer. He doted on his
wife throughout her sad decline; she passed away on September 20, 1999, at the age of eighty. Per her wishes, Joey and Larry
scattered her ashes in the Pacific Ocean. After that, they waited
nearly two months before announcing Sylvia's death.

As the author continued his discussions with Joey after Sylvia's
death, he noticed that the aging comedian seemed even slower
in his responses and often repeated stories in the same conversation. Still, he hung on. A newspaper reporter, in an attempt to
be nice to the eighty-one-year-old Joey, asked if laughter was the
thing that kept him young.

"*NO!*" Joey, ever the contrarian, said emphatically. "*Not* laughter—a sense of humor! If laughter kept you young, do you know
how old hyenas would be?"

Chapter 29
Imitation, the Sincerest Form of Thievery

Joey Takes on the Tribute Payers

The Rat Pack became the subject of an HBO mini-series in 1998. Pictured (left to right) are Joe Mantegna as Dean; Angus MacFayden as Peter; Ray Liotta as Frank; Bobby Slaton as Joey; and Don Cheadle as Sammy.

As Joey aged dramatically, the concept of the Rat Pack remained evergreen. *Ocean's 11* was reissued on DVD. Then, George Clooney, Brad Pitt, and Julia Roberts starred in director Steven Soderbergh's remake (this one using a word instead of a numeral, *Ocean's Eleven*) that premiered in 2001. Original cast members Angie Dickinson and Henry Silva had cameos. Joey was asked to do one as well but declined the offer.

"It's a bunch of bullshit," he contended. "In our film, we were all friends. Buddies. You can tell that. We had chemistry. Then they make this cheap remake. Crap. Make something original. They are just trying to cash in on something we had, but you can't recapture that. It's like a genie in a bottle...once in a lifetime."

Apparently, moviegoers didn't agree. The remake grossed over $450 million and spawned three sequels, with another one in the works.

For those who prefer their entertainment live and with a cocktail or two, Rat Pack cover groups continue to spring up in venues around the globe.

Deana Martin, daughter of Dean Martin, appeared at Michael Feinstein's club 54/Below with her brother Ricci Martin in a salute to their father and the Rat Pack in "His Son Remembers: Dean Martin's Music and More." Deana also tours the country doing her wonderful act in which she sings some of her father's songs.

When asked how the Rat Pack would fare in this #MeToo world, Deana said: "I think they would have, only because they were so cute at it, they were cool."

Deana agreed that much of the group's image was an "act."

"Dad came home every night. He wouldn't stay up with Uncle Frank and Uncle Sammy. He didn't want to do that...The cigarette, the womanizing, that was his *shtick*. Come to think of it, I really *don't* know how that would be received these days."[9]

Yet another Rat Pack tribute group features comic Sandy Hackett—son of the late Buddy Hackett—who plays Joey.

"Of course I knew Joey, as he was my dad's close friend," Sandy told the author. "I know his mannerisms and speech patterns."

9   As though to justify her trepidation, Dean's popular seasonal song, "Baby, It's Cold Outside," a holiday standard by Frank Loesser, has been banned by certain radio stations due to its seeming wink at date rape.

Comedy writer Monty Aidem (*The Tonight Show, Mama's Family*) appears as Sinatra in yet another ensemble. He recently took part in a Rat Pack Salute at the legendary Hillcrest Country Club, where Joey was a member.

"It's such great fun and there is still a strong response to Frank and the music of the Rat Pack," Monty told the author. "We try to capture the great fun they had."

Michael Starr, whose book resurrected a variation on the title Joey had for his unpublished memoirs, *A Mouse in the Rat Pack*, summed up Joey's life this way:

> A renewed fascination exists with the lives and times of Sinatra, Dean Martin, Sammy Davis Jr., Peter Lawford and the lone survivor of the pack, Joey Bishop, who could have explained a few things and corrected a few errors for the authors and artists, having actually been a part of that scene.
>
> If only someone had asked.
>
> "I guess you wouldn't want somebody with the facts coming in," Bishop says. "You'd rather go with the hearsay."
>
> He was there. He knows what really happened and what didn't.
>
> Sinatra was no myth to him. Frank was someone Joey was close to, someone with whom he is inextricably linked in life.
>
> At the funeral, he could have shared a few of those memories when Frank's friends began being brought up before the mourners to say a few words.
>
> If only someone had asked.
>
> A 9-hour marathon of The Joey Bishop Show will run on the TV Land rerun network Saturday, featuring episodes that aired between 1961 and 1965.

As would Jerry Seinfeld years later, Bishop had an NBC sitcom in which funny people would drop by his apartment.

Like when Buddy Hackett brings over a baby gift. Bishop deliberately kept himself in the dark so his reaction would be spontaneous when he opened the door.

"All I knew was that Buddy was bringing a baby present. I didn't know he'd bring a baby elephant."

In another episode, Leo Durocher has to listen to Phil Foster, a comedian and rabid Dodgers fan, bellyaching about the team leaving Brooklyn. It was back in the days that, in his Vegas stage act, Bishop would invite Don Drysdale of the Dodgers up to sing, then replace him with the relief pitcher Ron Perranoski for the final note.

Quite apart from his Rat Pack ties, Bishop had a stature of his own. His late-night talk show ran opposite Johnny Carson's. He also guest hosted The Tonight Show itself an astounding 207 times.

At a 1960 inaugural ball that he emceed, Bishop recalls asking John F. Kennedy, "To what do you attribute your success?"

"All you've got to do is get the facts," JFK replied.

That stuck with Joey, who can't understand why Rat Pack historians would rather print or film the lies than learn the truth.

Bishop takes pride in timing. He was lauded by the likes of Stan Laurel and Jack Benny for his. Higher praise there isn't.

On stage, Joey Bishop was no mere mouse among giant rats. He was a big part of the act. He can't understand why people diminish that. It reminds him of a show he missed because he was in traction. Carson, filling in, ascribed it to too much bowing to Frank.

"The joke's OK," Bishop feels. "All Johnny had to do was add, 'Get well, Joey.'"

It was a slight, like not being asked to say a few words at Frank's funeral. As the last of the pack, Joey says, "Don't you think you'd be at least acknowledged?"

What's done is done, though.

"Oh, well," he says. "I've got a Viagra joke. Want to hear it?"

On August 22, 1998, three months after Sinatra's death, HBO rolled out its Rat Pack biography film directed by Rob Cohen. It starred Ray Liotta as Frank, Joe Mantegna as Dean, Don Cheadle as Sammy (Cheadle also starred in the new version of *Ocean's Eleven*), Angus MacFadyen as Peter, and standup comic Bobby Slayton as Joey. Slayton was determined to get the part. He had his hair dyed black and cropped short and gave a convincing reading. The casting agents were impressed, although they were concerned that Slayton seemed too old for the part.

"*Too old?*" Slayton said. "I'm forty-two—the same age as Liotta and Montegna!"

He got the part.

Slayton wanted to make his interpretation of Joey as accurate as possible. He even sought out individuals who had known the comic personally, including Carl Reiner, Don Rickles, Buddy Hackett, and Regis Philbin. What he heard mostly was that Joey, despite his protestations of undying fidelity, fucked around on his wife. Don Rickles, despite his image as a vicious insult comic, was one of the nicest guys in the business. "I don't like to speak disparagingly about anyone," Rickles told him, "but in Joey's case I'll make an exception." Buddy Hackett didn't mince words either: "He was a fucking piece of shit." When Slayton asked Regis Philbin to sum up Joey in one word, Regis looked at him seriously and said, "*Evil.*"

Nobody, but nobody, had anything good to say about Joey Bishop—well, nobody except for Joey Bishop.

"You can't recreate what we did," he insisted. "There is just no fucking way."

Couldn't recreate it? Slayton thought. If you could bring dinosaurs back to life, you can certainly recreate five fucking idiots on a stage.

Someone else who was unhappy was Tina Sinatra. As the owner of her late father's image, she did not appreciate the fact that the Rat Packers' families weren't consulted about the casting process. This apparently made the suits at HBO nervous. As a concession to Ms. Sinatra, Larry Bishop was called in to read for the role of his father.

"*Larry Bishop*?" Slayton laughed. "He was seven feet tall and couldn't act worth shit."

Slayton was still the man who would be Joey—but only after nailing three auditions. When it was confirmed that the part really and truly was his, he went into research mode. He went to the Broadcasting Museum to watch archival tapes of his subject in his prime. After the first several minutes, he concluded, "This guy is just Jackie Mason without the timing! He's a zero. He stinks! He's the Zeppo Marx of the Rat Pack."

The script, it turns out, reflected the actor's opinion. Joey Bishop was essentially a bit player in the biggest event of his career. He was depicted as just some wise-ass comic who has such lines as:

"Frank, what do you have to say to a comic who can't shut up?"

"Shut up!" said Sinatra (Liotta).

"When I went to promote *The Rat Pack* film, I was doing a radio show in Chicago with a shock jock," Slayton told the author. "I thought it was just a one-on-one interview and was not aware that Joey was also going to be in on the call. We were both being sandbagged and neither of us knew it. Joey was already angry about the film since they never called him or contacted him beforehand. When Joey found out I was on the phone, he was angry. So, I tried to placate him. Trying to be nice, I told Joey that I respected him and heard he was quite a ladies' man—you know, the Rat Pack and all. Joey blew a gasket and started swearing and yelling at me, calling me a cocksucker, saying that he wanted to punch me out. After the show, they gave me Joey's home phone number and I called him to apologize and tell him that I was set up as well. Joey was fine then, and we talked. He sent me an autographed picture, which reads: 'Hopefully, some day they will get me to play *you* in a movie. Best, Joey.' I had that framed and hung it on my office wall."

Now that Slayton had proven to Joey that no malice was intended by his portrayal, he asked the aging comedian to be his guest for the film's debut screening. Joey turned him down flat, saying that HBO should have been the ones extending the invitation.

Joe Mantegna told the author, "I loved and idolized Dean, so it was great to have the opportunity to play him. It was a great honor. I'm happy Deana and family loved my performance."

In the film, Dean (Mantegna) tells Joey (Slayton), "The world is drunk and we're just the cocktail of the moment, pally. One of these days, everybody's gonna wake up with a heck of a hangover...and wonder what the hell all the fuss was about."

The film fictionalizes much of their story. Lawford has married Patricia Kennedy. Abandoning a notion to seduce Pat for his own amusement, Sinatra becomes more interested in her brother John Kennedy's ambitions. He sincerely believes Jack Kennedy would be a great president, but he also feels having a friend in the White House could benefit his own public image. Sinatra arranges for the entire Pack to perform at a JFK campaign fundraiser. Sinatra also knows Kennedy's infatuation with the opposite sex and introduces him to Marilyn Monroe, who begins seeing Kennedy unbeknown to her husband, baseball star Joe DiMaggio. JFK's pompous father, Joseph P. Kennedy, feels Sinatra's mob ties might hurt Jack's chances of defeating Richard Nixon in the election of 1960. He insists that Sinatra help the campaign from behind the scenes only; hypocritically, he also asks Sinatra to use those same mob ties to swing the West Virginia unions' support Kennedy's way. This is blatantly false, as Sinatra and the rest of the Pack campaigned out in the open for their candidate.

JFK is portrayed as a vacuous playboy who slept with mob moll Judith Campbell after being introduced to her by Sinatra.

A reporter asked Joey, "Did that really happen?"

"How would I know?" Bishop snapped. "If I don't see a guy doin' it with a broad, I ain't gonna say yes or no. But what does it matter? [Franklin D.] Roosevelt had a broad. [Dwight D.] Eisenhower had a broad who drove a jeep for him. I didn't hear anything about that."

Joey still allowed the occasional journalist into his inner sanctum, such as another of the author's good friends, Ed Bark, the television columnist of the *Dallas Morning News*. Eighty-year-old Joey would go through the routine of leading his guest up the stairs to his second-floor study to show off his memorabilia. One such item was a priceless framed poster advertising the Rat Pack's twenty-eight-night engagement at the Sands. Joey would also bring out the scrapbooks containing his yellowed press clippings and point out every plaque he had ever been given to him by the numerous service organizations citing his unwavering generosity. His comedy charity bouts with boxing greats were commemorated with pictures of Sugar Ray Robinson ("he was a sweetheart") and Rocky Marciano ("the greatest fighter that ever lived, ya hear?"). And over on the left, "that's Vietnam there. I took whatsername with me. From the movie *The Birds*."

"Tippi Hedren?" Ed Bark ventures.

"What's it, Tippi? Tippi Hedren," he replies. "There she is right there. That's us in Vietnam. See it?"

If the interview took place near the noon hour, Joey would take time out for lunch. He might make himself a chocolate shake to go with a hard-boiled egg and chocolate pudding from a sealed plastic cup. A gracious host, he offered the patient interviewer a soft drink, a ham sandwich, and pudding. Meanwhile, Joey's twelve-year-old cat Misty would sit on the table and watch them eat.

Then one day the interviews just stopped. Joey's friend and assistant Nora began to keep many of Joey's old friends, visiting journalists, and fans at bay. Joey, approaching ninety, began to repeat himself even more than usual. Sometime around 2004, his condition was diagnosed as Alzheimer's disease.

Joey passed away at his home on October 17, 2007, from multiple organ failure. As they had done with Sylvia, his ashes were scattered at sea.

Upon learning of Joey Bishop's demise, Rocky Kalish sent the author the following email:

Rick,

Bishop was not the most loved...and that was well deserved. Many of us never believed he was much of a funny man. He was never inventive. He did lines that everybody else did. He just played a tough guy role in life and that's what Frank liked about him. He came out of Philadelphia and was connected. He once punched out a writer, about fifty years older than he was. That writer was a friend of mine. His name was Milt Josefsberg (Benny, Lucy, etc.). Milt wrote for everybody and was well respected. He also was a fishing buddy and we caught marlin down in Mexico off Cabo San Lucas with Sheldon.

Bishop also ripped me off, stole stories from Irma and me. We never got paid. Five stories—and it was a time in my career when I needed the loot.

One time I was walking behind Joey, and Danny Thomas's daughter, Marlo Thomas, was on the lot where he was shooting his failed sitcom. He was barking at her, "I don't care who the fuck your father is, this is my show and you'll do what I say!" And Danny owned the show.

R.I.P. Joey.

But don't expect any flowers.

—Rock.

Joey went out quietly, hardly remembered at the time of his death. Having been married for fifty-seven years to Sylvia, most figured that was the end of the Joey Bishop story. What followed his death, however, was shocking to those who thought they knew him—and even to those who didn't.

Chapter 30
Post-Mortem

A Relationship Comes to Light

Joey and Nora Garibotti, c. 2002.

Joey Bishop spent his career in the spotlight doing everything he possibly could to avoid controversy. It is ironic, then, that controversy would sully his reputation now that he was dead.

As has been established in previous chapters, Joey watched his money carefully and was given sound advice by his financial planner. As a result, he left a generous estate of $8 million.

Everyone who knew Joey had an idea how that money would be allocated. There would, of course, be a sizeable chunk for his only son, Larry, and his children. Another, perhaps even more substantive portion, would likely go to Newport Beach's Chabad Center to benefit the charity's programs for special-needs children.

So it came as a shock to everyone when Bishop's Last Will and Testament stated that 70% of that $8 million would go instead to Nora Garibotti, described as Joey's "former golfing companion." The remaining 30% was to be divided between the comedian's agent, Ed "Hook" Hookstratten, who once represented Elvis Presley, and Bishop's financial advisor Myles Hymes. The story first broke in *The Daily Pilot*, a local newspaper for Newport Beach; the reporter was Brianna Bailey.

When the dust settled, a suit was filed by Newport Beach Chabad, naming Hookstratten, Orange County attorney James "Kimo" McCormick, Hymes, and Garibotti. The center was seeking damages in excess of $10 million for legal malpractice and breach of fiduciary duty, among other claims, according to court documents.

The lawsuit alleges that Bishop intended to leave part of his money to Chabad to benefit the charity's programs for special-needs children, but Hookstratten, Garibotti, Hymes, and McCormick took advantage of the Rat Packer's deteriorating mental faculties to usurp his estate. In the suit, Chabad claims Bishop's mental and physical health deteriorated over the final years of his life. It reached the point that the octogenarian had trouble remembering the names of his deceased wife, grandchildren, and his fellow Rat Pack members, according to legal documents. Bishop also could not identify Garibotti as his caretaker, and mistakenly identified her as a male assistant during an examination by a neurologist, the lawsuit claims. Garibotti's attorneys dispute the claim and contend that Bishop was alert and competent up until his final months.

Although Garibotti has claimed in legal documents that she was Bishop's longtime, live-in companion after the death of his wife, Sylvia Bishop, in 1999, Chabad claims in legal papers that Garibotti was only a housekeeper and caretaker. "Mr. Bishop became unable to distinguish between his personal and professional relationships, frequently characterizing anyone who visited him as 'a dear friend,'" the lawsuit alleges. "Mr. Bishop was acutely vulnerable to the suggestions of others and was no longer able to determine his own wishes and best interests and was subject to the exercise of influence by others."

Garibotti's attorney, Robert Julian, claims stacks of letters and cards sent between Bishop and his client show the pair had an intimate relationship that began when Garibotti was eighteen years old.

"They had a loving and caring relationship that lasted twenty years," Julian said. "When Nora walked into the room, Joey's eyes lit up."

Newport Beach Chabad's director Rabbi Reuven Mintz was a longtime friend and spiritual advisor to Bishop. According to Mintz, Bishop had expressly made known his desire to use his estate to form an entity called the Joey Bishop Foundation and fund a charitable program to help disabled children in Orange County. At Bishop's encouragement, Mintz traveled to Michigan in 2002 to meet with the founders of Friendship Circle, a program that offers support for children with special needs and their families. Bishop prominently displayed a proposal outlining the Friendship Circle program on his coffee table until Garibotti threw it out.

"Bishop, in the years before he died, set up another entity to have this children's organization started," said Steven Silverstein, an attorney for Newport Beach Chabad. "We have all kinds of emails and letters from attorneys to back up what they themselves made in their files. Whatever they did to change it was without Bishop's knowledge."

Bishop decided in 2005 that he did not want to leave his money to charity, Julian claims. He further avers that Mintz stopped visiting Bishop after the entertainer told him he no longer had any interest in setting up a children's charity.

"In my opinion, it's unfortunate that the rabbi has not apparently accepted Joey Bishop's decision that he did not want to provide any more to charity because he had already provided so much over the years," Julian said. "If the rabbi cared so much about Joey Bishop, why did he stop coming to his house?"

Bishop's attorney, James McCormick, began visiting the entertainer's home every week in 2004, "ingratiating himself" to Bishop, according to legal documents.

"During this period of time, Mr. Bishop was also subject to the direct and continuing influence of Garibotti, who controlled every aspect of Mr. Bishop's daily existence and who decided what persons would be allowed to visit Mr. Bishop."

"The case has absolutely no merit," McCormick's attorney, Adam Streisand, said. "It's completely frivolous and I expect it's going to be thrown out of court so fast it's going to make your head spin."

According to *New York Post* columnist Michael Starr:

> My 2002 biography of Joey, *A Mouse in the Rat Pack*,
> made no mention of Nora Garibotti—because, well,
> I didn't know she existed. When I visited Joey at his
> waterfront home in Newport Beach, California, in 1999,
> Nora was nowhere to be found—but Sylvia, Joey's wife
> of nearly sixty years, was there. Joey told me she was ill,
> and she died later that year. When Joey followed eight
> years later, his obituaries mentioned their long marriage.
> No one mentioned Garibotti."

Still, Garibotti's fight to claim Joey's millions became the centerpiece of an episode of *The Will: Family Secrets Revealed*, which aired on the I. D. network.

In order to get her money, Garibotti had to prove that she was more than Joey's nurse, since she couldn't legally inherit any money as his caretaker.

She also claimed that his longtime attorney, Ed Hookstratten, lawyer James Kimo McCormick, and Joey's accountant schemed to siphon his money by convincing the failing comedian to alter his will in their financial favor.

Thrown into the mix was Rabbi Reuven Mintz, who claims he was Joey's "spiritual advisor"—and who later sued when Joey cut Mintz's Chabad children's charity out of his will (the suit was tossed).

The program consists of re-enactments and interviews with Garibotti, Sandy Hackett (Buddy's son), and Joey's neighbors—each of whom gives different versions of the Joey-Garibotti relationship.

To quote Joey's catchphrase: "Son of a gun."

In interview after interview, those who knew Joey would say, "He was quite the ladies' man." After we learned the truth about the nature of Joey and Nora's relationship, Don Sherman told the author, "During the years of his sitcom, Joey regularly had women visit him in his dressing room or on the set and often hired them as performers on the show. Joey had several long-term female companions. Trustin Howard, a writer for Joey's talk show, also corroborated that allegation.

The author reached out unsuccessfully to both Ms. Garibotti and Larry Bishop for their thoughts and comments. Our sources for the following information are limited to media reports and the television documentary. Although Garibotti appears to have been a willing participant in the *I. D.* program, she must have had second thoughts when she saw the edited version the night it aired. She sought damages for fraud and defamation and contended that she had been tricked into appearing in the documentary and for being falsely portrayed as a gold digger. Statements were made in the documentary by neighbors of Garibotti—without revealing they had been engaged in litigation with her—who "made statements which impugned plaintiff's name and character, put her in a false light, and accused her of trying to obtain money from Bishop's estate, which they claimed she was disqualified from obtaining," the complaint reads.

The court declined to hear the case based on technical reasons and did not address the merits of Chabad's case. Attorney Bob Weinberg, who represents Chabad, told the press, "Mr. Bishop was the victim of elder abuse. The lawyers and accountant and the housekeeper got Mr. Bishop's money despite Mr. Bishop's repeated statements that he wished the bulk of his estate to go to charities run by Chabad."

Chabad is still weighing its legal options, and the fight is far from over, Weinberg said. "Chabad is going to continue to fight for the vindication of Joey Bishop's wishes."

Garibotti said in the statement that "Rabbi Mintz has caused tremendous monetary costs to Joey Bishop's estate and to me and may have a lot of explaining to do in the future. Sadly, Rabbi Mintz probably caused Chabad, which is an organization that involves itself in good deeds, to pursue what I believe to have been a wrongful course of litigation without a proper basis, which was likely at significant expense to them."

Garibotti went on to claim that Rabbi Bernie King, who is retired from Congregation Shir Ha-Ma'l in Irvine, was Bishop's rabbi in his last years, not Mintz.

"Rabbi King was a wonderful human being to both of us, good hearted, with no motives, and genuinely there for Joey. Rabbi Bernie King visited us at our home, was there for Joey when he became ill, visited him at the hospital regularly, gave Joey his last rites in the last hour of his life, and conducted his funeral services for a private gathering," Garibotti said in the statement. "I want to make clear that Rabbi Reuven Mintz, in my opinion, was adverse and hostile to Joey's trust and estate and to me. He does not deserve to have his name associated with Joey Bishop, in my opinion."

The following is from the front page of the *Metropolitan News-Enterprise*, Thursday, December 31, 2015.

The Court of Appeal has reinstated a $488,448.29 judgment in favor of the late comedian Joey Bishop's live-in companion because the judge who purported to vacate a default and revise the judgment failed to act within the statutory period.

The plaintiff in the case is Nora Garibotti, who, according to a 2010 column in the *New York Post*, claimed she was Bishop's "lover for nearly twenty-five years—they met when she was sixteen and he was sixty-six."

The opinion, filed late Tuesday, notes: "She lived with him in his home on Lido Island in Newport Beach for the last ten years of his life. Bishop died in October 2007, and Garibotti was one of his estate's major beneficiaries."

The plaintiff obtained a default judgment against Bruce Hinkle, an unlicensed contractor, after his answer was stricken in 2011 as a sanction for repeatedly failing to show up for his deposition. She offered proof that work he performed at the residence—purportedly to fix it up, preparatory to it being sold—was shoddy, and that items he removed from the home, and was to store, were stolen by him. Many of the items were Garibotti's property. The opinion describes those that belonged to the comedian as "irreplaceable and priceless jewelry, paintings, antique furnishings, and other personal property, mementos, trophies, and memorabilia Bishop acquired over a lifetime in show business and as a member of Frank Sinatra's 'Rat Pack.'"

Under the judgment, Garibotti was to receive $310,650 for the value of the purloined personal property, $52,234 for the work performed on the premises, $15,154.29 in prejudgment interest, $100,000 in punitive damages, and $10,410 in costs.

Hinkle filed a motion to vacate the default judgment on March 18, 2013. Orange Superior Court Judge Franz E. Miller granted it on June 12, 2013, paring the judgment to $25,000 in damages for the personal property, $9,198.80 in prejudgment interest, $10,410 in costs, and no punitive damages, for a total of $44,608.80.

The Court of Appeal reversed in an opinion by Richard M. Aronson of the Fourth District's Div. Three.

Miller's post-judgment decisions were void for lack of jurisdiction, he said, noting that the jurist acted "nearly 90 days" after Hinkle's motion was filed. Under Code of Civil Procedure §663a(b), the time limit for ruling, Aronson declared, was 60 days.

He wrote:

"That statute provides a trial court's power to rule on a motion to vacate judgment expires 60 days after service of notice of entry of judgment or service of the first notice of intention to move to vacate, whichever occurs first. The statute further provides that the trial court's failure to rule within that period automatically results in a denial of the motion without further court order. In drafting section 663a, subdivision (b), the Legislature used the identical time frame and statutory language it adopted in section 660, which established the deadline for a trial court to rule on a new trial motion. California courts long have held that section 660's time frame for ruling on a new trial motion is mandatory and jurisdictional, and any order purporting to rule on a new trial motion after the period lapses is beyond the court's jurisdiction and void. Section 663a, subdivision (b)'s plain language and legislative history establish the Legislature intended the deadline for ruling on a motion to vacate judgment to have the same legal effect."

He went on to say:

"The statute's plain language therefore compels the conclusion Hinkle's motion was denied by operation of law before the trial court ruled on it, and when the court entered its order purporting to grant the motion the court's power to do so already had expired."

Hinkle contended that Garibotti is estopped from challenging the court's jurisdiction because she had obtained a continuance of the hearing on Hinkle's motion to a date beyond the 60-day period.

"Estoppel, however, may not extend a trial court's jurisdiction to rule on either a new trial motion or a motion to vacate judgment," Aronson responded, adding:

"Here, the trial court lacked subject matter jurisdiction to grant Hinkle's motion to vacate once the 60-day period for the court to rule lapsed, and that jurisdiction cannot be renewed or extended by principles of estoppel."

The action, filed in the Orange Superior Court, was dismissed on August 31, 2012, pursuant to a settlement.

On May 8, 2008, Garibotti sued the law firms of Hookstratten & Hookstratten and Matkins Leck Gamble Mallory & Natsis, LLP, as well as individual attorneys, for legal malpractice. She contended the lawyers engaged in "despicable and fraudulent conduct" and failed to "handle, draft and administer" Bishop's trust in a manner consistent with his intentions.

At one point, Los Angeles Superior Court Judge Ralph Dau made a tentative ruling permitting the Hookstratten firm to file a cross-complaint against Garibotti for "financial elder abuse," but changed his mind in response to legislation that was signed by then-Governor Arnold Schwarzenegger clarifying the definition of that term.

The proposed cross complaint alleged that Garibotti in 2007 persuaded Bishop, who was suffering from dementia, to write out holographic notes bequeathing the residence and $60,000 in cash to her.

The proposed pleading averred:

"These handwritten notes were the direct result of undue influence exercised by the caregiver, Garibotti, on the severely demented and incompetent Joey and therefore constitute financial elder abuse."

That case was also settled.

Acknowledgments

First, I wish to thank my stepson Jason, daughter-in-law Sonja, and my beautiful grandchildren Andrew and Alyssa for their support. My late wife, Diana, was my greatest cheerleader; it is to her that this book is lovingly dedicated. My late sons, Matthew and Tommy, were also important inspirations. My beautiful partner, Kathleen (Kathy) Anderson Lindsey, is my source of strength and love. Emmy Lindsey, Kathy's daughter, is brilliant, beautiful, and successful.

My dear friend, brilliant writer and etiquette guru Ellen Easton, is a great source of support and guidance. Another good friend, Marie Elana, was of great assistance concerning transcripts. Thanks to Nick Santa Maria, Jeff Abraham, and Jordan Young. And a big thank you to famed *New York Post* columnist Michael Seth Starr for sharing his info from his outstanding biography on Joey Bishop. Thanks are also in order for Melinda Cummings Cameron and her husband, Professor Kim Cameron; William J. Birnes and his wonderful wife, writer Nancy Hayfield Birnes; and the late C. David Heymann for his guidance.

My sincerest thanks to Robbie Adkins for her elegant design work, and to one of my favorite writers, Steve Stoliar, for his assistance with proofreading. Scott H. Reboul was a great help as well.

I greatly appreciate my co-author and friend Lon Davis (and his terrific wife, Deb) for his editorial guidance, knowledge, and support.

And, of course, a great debt of thanks to that Son-of-a-Gun, Joey Bishop. His hours of conversation and his contribution of his materials made this book possible.

Sources

Although the majority of the information in *Deconstructing the Rat Pack* derives from the interviews conducted by Richard A. Lertzman over a five-decade period, there were some books, magazines, and newspaper articles that were most helpful.

Books

Besser, Joe, with Jeff Lenburg and Greg Lenburg. *Once a Stooge, Always a Stooge: The Autobiography of Hollywood's Most Pro- lific Funnyman.* Revised edition of 1988 book. Litchfield Park, AZ: Moonwater Press, 2020.

Doll, Susan, Ph.D. *Elvis for Dummies.* For Dummies, 2009.

Levy, Shawn. *Rat Pack Confidential: Frank, Dean, Sammy, Peter, and Joey and the Last Great Show Biz Party.* Garden Grove, NY: Doubleday, 1998.

Lewellen, Scott. *Funny You Should Ask: Oral Histories of Classic Sitcom Storytellers.* Jefferson, NC: McFarland & Co., 2013

Lewis, Brad. *Hollywood Celebrity Gangster: The Incredible Life and Times of Mickey Cohen.* New York: Enigma Books, 2009.

Mickey Cohen: In My Own Words, As Told to John Peer Nugent. New York: Prentice-Hall, 1975.

Parr, Jack. *My Saber is Bent.* New York: Trident Press, 1961.

Spada, James. *Peter Lawford: The Man Who Kept the Secrets.* New York: Bantam, 1991.

Starr, Michael Seth. *A Mouse in the Rat Pack: The Joey Bishop Story.* Taylor Trade Pub., 2002.

Weisman, Eliot, and Jennifer Valoppi. *The Way It Was: My Life with Frank Sinatra.* New York: Hatchette Books, 2017.

Wilde, Larry. Interview with Joey Bishop in *The Great Comedi- ans Talk About Comedy.* Updated edition of 1968 book. Laugh. com, Inc. 2013.

Magazines

Apatow, Judd. "Our Mr. Brooks." (Interview with comedian/film-maker Albert Brooks) *Vanity Fair* (Jan. 2013).

Crisafulli, Charles. "Sin-a-tra City: The Story of Frank Sinatra and Las Vegas." *Medium Magazine* (Dec. 2, 2015).

Handy, Bruce. "And Then There Was One: Joey Bishop, the Sole Surviving Rat Packer, Fights a Losing Battle Against Myth." *Time* magazine (June 6, 1998).

Kluth, Andreas. "The Catastrophe of Success." *The Harvard Business Review* (Feb. 17, 2002).

Whitney, Dwight. "Sick, Sick, Sick.": All's Not Well with Joey." *TV Guide* (Feb. 20, 1965).

Newspapers

Bailey, Brianna, "Appeal Rejected in Dispute Over Bishop Estate," *The Daily Pilot* (Newport Beach, CA), Jan. 15, 2010.

Bark, Ed, "Joey Bishop: 'Anybody Tells You You're a Good Audience, Punch 'em Right in the Mouth,'" *Dallas Morning News*, Aug. 16, 1998.

Buckley, Tom, "'Sugar Babies' with Joey Bishop," *New York Daily News*, Feb. 2, 1981.

Gould, Jack, "Television: Joey Bishop Begins a Situation Series; Plays Milquetoastian Aide of Press Agent; Channel 4 Premiere is Same Old Fluff," *New York Times*, Sep. 21, 1961.

Humphrey, Hal, Column on Bishop show rancor, *New York Post*, April 26, 1963.

Kraushar, Jonathan P., "Bergen: Comics' Haven," *New York Times*, March 21, 1976.

Krebs, Albin, and Robert Mcg. Thomas. "'Sugar Babies' As Seen Through the Eyes of Joey Bishop," *New York Daily News*, Feb. 2, 1981.

Lieberman, Paul, "A Bullet Between the Eyes at Rondelli's, *Los Angeles Times*, Oct. 31, 2008.

McNamara, Mary, "John F. Kennedy is Too Complicated to be Idolized," *Los Angeles Times*, Oct. 25, 2013.

Thomas, Bob, "'The Joey Bishop Show' Keeps Name, Rest is Changed," *Associated Press*, Aug. 5, 1962.

Interviews

The journey to write this book began over thirty years ago and includes nearly fifty years of interviews. Starting in 1972 and as a cinema student, I was able to meet and interview some very fascinating people, some of whom I have included in this volume, and many of whom have since passed on. In no particular order, they are: Moe Dalitz owner of the Sands, the Sahara, the Dunes etc.; president of the Sands Casino Carl Cohen; television comedy writers Rocky and Irma Kalish; Las Vegas entertainer Debbie Reynolds; comedian/actor Bobby Slayton, who portrayed Joey Bishop in the 1998 HBO mini-series *The Rat Pack*; Dean Martin's daughter, singer Deana Martin; Frank Sinatra's daughters, actress/singer Nancy Sinatra, and executive producer of the 1992 mini-series *Sinatra*; Tina Sinatra; actor/producer Max Baer Jr.; actor Adam West; actress/dancer Julie Newmar; former chairman of the William Morris Agency Norman Brokaw; Johnny Carson's attorney, Henry "Bombastic" Bushkin; television game-show host Monty Hall; *Ocean's 11* writer George Clayton Thomas; singing superstar Julie Budd; comic and *Joey Bishop Show* regular Corbett Monica; Head Stooge Moe Howard; actress Marlo Thomas; television writers Bill Persky and Sam Denoff; writers Saul Turtletaub and Bernie Orenstein; writer Phoef Sutton; writer Mark Dawidziak; TV critic Ed Bark; writer Monty Aidem; writer Irving Brecher; producer Terry Allen Kramer; television icon Art Linkletter and his wife, Lois; singer Andy Williams and his press agent, Paul Shefrin; actor Roscoe Lee Browne; film star Tony Curtis; publisher Larry Flynt; writer/producer Del Reisman; film editor Stanley Frazen; actress Ann B. Davis; actress Linda Kaye Henning; Hank Messick, author of *The Silent Syndicate*; mob boss Max Diamond; author/commentator Gore Vidal; actor Joe Mantegna, who played Dean Martin in the HBO mini-series *The Rat Pack*; actor Warren Berlinger, who played Joey's brother on *The Joey Bishop Show*; actor/producer Sheldon Leonard; mobster Mickey Cohen; comedian Jerry Seinfeld; TCM host Robert Osborne; singer Eddie Fisher; film director John Waters; Sands Casino owner Jack Entratter; actor Mickey Rooney and his wife, Jan; comedy writer Carl Kleinschmitt; actress Abby Dalton, who played Joey Bishop's wife on his eponymous sitcom; comic actor Joe Besser, who played a supporting role on *The Joey Bishop Show*; television producer Robert "Bob" Finkel; movie producer Robert Evans; television personality Regis Philbin; comedy writer Trustin Howard, better known as Slick Slavin; comic and comedy writer Don Sherman (*The Joey Bishop Show*), and the father of actress Amy Sherman Palladino (*The Marvelous Mrs. Maisel*); television columnist Ed Bark; television comedian Sid Caesar; writer/producer/director Mel Brooks; writer/actor/producer/director Carl Reiner; actor/comedian/director Jerry Lewis; his sons Anthony, Gary, and Chris; film critic and author Leonard Maltin; writer/director Garry Marshall; columnist/author Michael Starr (*A Mouse in the Rat Pack: The Joey Bishop Story*); author Shawn Levy (*Rat Pack Confidential*); daughter of Charlie Morrison, Marilyn Morrison; producer/director Steven Spielberg; comic Shecky Greene; comic Jack Carter; television director Howard Murray, the son of comic Jan Murray; comedian Buddy Hackett; his son, comic Sandy Hackett; television director Charles Dayton, son of comic/actor Danny Dayton; television talk show host/author Steve Allen; television talk-show host Dick Cavett; mobster Shondor Birns; and Joey Bishop.

About the Author

Richard A. Lertzman is the co-author (with William J. Birnes) of the bestselling, widely acclaimed biographies *Dr. Feelgood: The Shocking True Story of the Doctor Who May Have Changed History by Treating and Drugging JFK, Marilyn, Elvis, and Other Prominent Personalities* (2014); *Mickey Rooney: His Life and Times* (2015, Simon & Schuster); *Beyond Columbo: The Life and Times of Peter Falk* (2017); and *The Dr. Feelgood Casebook* (2020). Richard's next book will be a comprehensive look at comedian/filmmaker Jerry Lewis, written with Lon Davis.

About the Editor

Lon Davis is the co-author (with his wife, Debra) of several books on some of the major figures of the silent film era. Lon has also edited hundreds of academic books on every aspect of the performing arts. In 2021, Flicker Alley will release the Davises' documentary film *This is Francis X. Bushman*, produced in connection with the Niles Essanay Silent Film Museum. *Reconstructing the Rat Pack* is Lon's first collaborative effort with Richard A. Lertzman. Their next book (on Jerry Lewis) is already in the works.